Planned Relocation

Planned Relocation

Philip Schorr
Relocation and Management
Associates, Inc.

Lexington Books
D.C. Heath and Company
Lexington, Massachusetts
Toronto   London

Grateful acknowledgment is made for use of material reprinted herein: Table 1-1, "Industrialization—Economic Aspects" by J.R.T. Hughes, reprinted with permission of the publisher from *International Encyclopedia of the Social Sciences*, David L. Sills, editor, Volume 7, page 252, Copyright © 1968, Crowell Collier and Macmillan, Inc.; quote on page 103 from feature story in *New York Post*, reprinted by permission of *New York Post*, © 1958, New York Post Corporation; quote by Jack E. Woods on page 111, © 1959 by the New York Times Company, reprinted by permission.

Library of Congress Cataloging in Publication Data

Schorr, Philip.
  Planned relocation.

  Bibliography: p.
  Includes index.
    1. Relocation (Housing)—United States. 2. United States—Social policy. 3. Urban renewal—United States. I. Title.
HT167.S28   301.5'4   74-25069
ISBN 0-669-97378-5

To My Wife Hannah

Who inspired me to try to understand our
society besides simply coping with it.

Contents

x

List of Figures

List of Tables

Acknowledgments

My deep thanks and appreciation are extended to the many people who played vital roles in the development and completion of this work.

I would like to indicate my indebtedness to the academic community at New York University, Graduate School of Public Administration, and most especially to my long-time friends and counsellors, Professors Herman D. Hillman and Herman Berkman, without whose judgment, wisdom, and guidance, this study would not have been accomplished.

I also wish to express my gratitude to the Honorable Robert Weaver, the first Secretary of the Department of Housing and Urban Development and now Distinguished Professor of Urban Affairs at Hunter College, City University of New York, for his comments and insights on the issues surrounding relocation in the turbulent sixties. Dr. Robert Lipsey, Vice-President of the National Bureau of Economic Research and Professor of Economics at Queens College, City University of New York, guided me through the implications of economics in relocation. I also owe a great debt to Professor Irwin Talbot of Fairleigh Dickinson University who critically reviewed the manuscript. Mrs. Marian Sameth, Associate Director of the Citizens Housing and Planning Council of New York, who opened the library resources of that organization to me, was very helpful as well.

I cannot overstress my gratefulness to my dear and patient wife Hannah who sacrificed much of her time on my behalf. I hope her philosophical and behavioral insights are reflected throughout these pages.

I also wish to express my thanks to my children, Brian and Beth (and Taffy and Mickey as well), for their patience and forbearance. I have no way of repaying those "lost weekends" apart from the family.

In addition, the professional community and the relocatees with whom I have worked over the years have all contributed their special insights and observations here. This includes Melvin Geffner, Deputy Director, Relocation and Development Services Division, Community Planning and Development, Department of Housing and Urban Development; Joseph D. Cohen, Executive Secretary, Relocation Assistance Implementation Committee, Office of Property Management, Office of Federal Management Policies, General Services Administration; and George T. Jefferson, Chief, Payments and Services Branch, Federal Highway Administration, Department of Transportation.

And finally my appreciation to Marion Kurtz and Cass Ball who had the unenviable task of typing from my handwritten notes, and to Mollie Novick, my secretary, who maintained a semblance of order at work, thereby enabling me to complete this endeavor.

None of the people mentioned bear any responsibility for what I have written or for my judgments or conclusions. This responsibility is solely mine.

Introduction:
The Transformation of
Relocation

Relocation Dichotomy

Processes of urban growth and change have been part of man's environment since the beginning of recorded history. Although the rate of change may differ from one society to another, nevertheless the phenomenon is a real one.[1] Implicit to this notion is the movement of peoples, either as a result of individuals' voluntary decisions or as the result of public policies requiring their involuntary relocation. Both patterns—voluntary and involuntary relocation activities—have occurred in the United States since its establishment. In analyzing such movements, two congruent themes are of special concern to this study. One is the ever-increasing intervention of the state (in this case read federal government) in the social processes affecting society; the other is the existence of democratic and authoritarian relocation models and their effects on social democracy and the growth of the individual. That the first theme—the increasing involvement of the state—is not merely a recent phenomenon is demonstrated by an event that occurred during the early days of the nation in the administration of Thomas Jefferson.

The agrarian-rooted Jeffersonian model of government adopted by the newly formed Democratic party espoused a limited role for the state in the regulation of the affairs of men. In 1800, the political strength of the Democrats was concentrated in the egalitarian frontier and rural environment west of the Alleghenies.[2] Jefferson, in his first inaugural address in 1801, outlined his understanding of this limited role thusly: "Still one thing more fellow-citizens—a wise and frugal government, which shall restrain men from injuring one another, shall leave them otherwise free to regulate their own pursuits of industry and improvement, and shall not take from the mouth of labor the bread it has earned. This is the sum of good government and this is necessary to close the circle of our felicities."[3] But Jefferson was faced with the "realpolitik" probability that if France were to acquire Louisiana from Spain, a strong French army would be replacing a weak Spanish force on America's borders in Louisiana. He was also receiving increasing pressure from his settler supporters for more and more land in that area. These factors pushed him to purchase Louisiana in 1803. This act was in fact a modification of his theoretical model of a limited role for government.[4]

The second theme, the dichotomous and sporadic nature of the movement towards enhancing social democracy in America, is illustrated by two case studies of involuntary relocation and one of voluntary relocation programs. By the Removal Act of 1830, about 100,000 Indians were forced to migrate westward from the Mississippi Valley to provide this land for white settlers.[5] And during the first days of World War II, some 110,000 West Coast Japanese were involuntarily relocated to various camps—ostensibly to protect the nation from sabotage and subversion.[6] Both cases are sorry social chapters in American history that reveal an inclination by the federal government to bypass the Fourth Amendment and other legislative guarantees of the Constitution and the Bill of Rights.[7] This bleak record is somewhat mitigated by other acts designed to encourage settlement of the land during the nineteenth century. The disposition of the public domain, culminating in the Morrill and the Homestead Acts of 1862, provided public lands to the states and to about 1,500,000 families. These Acts have been hailed by some as examples of American Democracy and social justice.[8] The Uniform Relocation Assistance and Real Properties Acquisition Policies Act of 1970, although not of the same nature or magnitude, can also be considered a positive landmark in the area of relocation legislation.[9]

The realization of social democracy and individual social development is therefore neither steady nor guaranteed as evidenced by the irregular development of relocation policies and programs of the federal government. Put another way, there has been no consistent, sustaining philosophy toward the goal of enlarging social justice via the legislative or administrative process affecting relocation.

The two themes—the increasing involvement of the state in society and the erratic, pragmatic mixed-model of social democracy—reflect an America in perpetual flux as it evolved from a frontier society into a rural society and then to an urban, technologically oriented nation. This increase in societal scale required changes in the nature of governmental intervention as well. In a frontier and rural milieu, broad "macro" policies of land acquisition and disposition, which included the removal of the Indians, served to "manifest the nation's destiny." But a disappearing frontier in an urbanizing industrial America modified the nature and scale of government interest in migration, mobility, and relocation. Eventually the increasingly complex level of society necessitated public intervention, including specific relocation programs and processes on a "micro" level. For example, the planned rural resettlement programs of the Resettlement Administration in the Department of Agriculture were initial "micro" responses to the depression of the 1930s. Program counterparts in urban areas included public housing and slum clearance, first under the Public Works Administration and the United States Housing Authority and later under the Housing and Home Finance Agency.

Trends in Relocation

Over the long term, the changing scale of societal problems require a more formal bureaucratic and interventionist organizational process. This is in response to the dilemmas created by an everincreasingly complex social environment.[10] The trend of such changes has been towards the gradual enhancement of social equity in the United States. It is suggested here that a continuation of the physical redevelopment of urban areas is inevitable. However, the rationalization and general acceptance of this process will be increasingly dependent upon the creation of socially oriented relocation models that support and enhance individual social development in new physical milieus.

Relocation and the New Deal

The original limited and rudimentary experimental approaches to planned relocation activities in rural and urban environments demonstrate the differing strengths and weaknesses of these early relocation systems. Although the New Deal rural resettlement programs originally tried to incorporate an enhanced social vision[11] as well as physical redevelopment activities, they failed in their basic objectives for relocating depression-struck farmers and city dwellers into rural subsistence homesteads. These programs were phased out because of philosophical objections by Congress to the communal life patterns espoused by key administrators of the Resettlement Administration. Furthermore, they did not produce a sufficient number of dwelling units to make a dent in relieving the living conditions of the poor. Finally, the onset of World War II required increased agricultural production and manpower, and these needs ran counter to the depression-born economic policies of limiting farm land and farm productivity. One commentator further notes that besides wartime reasons for the demise of the rural resettlement programs, another vital issue helped cause their termination: the conflict between the classic American portrayal of the rugged, individualistic farmer with his ethic of private land ownership versus the new view of a rural communal, cooperative lifestyle envisioned by some social scientist-administrators.[12] Even the Tennessee Valley Authority, generally acknowledged to be one of the most far-reaching and innovative economic and social experiments in America, failed to develop an effective social model for its relocation activities. Its avowed general goal of participatory democracy was little in evidence in the planning and physical redevelopment programs that required the relocation of families and businesses.[13]

The depression of the 1930s transformed the nature of federal intervention. Urban, as well as rural, economic and social programs were adopted to create new physical facilities and to encourage employment and individual security. Thus, the original conception of slum clearance and public housing had as one of its social objectives the elimination of those "breeding grounds for social problems" to be replaced by new dwellings to house the impoverished.[14] Relocation per se was not much of a public issue during this period since depression-induced dwelling vacancies in the large cities were sufficient to accommodate the displaced slum residents.[15]

Relocation Following World War II

The advent of World War II, which required the deployment of building materials from housing construction to war goods, also resulted in a shortage of dwelling units at the cessation of hostilities. Subsequently, a political alliance was brought together that included underhoused war veterans, economists fearing a postwar recession, public housing advocates, and politicians striving to develop strong urban constituencies. This coalition secured the passage of landmark urban redevelopment legistration, the Housing Act of 1949.[16]

This Act and especially Title I, which dealt with urban renewal activities, eventually formalized the relocation process. But the uniqueness of its processes and goals—combining public land acquisition with private and public redevelopment of cleared slum areas—contributed to a slow start for urban redevelopment programs. From this seminal beginning, relocation problems grew, slowly at first and then to a crescendo. This led to successive legislative attempts to grapple with the mounting protests of the new urban dispossessed, the relocatees. Relocation activities, originally considered a by-product of community building programs, nevertheless had a ripple effect adverse to the interests of all the impacted groups, particularly the small businessman, the elderly, and the black and white urban poor. These disparate groups were forced to give up their livelihoods, their homes, and their neighborhood communities for the benefit of the politically more powerful including large central city-oriented businesses and the upper and middle classes.

Social Protest and Government Response

The relocatees objected vociferously—so much so that in 1964 a special congressional investigating committee undertook an exhaustive study of their condition.[17] The protests were all part of the erupting social scene of the 1960s, and in their demand for greater social justice in American life,[18] the protestors descended in force on the relocation process. This social action finally led to the passage of the Uniform Relocation Assistance and Real Property Acquisition Policies Act of 1970, which codified the widely disparate and limited relocation benefits of various federal and federally aided programs. The Act also provided for a quantum increase in federal financial assistance to relocatees, mandated relocation planning studies, and required housing to be provided or developed by all agencies whose activities required the relocation of households.

Although the Uniform Relocation Assistance Act includes enlarged financial benefits, it does not address itself directly to many of the relocation problems, including the major social issues that forced its enactment in 1970. Before suggesting a transformation in current relocation concepts and practices, it is useful to consider the criticisms levelled at relocation programs during the past few years. In so doing, we can evaluate their validity and attempt to overcome the errors and omissions of the recent past. Thus, we shall consider problems such as the lack of adequate financial aid and business advice to small businessmen, inappropriate and inadequate housing resources for the elderly and poor, the effects of relocation programs on minority groups,[19] and the extent of social damage to relocatees and neighborhoods subject to the relocation process.[20] Administrative issues that will be reviewed include the adequacy of the data base along with several models of relocation organizations. We shall also consider the economic effects of displacement on the community and attempt to draw some conclusions relative to the benefits and costs of such programs.[21]

Transforming Relocation

Upon identifying the weaknesses of earlier relocation models, a comprehensive, transformed, relocation system may then be designed to provide essential social and housing programs as well as the financial resources required to meet the needs of the impacted peoples.[22] The social component would include education, good health, on-the-job training, and related social programs. Unless this transformation occurs, the relocation process will remain counterproductive as a vehicle for enhancing one's life opportunities, and it will still be regarded as the "Achilles heel" of physically oriented community development programs.

The aim of this study will be, therefore, to develop a relocation model planned to transform the present system to enable it to provide a full bundle of social services to meet the needs of the relocatees and the community. Such a model should be rigorously tested so as to evaluate and establish its effectiveness for enhancing the growth capabilities of the relocatee and thereby enriching the nation's social and human capital. An ancillary benefit would be a reduction in conflict and turbulence in our total environment. Planned relocation then becomes the instrument for enlarging the social and economic capital of relocatees. It does so by providing them with sufficient and necessary social, physical, and fiscal resources and services. Its goal is to be individual oriented— that is, to enable each person to join the mainstream of human endeavor through decent education, productive work, good health, and decent shelter, within a revitalized physical environment.

This author also posits that the above objectives are more readily achievable by providing for the early participation of locally impacted groups in decision-making processes regarding the selection of sites for community development and the nature of the bundle of social services needed to enhance earning capacities, lifestyles, and housing accommodations. By enlarging its scope, purposes, and focus, a planned relocation system can more fully benefit the individual by providing him the means for overcoming his environmental and social handicaps. This broadened social purpose also comes under the rubric previously noted: the increasing intervention of the state in the relocation process and the irregular but gradual expansion of social justice and equality in America.

Another policy consideration is the necessity for an overriding "Declaration of National Social Policy" by Congress as a touchstone for all governmental activities and programs designed to serve the citizenry. Unless this enlarged "macro" national social framework is proclaimed, many "micro" social programs, although conceived with the best of intentions, may fall short of fulfilling their goals for failure to fit within a declared federal social policy framework. And finally, community development programs must be designed so that the primary beneficiaries are the impacted groups as well as the rest of the community while the costs are redistributed equitably among all the polity. In this way, the relocation process can be transformed from "grief to gratification."

Part I:
The Dynamics of Natural
Relocation and Urban
Growth

1 Relocation in the Urban Context

The Pre-Industrial City

The evolution, growth, and changing functions of cities reflect the interrelationships between urban change and relocation as a natural process. This involves the free movement of individuals or groups of people from one area to another. Archeological evidence such as flints, flakes, and stone cores support the assumption that modern man's predecessors voluntarily relocated over several continents in search of congenial physical living environments during and after the Ice Age and into the Paleolithic period.[1]

Although it is not the purpose of this study to analyze in great detail these voluntary movements of prehistoric people and their successors, a brief review of this activity is useful in providing the necessary perspective for recognizing the possibilities of individual and group growth and fulfillment via planned relocation processes. It is suggested that an understanding of modern urban society is best characterized by a model of change and instability and these elements are rooted in the development of civilization itself.

Neolithic Cities

Neolithic villages of Western Europe, the Nile Valley, and those between the Tigris and Euphrates Rivers in Mesopotamia were among the earliest civilizations preceding pre-industrial, metal-using societies and cities.[a] These cultures appeared to have been formed on the basis of clanship as indicated by the worship of similar totemic images as the elephant and falcon by inhabitants of several adjoining villages. The establishment of new villages in close proximity to the original settlements is inferred by the discovery of similar stone artifacts near each other. The offspring of the residents of older villages apparently relocated to new communities nearby those from which they sprung. This phenomenon seems to be a recurring one in the relocation patterns of people.[2] Despite the ready availability of land, the size of these villages was probably no greater than one acre.[3]

From about 6000 to 3000 B.C., the nature of civilization underwent a series of major changes as man learned to use animal and wind power, invented the

[a]Although cultures also existed simultaneously in the Indus Valley, since they influenced Eastern rather than Western societies, they are not considered here.

3

plow, the wheel and sailboat, developed a solar calendar, and discovered the chemistry of smelting copper ores, all of which are preludes to an urban life. It appears reasonable to conclude that these burgeoning technologies led to the development of new transportation forms, which when coupled with the growth of communal organization, provided the basis for the urban revolution following the neolithic era.[4]

By 3000 B.C., the plains and valleys of the Middle East were hosts to three somewhat related regional civilizations: Sumerian, Egyptian, and Indian. Gordon Childe notes the development of the city as a centralized meeting place as a common characteristic of these early Bronze Age societies.[5]

In moving from prehistory to history, man shifted from a hunting and nomadic cave-dwelling existence, to either a land-rooted pastoral and communal village phase or a pastoral-nomadic economy, and then into an urban society that included agricultural, commercial, manufacturing, and communal activities.[6] Work became more organized, more group structured, and more ritualized. The accumulation of food surpluses apparently served to encourage population growth with the resulting diffusion of excess peoples into the surrounding areas. Technological improvements when joined with new forms of transportation encouraged emigration as well as the stimulation of trade. As the sail earlier opened the waterways to travel, so the wheel and cart now opened the landways.

There are several schools of thought concerning the reasons for the development of the early pre-industrial city. Gideon Sjoberg states that technology is the key independent variable since it requires and makes possible certain forms of activity—for example, population mobility, differentiation of population based on class, and the establishment of economic, social, and political power bases. Each city, however, developed along different lines, based upon its own cultural values, its early history, and its particular form of social and political power.[7]

Egyptian history records a flow of invasions, wars of conquest, the taking of slaves, and drafting of men for military service. Although Egypt was long unified under the Pharaohs (Thutmose III, who ruled about 1479 B.C., conquered Assyria, Canaan, (Palestine), Phoenicia, Syria, and the Hittite Kingdom), the Egyptian empire, like Mesopotamia thirteen years earlier, ended with the Persian invasion in 525 B.C.[8] Childe believes these Persian conquests were of great significance since they led to a pooling of population, knowledge, and experience, which thereby led to the development of cosmopolitan cities.[9]

Lewis Mumford theorizes that the neolithic village, with its cluster of from six to sixty families, served as a container for a civilization about to be born. The city began as a religious meeting place and served as a magnet for encouraging human intercourse to which people periodically returned. He suggests this early religious role is fundamental to the beginning of a city. The city as an economic center developed later.[10] The key to understanding the development of the city is not merely a change in its size and shape but, more importantly, a change in its purpose such as a transfer of priestly power from the village to the city.[11]

The preceding paragraphs describe the transition from prehistoric village societies to city civilizations in terms of changing technologies, territorial aggrandizement through colonization and warfare, and the interactions and interdependence of various peoples and forces for new and different purposes, all of which imply the concept of population mobility. This notion is further supported by the invention of the wheel, chariot, and sailboat. Sumerian art, dated at about 3000 B.C., shows a wheeled cart or chariot drawn by a horse or donkey. Egyptian drawings of sailboats navigating the Mediterranean are placed at about the same time.[12] Thus, the new forms of transportation were revolutionary changes that very likely served to accelerate the relocation of populations from place to place. This mobility was an essential factor in the growth and transition of the neolithic village to the early city.

Medieval Cities

That this natural relocation process was also extant in medieval cities is evidenced by their growth; during the tenth to the fourteenth centuries, 2,500 new cities were established by peaceful colonization throughout Germany alone. Other European cities—such as Paris—grew from 100,000 inhabitants at the end of the twelfth century to something like 240,000 by the end of the thirteenth, while Florence, which in 1280 had 45,000 inhabitants, increased to 90,000 by 1339.[13]

What led to the growth and development of the medieval city was a new found purpose—industrial activity—states Mumford. Processes—such as capital accumulation through banking, trade, mechanization of production, and new forms of business organization—when combined with the newly established guarantee of rights of personal freedom to former serfs—who had lived in a corporate town for at least a year and a day—resulted in a population explosion as villagers moved to the burgeoning cities. The grant of freedom and citizenship to these new migrants encouraged their individual mobility that had previously been denied them in their former status as serfs bound to the land. It may be concluded that "... town building itself was one of the major industrial enterprises of the Middle Ages."[14]

The pre-industrial city of the medieval period is identified by the development of trade as its economic mainstay and the social and political alliance of upper-class churchmen and noblemen. Class stratification became embedded in this society with an emphasis on birth and kinship as the major determinants of one's place in city life. Spatial segregation in the form of the ghetto and the location of trades in specific districts served to further rigidify city life in this time. Nonetheless, the city became the new mecca for the country folk, for it was here that one could gain freedom from serfdom and a life of unremitting and unrewarding agricultural toil. By serving as an apprentice in town, one could learn a trade in a small shop. Furthermore, military service could be avoided since a pledge of fealty to a noble was much more difficult to enforce in a typical bustling city or town with anywhere from 1,000 to 35,000 residents than in the countryside.[15] Thus, the combination of technological, political and social forces resulted in the growth of a new type of society—mobile rather than static, and aggressive rather than passive—and in some ways was an incubator for the industrial city to follow.

The Industrial City

The development of the industrial city was as significant a transformation in society as the change from the neolithic village to the medieval city. The phrase "Industrial Revolution" encapsulates this vast change. "A civilization based on the plough and the pasture perished—in its place stood a new order, resting, perhaps dangerously, on coal, iron and imported textile materials."[16] The population growth in England and Wales, exemplars of the Industrial Revolution, demonstrates the magnitude of this transformation. In 1801, their combined populations were 8,892,000, of which some 6,600,000 lived in rural areas with under 5,000 people, while 2,300,000 lived in towns and cities. By 1851, just fifty years later, total population had more than doubled to almost 18,000,000. While the rural areas grew half again as much to 9,900,000, the towns and cities quadrupled their size to about 8,000,000. By 1891, the total population had increased nearly 11,000,000 to 29,000,000. Rural places, however, decreased by approximately 700,000 to 9,200,000, whereas urban populations grew by almost two and one-half times to 19,800,000. During a ninety-year span encompassing the beginning and growth periods of the Industrial Revolution, about eighty percent of the population increase in England and Wales occurred in cities and towns.[17]

The rapid growth of urban populations is a concomitant of societies in transformation from craft and trading centers to industrial communities. For example, in the nineteenth century, sailings from Europe to the United States, which was entering its industrial era, brought in some 35,000,000 immigrants in little more than one hundred years, which constitutes the largest voluntary relocation of peoples in history.[18] Table 1-1 illustrates the percentage redistribution of labor from agricultural activities to manufacturing trades and other pursuits in England and the United States during a one hundred-year span of industrialization.

The voluntary movement of populations was accompanied by the phenomenon of urbanization as exemplified by the adoption of industrial processes throughout many areas. In Europe, cities moved beyond their medieval walls to incorporate the surrounding countryside. In walless America, this movement took the form of the birth of cities devoted to the new manufacturing activities. In England, the growth of Birmingham, Wolverhampton, York, Leeds, and Liverpool resulted in the enlargement of their original boundaries to include

Table 1-1

Percentage Labor Distribution Patterns, United States and England, Industrialization Period

	England		United States	
Activity	1801	1901	1820	1900
Agriculture	35.9	8.7	71.8	36.8
Manufacturing and Trades	29.7	46.5	12.2	21.8
"Other"	34.4	44.8	16.0	41.4
Total	100%	100%	100%	100%

Source: J.R.T. Hughes, "Industrialization—Economic Aspects," *International Encyclopedia of Social Sciences*, Vol. 7 (New York: Crowell, Collier and Macmillan, 1968), p. 257.

their suburban areas, while in the United States, the Industrial Revolution spawned new cities such as Cincinnati, Columbus, Chicago, Indianapolis, and Detroit.[19]

Tremendous population increments resulting from migration, increased life spans, and increases in fertility were some quantitative indicators associated with industrialization, but equally important was a qualitative change in man's response to his new urban environment. What emerged was the development of urbane man—a pragmatic, cosmopolitan, and rational individual, receptive to risk-taking and change and interested in the pursuit of money and wealth. The birth of the industrial city was coupled with the birth of economic man who replaced his sackcloth of neotechnic and medieval divination and mysticism with the gown of talent, technology, and science.

Unfortunately, there is no one elegant theory to explain the reasons for the Industrial Revolution. For purposes of this study, none is needed. Its significance here is in its existence and its effects on urban places in the United States. The Industrial Revolution not only spawned a new man and a new spatial city configuration clustered about an industrial core, but a host of social relationships and problems: the quantum demographic growth resulting from increased birth rates and life spans; the surplus of farm labor due to the mechanization of agriculture; city growth and change related to the technologies of the Industrial Revolution, which created particular spatial patterns and demands for labor; and the intensification and identification of social problems among those people who, in their quest for economic betterment, moved from closed village and folk societies into more open and alien urban industrial milieus. The transformation from rural to industrial societies in many parts of the world has unleashed the processes of natural relocation on a scale heretofore unknown to early agrarian societies and the commercial and trading cities of the Medieval period. Some would say that we have already moved beyond the Industrial City and that we are spawning still another urban lifestyle and form.

The Post-Industrial City

Several writers suggest that during the past thirty years American society has changed from a mechanical/electrical industrial base to a more intellectually demanding technological form. Electronics, cybernetics, atomic energy, and advanced forms of communications and knowledge transfers have, in short, modified our nation from a blue- to a white-collar society. If this is so, how does this new technological society affect American cities and influence their processes of growth, change, and population mobility?

Daniel Bell begins an essay by stating: "The post-industrial society is a society in which business is no longer the predominant element but one in which the intellectual is predominant."[20] He cites three elements that are leading towards a transformation of society: (1) the exponential growth in science, (2) the growth of the intellectual technology, and (3) the growth of research and development activities.[21]

Peter Drucker, in *The Age of Discontinuity*, talks of the revolution of our times in four areas: (1) genuinely new technologies, (2) development of a world economy, (3) creation of a new pluralistic, institutional society, and most importantly, (4) knowledge as the crucial resource of the economy.[22]

Victor Ferkiss says esoterically, "To the Stars!", for "today after uncountable millenia of existence bound to the surface of the planet we call earth, humanity is taking its first feeble steps toward the conquest of outer space."[23]

While some analysts fantasize about future man-machines, or "cyborgs," Zbigniew Brezezinski offers a somewhat more sober interpretation: "the transformation that is now taking place, especially in America is already creating a society increasingly unlike its industrial predecessor. The post-industrial society is becoming a 'technotronic' society; a society that is shaped culturally, psychologically, socially, and economically by the impact of technology and electronics—particularly in the area of computers and communications."[24]

Moon flights, TV satellites, computer technology, missile warfare, the ability to alter the biological and mental composition of man, and the substitution of communications for physical work as the foundation of the technical system are some current indicators of society's seeming move toward its third major technological revolution.[b] A concomitant social and economic revolution may also be discerned. According to Charles Reich, this social transformation is a "... movement to bring man's thinking, his society, and his life to terms with the revolution of technology and science that has already taken place. . . . At the heart of everything is what we shall call a change of consciousness . . . [which]

---

[b]According to Childe, the first revolution occurred between 6000 B.C. and 3000 B.C., with the invention of the plow, wheel, sailboat, solar calendar, and copper smelting; the second was the Industrial Revolution. See V. Gordon Childe, *Man Makes Himself* (New York: Mentor Books, 1951), pp. 37-42.

seeks a new knowledge of what it means to be human, in order that the machine having been built, may now be turned to human ends, in order that man once more can become a creative force, reviewing and creating his own life and thus giving back life to his society."[25]

A restricted interpretation of Reich's thesis—the evident frustration and discontent of various social groups with the social rigidities and economic inequities of present American society—is well taken. The rhetoric of social revolution led to a crescendo of violence and flames in America's cities in the mid- and late-1960s. Blacks vented their pent-up hostilities against what they perceived to be an unyielding white industrial society. They, along with students, protested against an unresponsive "establishment" that refused to equitably share economic and social benefits and instead maintained segregation in housing and schools and discrimination in employment and education.[26]

The present era furnishes additional evidence of significant social economic and demographic changes, including the tremendous worldwide population explosion, the relocation of peoples from rural to urban areas, the development of "Megalopolis" along the eastern seaboard of the United States and possibly elsewhere here and abroad. Furthermore, the simultaneous urbanization and metropolitanization movements continue to transform the social, ethnic, political and economic mixes of America's cities. Perhaps the most important feature of our present society and its "Megalopoli" is not the increase in the physical area, but rather the vast number of inhabitants and the intensive use to which they put the land, and the constant churning and internal movement of people and industries within the regions.[27]

A highly significant note is struck in one study concerning the issue of ethnic distribution in America. By 1985, ". . . although there would be some decentralization of nonwhite population within SMSAs, 75 percent of all nonwhites in metropolitan areas will still be residing in central cities and only 25 percent in the suburbs," thereby resulting in an increasingly ethnically stratified society now reinforced by geographic as well as social and economic separation.[28]

Another element of the change affecting cities is the nature of their economic "mix." The central cities are losing their relative and absolute position as metropolitan magnets. They are no longer the place for almost everybody and, as is generally known, have yielded much of their earlier, unrivalled predominance as retail, wholesale, manufacturing, and population centers to the suburbs. Many secondary and tertiary activities—such as processing, manufacturing, wholesaling, and research and development—are performed just as satisfactorily in the suburban ring, although some cities are expanding in such tertiary functions as banking and finance, government activities, real estate and insurance, advertising, and law. They are also serving as the "front offices" for major industries and businesses.[29] According to *The New York Times*, the patterns of resettlement to the suburbs "...are reflections of an 'outward movement' in this century that ranks in importance with the Westward movement of the last."[30]

In many respects, the changing population and economic patterns described above have had serious consequences for the cities. A declining white, middle-class base is being replaced by an increasing nonwhite population handicapped by economic, educational, and social disparities. This has resulted in polarizing the social classes in the cities as the latter groups push for a larger share of a smaller economic and political pie. Although the newcomers require more public services, the economic base of the cities is declining, which has resulted in an erosion of the ability of cities to provide responsive public services and suitable physical plants.[31] Besides the negative social, economic, and physical impact on cities, the increasing polarization of the races negates the democratic credo of equal opportunity for all,[32] for the largely white suburbs are increasingly the places where new jobs are to be found. Thus, a major function of the American city—post-industrial or otherwise—as an environment for individual growth and economic betterment through an enhancement of the social processes, is now vitiated by the scarcity of economic resources.

Summary

The preceding analysis of various societies reveals several interrelated phenomena as we move from the industrial age into the post-industrial society. Sjoberg, in analyzing earlier cities, points to new forms of transportation, which, when coupled with the growth of society, served to accelerate the urban revolution following the neolithic period. Mumford offers another approach: changing needs bring forth more complex forms of society. The more complex the technology of a specific society, the more complex are its social processes, including government intervention. Thus, the degree of sophistication of voluntary and planned relocation processes reflect the relationship between the level of technology and social progress.

Accordingly, the changing scale of society leads to changes in the nature of man's relationship in society. (This theme will be discussed more fully later.) The changing role of the state, therefore, is accompanied by its assumption of increased responsibility and its institutionalization of authority. The interdependence of the growth of technology and the increase in societal scale and social processes, including government intervention, is shown in Figure 1-1.

This interrelated growth process is evident in the descriptions of the characteristics of the various periods in the development of Western society, and it is reasonable to suggest that as we enter the post-industrial era, the heretofore relatively simplistic nature of amorphous, voluntary, and planned relocation programs of the industrial era will be replaced by more sophisticated relocation systems. These new systems will incorporate the provision of opportunities for individual fulfillment through social development and social justice as an integral function of the process.

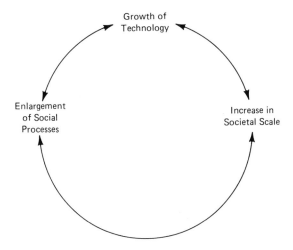

Figure 1-1. Interrelated Growth Processes.

2 Theories of Urban Growth

Ecological Views of the City

Urban growth processes may be considered one of the components of the broader process of social change. This view is expressed by Eric Lampard who defines urbanization ". . . as a process of population concentration that results in an increase in the number and size of cities and social change as an incremental or arhythmic alteration in the routines and sequences of everyday life in human communities."[1] The urbanization of society as a manifestation of social change is implicit, while social change is a modification of the stable elements of life-sustaining systems in societies. In this context, urbanization is viewed as a dynamic process.

Lampard goes on to say that there is no single approach to explain urbanization but suggests three fruitful salients: the demographic, the structural, and the behavioral. The first deals with population growth and its distribution in space; the second, with the organization of communities and society; and the third, with the conduct of individuals. But Lampard also states: "The broadened perspectives on urbanization and social change . . . form no more than a partial framework of explanation."[2] Accordingly, other typologies are possible within the dynamics of urbanization including the ecological, demographic, and work and life processes with their concomitants of growth and change.

Amos Hawley defines human ecology ". . . as the study of the form and the development of the community in human population."[3] Although he recognizes a close relationship between human ecology and demography, he draws a distinction between the two; the former discipline concerns itself with qualitative relationships whereas the latter deals with quantitative ones.[4]

In considering work and life processes, we are dealing with essentially aspatial approaches to urban places that transcend the limits of land-bound physical processes. These include such sociological phenomena as social stratification and social mobility, the use of communications that supersede the narrow confines of present political and geographic boundaries, planning theories regarding communities of interest, and the economics of urban regions. These processes have as their unifying theme the notion of change and its derivative, the process of mobility or natural relocation. They are representative rather than inclusive and serve to demonstrate the nature of urban change and mobility. Although some of the theories are limited by their lack of general applicability, this problem is secondary to our major purpose, which is to indicate the universality

13

of natural relocation processes and to derive some insights for use in planned relocation systems.

According to Robert E. Park, primary instruments in the ecological organization of the city include the means for transportation and communication, such as trolley cars, elevated lines, and telephones, as well as newspapers and elevators. As he sees it, the city is "... a kind of psychophysical mechanism," through which public and private interests find expression.[5] He conveys a sense of mobility, dynamism, strength, and intensity, which are all characteristics associated with the Chicago he analyzes. He also asks questions about its people: where they come from, how they reproduce themselves, the proportion of native and foreign stock, their natural areas of abode, and whether the population is increasing or declining in the neighborhoods. To this point, his concern is primarily demographic. He is very much aware of the continual movement and instability of certain natural areas or neighborhoods that shelter floating populations of nomads, hoboes, gypsies, and people who rent or live in hotels. Still other areas provide too much isolation, such as the ethnic ghettos that serve to intensify racial prejudice and class interests.[6]

Park concludes that industrial organization has a collateral effect of increasing the mobility of the population. Under the conditions created by city living, the laborer and artisan are "... compelled to move from one region to another in search of the particular kind of employment which they are fitted to perform."[7] This compulsory movement for laborers and artisans is in contrast to the movement of the tradesman, manufacturer, or professional man, who seek out their clients over an increasingly broad geographic area as travel and communication become more common. He then enlarges the concept of mobility beyond its physical or social connotation to include an intellectual facet, namely, communication. The ability to read and write, to use money and to achieve a college education, he says, may result in increasing one's mobility.[8] One may say that Park views the city as a laboratory for collective behavior that includes physical and intellectual mobility as two of its basic ingredients.

Another early ecologist, Ernest W. Burgess, considers the phenomenon of city growth beyond the original political boundaries.[9] He identifies a series of "successive zones" or concentric circles surrounding a central city core. This ideal construct begins with the central business district of "The Loop" (I), the place from which the city expands radially. Surrounding the "Loop" is an area in transition—the Zone in Transition (II)—which is under invasion by business and light manufacturing. The next ring is the Zone of Workingmen's Homes (III), occupied by those who have escaped from the deteriorating transitional area. Beyond the worker's quarters, there is the high-class apartment house or "restricted" single-family home areas of the Residential Zone (IV). And finally, past the Residential Zone there is the Commuters' Zone (V), or the suburban areas surrounding the city.[10] Urban expansion, he states, is the result of the tendency of each zone to expand its boundaries by "invasion" of the next zone through a process of succession. In addition to these outward movements of activities and people, he identifies the processes of concentration and decentralization with the former exemplified by the convergence of transportation into the core of the city, and the latter by peripherally located satellite shopping centers.

Burgess views the city essentially as a growing organism that continually "... sifts and sorts and relocates individuals and groups by residence and occupation ... " into natural areas such as the "mainstem," "hobohemia," Little Italy, Chinatown, and the Black Belt. He identifies such growth as a result of the invasion of the city by immigrants along with concurrent internal movements that speed up expansion, industrial growth, and slum formations.[11] The voluntary migration of people and their subsequent relocation activities from one zone to another is viewed by Burgess as a natural process of organic expansion of the city. He further attributes to the city such vital characteristics including change, movement, decay, and growth in a continuing, cyclical process.[12] Although the Concentric Circle theory has been subject to serious criticism, the interest here lies not in its reliability or universality but in its use of concepts such as urban growth and neighborhood change.[13]

One of the later challenges to the Concentric Circle theory is Homer Hoyt's Sector theory. This work attempts certain generalizations about city structure and growth in terms of the arrangement of land uses and residential neighborhoods.[14] Hoyt explains that occupancy patterns are formed by residential districts on the basis of rent differentials. His study of 142 cities reveals a hierarchy of rents ranging from the highest near the city's periphery to the lowest in the slums and forming no solid geometric patterns. In many cities a pyramid exists within a few blocks; the apex forms where the highest rental area is located, and the rents of all the other blocks slope downward. Apparently each income group tries to get as close as possible to the next higher group in the economic scale.[15] Through the use of maps that trace the locations of fashionable neighborhoods over time in several cities, Hoyt develops his basic concept of neighborhood growth; the sequential location of the various rent districts in a city is in accordance with a definite pattern. This movement is best understood by visualizing the city as a circle with radial lines emanating from its core. The various rent sectors spread along these radii until they reach the arc of the circle at the edge of the city. The high rent district serves as a magnet in its ability to attract the growth of the city in its direction. The highest income group generally moves to the outskirts of the city from its origin near the retail and office center, and since this group is the pole or center of attraction, it pulls the other income groups towards it.

The assumption underlying the Sector Theory is that the process of city growth and population movement can be identified according to a specific pattern that is governed by the locational pull of high-rent districts. This theory has been criticized for being too simplistic in its undue consideration of the role of the upper class as the catalytic force in urban development and its narrow social perspective regarding the needs, desires, and roles of other groups in society.[16] Nonetheless, it does describe the dynamic, mobile processes of city life and the natural push of population toward new places. Does this dynamic concept apply to other areas such as ghettoes?

Two ghetto studies will be considered to determine the degree to which they are characterized by social and population mobility and social change. The use here of the term ghetto applies to a specific cultural settlement, which over the course of time through a natural process of voluntary selection, has attracted a specific cultural or ethnic group.[17] It is an adjustment mechanism for immigrant peoples. Louis Wirth states the American ghetto serves three major purposes: (1) as a means of accommodation between different populations in which an alien group subordinates itself to the larger society, (2) as a form of toleration or *modus vivendi* between conflicting groups, and (3) as an administrative instrument of control.[18]

Wirth's study of Jewish immigration to Chicago is a chronicle of the different social and residence patterns of the Jews according to the time of their arrival, the form of Judaism practiced (Orthodox, Conservative, Reform), and their economic and social status.[19] The first Jews settled primarily in the "Loop." As a result of the Chicago fire in 1871, many of these Jews were forced to move to the West Side of the city. This area was later sought out by Jewish immigrant— victims of the Russian pogroms of 1882—which thus increased the density and size of the West Side ghetto. By the time of World War I, the occupancy of this ghetto had changed to a non-Jewish area as new Jewish settlements, indicative of a newly achieved social status, were established in high-class residential districts on the outskirts of the city.[20]

The significance of the ghetto, according to Wirth, is its attraction to people of like economic status and cultural background who come into a strange and often hostile environment: ". . . each seeks his own habitat much like the plants and animals in the world of nature, [but] . . . human beings are more mobile, and through locomotion can seek those areas in which they can most satisfactorily gratify their fundamental interests and wishes."[21] Even within the unwalled bounds of America's cultural ghettos, there seems to be a constant sorting, sifting, and segregating of peoples based upon similar economic resources and social and cultural likenesses.

Boston's West End was characterized by Herbert Gans as an urban village: a low-rent district in which population patterns changed over a period of generations, from Yankee to Irish, to Jewish, and then to largely first- and second-generation Italian occupants. The Italians came as families during the 1930s, and their children, upon marriage, remained in the area because it was a close-knit social community that was also convenient and economic. "In any case," states Gans, "almost all of the West Enders came to the area as part of a group."[22] The continued physical presence of second-generation Italians in the area was largely dependent upon their rejection of middle-class lifestyles, their low opinion of suburbia, a disregard for college education and white-collar employment, a rejection of the culture of the middle class, and their strong need for the kind of social reinforcement found only among one's peers and relatives.

According to Gans, the relative lack of social and spatial mobility among the residents of the West End was related to the desire of this group to transmit and maintain a lifestyle that rejected middle-class, object-oriented relationships in favor of an interpersonal, peer-oriented society. Despite their self-imposed limited social and economic mobility, Gans expects that over the years there will be an increase in their mobility as more and more of the younger generations seek out the differing cultures in a pluralistic society.[23]

These two studies of ghetto life suggest that the rates of social and physical mobility are dependent upon the desires and abilities of the group and the individual to break from the ghetto confines.[24] Most interestingly, they do not picture the ghetto as a permanent, monolithic society, but as one that is subject to change over a period of years. Thus, the forces of the outside world impinge on ghetto life and cause ruptures and fissures within the sheltered environment.

R.D. McKenzie also utilizes the ecological approach toward cities and likens their growth processes to that of plant ecology as they evolve from the general to the particular. Not only is there population growth, but with it there occurs a process of differentiation and segregation. Residences and institutions move centrifugally, away from a central location, while business responds in a centripetal movement around the point of highest land values. As a community grows in successional sequences to about ten or twelve thousand, its structural growth becomes fairly well differentiated. "And just as in plant communities successions are the products of invasions, so also in the human community the formations, segregations, and associations that appear constitute the outcome of a series of invasions."[25]

McKenzie next classifies neighborhood invasions by three stages: (1) the initial stage, which reflects an advance in land values along with a decrease in the value of the buildings that may be put to a parasitic use such as for vice, (2) the secondary or developmental stage, in which old uses and businesses compete fiercely with the invaders (as the process continues, similar types of business invaders cluster to form their own market, e.g., used car dealers, financial districts), and (3) the climax stage, in which the dominant type of ecological organization emerges, capable of withstanding an invasion from others. The end result is the formation of natural areas of the city.[26]

These various ecological constructs of city development, growth, and change share one element in common: the physical mobility of groups or individuals. These theories have only partial validity to the degree that a city limits the voluntary mobility of a minority group either through legislation or by custom. Significantly, however, their major focus is on neighborhood change as a natural process of community development that is closely akin to the cyclical, rhythmic changes found in nature. Even the most stable neighborhoods are subject to population changes over a period of years as life values and lifestyles are modified. Thus, what one sees at any point in time is but a snapshot of a continuing process of neighborhood birth, growth and maturation, and senescence.[27]

Demography and Urban Growth

Demography is concerned with fertility, mortality, family formation, and migration as indices of change and mobility in society. Its basic tools are census data and registration data based upon recordings of births, deaths, and marriages.[28] Because of the varied uses for this subject matter, it serves primarily as a handmaiden for sociologists and social scientists. There are some who broaden its concerns beyond the measurement of physical movement to include social movement as well.[29] Although the consideration of social mobility is not included in most demographic studies, this is merely a matter of convention.[30]

Of greater moment to this analysis than the definitional scope of the demographic discipline is that both spatial and social mobility include such concepts that apply to natural relocation processes as:

1. Migratory pushes, pulls, and economic opportunities. These are evidenced by the centrifugal movement of job-seeking immigrants into cities and the centripetal, outward flow of space-seeking populations to the suburbs.
2. Intervening opportunities. In this hypothesis, the number of persons willing to travel a given distance is directly proportional to the percentage increase in job or other opportunities at that distance.
3. Reverse migration. This concept embodies theories relating to the return of emigrés to their home base.
4. Selective migration. People move according to individual social characteristics such as age, sex, or family status.
5. The exhaustion of pools of potential migrants.
6. The distinction between migration and residential mobility. Migration applies to population movements between different geographic and political areas while mobility refers to intracommunity movements.[31]

These quantifiable concepts are all indicators of natural population movements. While numerous studies on migration could be cited to demonstrate the interrelatedness of that subject and natural relocation processes, the following observations are based on one demographic study that serves as a surrogate for others of a somewhat similar nature.

Amos Hawley, in an analysis of physical mobility in metropolitan areas in the United States, concludes that around 1900 the population growth in the country's central cities started to decline as compared to the suburban areas because the cities were no longer capable of serving as "population pulls." He also theorizes that maturation of urban areas is a requisite for the later settlement and expansion of adjoining suburban areas. Starting in the 1920s, the reductions in the growth rate of the larger cities reflects both the decrease in foreign immigration, which resulted from restrictive federal legislation, and the dispersal of population, which was aided by the expansion of the highway system and the use of automobiles, to increasingly accessible geographic areas in a ten to a thirty-five mile radius around core cities. Nevertheless, the overall growth of urban population, whether in core cities or suburbs, was at the expense of rural areas, which is ". . . one of the most conspicuous features of the population movement in the United States in the first half of the twentieth century."[32]

Another characteristic of spatial mobility is the deconcentration of manufacturing cities as a result of the greater inclination of factories to locate outside central cities sooner than other types of industries and businesses. Hawley concludes that there is some relationship between industrial movement and the relocation of the metropolitan population from the core to the interstices and the periphery.[33] The policy implications of population shifts and changes in the ethnic make-up of cities and suburban areas were discussed previously. We note here that demographic data provide much of the necessary technical support for decisions involving public planning and policy.

In addition to a physical or spatial connotation, mobility has a social connotation. As mentioned previously, social mobility can be viewed as a change in social status that may be evinced from descriptive evaluations or from statistical data concerned with occupation, education, and income. The "rags to riches" Horatio Alger stereotype of the 1890s has been replaced by the "upward mobiles" of the present era, or by those who have reacted positively to opportunities for self-advancement available to them in a bureaucratic milieu and have succeeded.[34]

The concepts of social stratification and social mobility merit some attention here for they too function as indicators of growth and change in society. Social status is achieved by a combination of personal factors that are convertible into economic assets. These in turn may cause one to move from one place to another, and, under these conditions, may be considered as another component of urban change.

The technique of social areas analysis developed by Eshref Shevky and Wendell Bell includes both an index for social rank that is based upon occupation, means of schooling, and rent paid and an urbanization index that measures the degree of fertility, the number of working women, and the number of single-family dwelling units in an area under study.[35] Without considering here the validity of the Shevky-Bell analysis, we can summarize their work on the basis of its merits as a tool for describing and comparing areas of a city or regions of a country at a specific point in time and for evaluating changes over successive periods in social status in such areas.

In viewing the city or urban place as an area of growth and change, demographic concepts such as physical mobility and population changes tend to support the view of urban environments as dynamic and changing locales. Social concepts of status, mobility and stratification are indirect indicators of change. Combined with studies of population and places, they provide some understanding of the kaleidoscopic nature of our urban milieu.

Work and Life Processes

So far the city has been viewed as a physical entity that is circumscribed by a given size, shape, density, and population and is located within a politically bounded space and bounded facilities. We now add another dimension to this emphasis on spatiality and location—process—thereby demonstrating the declining importance of politically bounded city space as the major critical element in urban society.[36]

Some students of urban affairs today consider the urban region as the only viable physical entity for dealing with physical and communal processes. They are concerned with understanding how certain activities and processes take place and how they work. Mobile *flows* of people, information, boundaries, income, and commodities, for example, replace fixed *stocks* of buildings, goods, and wealth as shapers of opportunity and growth. "Our new perspective is helping to distinguish the urban subsystems by their social and economic functions—by the roles they play and the purposes they serve—rather than to define them merely by their locations or by their administrative organization."[37] Each subsystem is open to the flows of information, money, and goods from other subsystems on which it depends. This new approach contains two important implications: the view of a city as an open economic and social system transcending politically delimiting boundaries to encompass an urban region or field, and the mobility of events, activities, and flows that, in turn, galvanize people to change their residences. Now for some, the residence as a nesting place has been replaced by the residence as a way station; a place of allegiance has been replaced by one of convenience.

In the "Post-City Age,"[38] Melvin M. Webber says that the social processes of urbanization are freeing us from the locationally fixed city and region. No longer do urban dwellers live only in cities and rural people in the hinterlands. Instead, he sees an urban society that is replacing the geographic city. The new turf is the nation, supplanting the neighborhood, the city, and the region, since territoriality is no longer a necessary condition in the post-city age. This is so because of the creation of a new social class who trade in information and ideas that cut across political boundaries. This highly educated intellectual elite is comprised of businessmen, educators, scientists, political leaders, and the like, who are the new cosmopolites concerned with esoteric specialities. Their attachment to a specific place is limited since they belong to a series of world cities or realm spaces that are interconnected by networks of communications and their own system of shared values. To these purveyors of information and ideas, the city functions as ". . . a massive communication's switchboard through which human interaction takes place."[39] In this view, the place-oriented community is replaced by the interest community that cannot be defined by area. This "non-place" is the urban realm that is ". . . neither an urban settlement nor territory, but heterogeneous groups of people communicating with each other through space."[40] It is this kind of interaction that is the essence of city life today, rather than the accident of location or place, states Webber.[41]

Richard Meier postulates a communications theory that relies upon the use of time and transactions as new social indicators and as a means for defining city growth and change.[42] He describes an urban time budget that establishes the proportion of time urban residents spend in various activities such as working, attending school, travelling, reading, playing, taking care of personal services, and sleeping. The variety of the activities and the time spent in performing them yields an index of urbanity.[43] Total time spent per public social activity is shown to be highest in urban places, which leads Meier to conclude that the most urbane communities support a wider range of human activities than others. Meier is also concerned with human transactions and their frequency. Each transfer of information, by telephone, letter, or direct mail advertising, becomes a completed transaction from the sender to the receiver. Since cities evolved primarily to facilitate human communication, an increase in the transfer of images is characteristic of urban growth.[44] Meier's picture of the metropolis is a stream of action sustained by a type of population he considers to be assets—that is, those who are self-motivating, self-maintaining, and self-repairing—for, he says, the competition among metropoli is to recruit the young with talent who demand rich cultural and innovating, communications-oriented environments.[45] This theoretical approach posits a society in motion—electronic and physical—in which a city's survival is related to its ability to increase its communication transactions and its capability for attracting young elites from other places as well as permitting it to hold on to its own. These esoteric and stimulating approaches toward mobility are followed by more conventional views of this construct.

The concept of a Standard Metropolitan Statistical Area is tacit recognition that the present American city is no longer the key geographic area but is a node in a region with a continual flow and enhancement of people, information, and commodities. The older cities, along with their outer cores or peripheries, comprise the new spatial units or "urban fields" of post-industrial America. This view incorporates a broadened spatial or physical area, increasingly drawn together by technology, economics, shared interests, and a shared environment.

This fusion encapsulates a minimum population of 300,000 within a travel time of two hours from the core city to its circumference. The interstices along the eastern shores still have space, scenery, and settlements that hark back to colonial village societies with their rich lode of rural folkways, but people with more money, more time, and more mobility are creating a demand for such areas as places for second homes and weekend recreational spas.[46]

The sense of population fluidity portrayed thus far has its counterpart in the institutions of government as well. Shifting populations result in shifting service demands as administrators are forced to find new ways to meet the pressures for more effective public sector performance. The metropolitan area, as a homogeneous public service area, is slowly becoming more of an administrative reality. The more urbanized the area, the greater the apparent need and demand for some functions and processes that extend beyond local political boundaries. Illustrative cases abound as political theory yields to administrative practice.

General and special service units of government have been established to meet the needs of the residents of metropolitan areas. One example of general services is found in the Lakewood Plan whereby Los Angeles County serves as a contractor to neighboring towns and villages for a package public services including police, fire, libraries, and the like. Another is the area of Metropolitan Toronto, a federation of thirteen local governments recently incorporated into a centralized Municipality of Metropolitan Toronto, in which public functions and services are shared by the local communities.[47] In Indiana, the consolidation of Indianapolis and Merian County ("Unigov") in 1969 created a new metropolitan entity of 820,000.[48] Special-purpose authorities are adaptive approaches designed to meet the demands for service occasioned by population shifts within metropolitan areas. According to York Willbern, "most Americans are in reality members of many overlapping communities. . . . This is a mobile, shifting society . . . and a man is as likely to put down roots in a corporation or a profession as in a locality."[49] His concluding sentence is the capstone to this interpretation of organizational response to urban change: "As we adapt our institutions to our changing styles of life it seems likely that both the sense of community and the government arrangements for communities will become more fluid and more diverse than they have been in the past."[50]

Economics provides still another approach to the city as a process, especially that aspect concerned with issues of growth. Macroeconomics is the study of the total activity of an economic society and its participants.[51] One of the tools is the economic base analysis that attempts to explain what share of a national product a given community produces and whether this share is increasing, is stable, or is decreasing. This is useful in understanding the relationship and interdependence of the local economic system to the national system. Since population flows are related to the economic activity and the growth of an urban area or city, a study of the direction of a community's economic base can serve as an indicator of local urban change and population mobility.

Whether one views the city spatially and organically as do sociologists, or as a geographic area for purposes of studying various population movements as do the demographers, or as a bounded or nonbounded work and life process as conceived by some planners and social scientists, each of these approaches assumes the voluntary, unplanned, continual movement of people in dynamic urban environments as compared to the relatively static nature of rural environments. More recent studies of the urban realm—such as those emphasizing communications theory, the metropolitan region, metropolitan government, and economic base theory—also share this viewpoint of our urban society as one containing a highly mobile, fluid population not necessarily bounded by space. Thus, political and historic geographic divisions become less meaningful as people acquire greater physical and social motive power. New means of transportation and communications and new political and administrative structures are overcoming the limitations of fixed social and political traditions. An increasingly urbanized country tends to encourage and support the natural relocation processes of freely moving people who are the most essential element in our mutable society. Furthermore, as several commentators have pointed out, increasing state intervention in the natural processes of population movement appears to be an inevitable concomitant of urbanization and the changing scale of society.

The Role of the State

The changing role of the state as society moves from natural to planned relocation processes has its analogues in the works of several sociologists. Ferdinand Tönnies' notion of the dichotomy between community and society and Max Weber's analysis of charismatic and bureaucratic authority are two such antecedents. Another is Park's analysis of "primary" and "secondary" social relationships in which he concludes that the element of social control, originally dependent upon communal mores or informal restraints, is replaced by formal, positive law in a city environment. Wirth states that one effect of urbanization is the change from "primary" to "secondary" societal relationships, while Scott Greer notes that the transformation of societal processes towards more formal organizational patterns results from the dynamics of an increase in scale.

Tönnies defines *Gemeinschaft* as "community" or fellowship among a small clan or kinship group in which the blood bonds or ties are primary, which results in an integrated value system. Social organizations evolved from these natural relationships of mutual dependence of a folk, tribal, or agrarian civilization. The individual is affirmed through his role in the social organization or group. As the necessity for a common defense and peacekeeping grew, people not related by blood who assembled in the towns and villages required the formation of a political community either under the rule of a lord or as a group of independent citizens with equal rights. In this way, the town or village was transformed into a state.[52]

Tönnies then goes on to say that in an evolving capitalistic environment, this heterogeneous, burgeoning group developed a new social form or characteristic that was based upon individual, impersonal, and socially differentiated values. This new phenomenon, which replaced the original closely related group, is known as *Gesellschaft*, or "society," which is identified by its cosmopolitan, impersonal, and urbane attitudes. Under these conditions self-interest replaces communal interest; individualism supplants collectivism. The affirmation of each person's existence through the reciprocity of rights and duties in a "community" is replaced by the impersonality of the exchange of goods and services in a "society," which thereby requires more and more people to turn to the state as the means for bettering their condition. The state replaces the group as the instrument for attaining honor and status and for insuring the protection of its citizens.[53]

Weber views the progression of authority from a charismatic to a bureaucratic form as part of an erratic societal process leading towards the rationalization of historic trends. He defines charisma, meaning literally "gift of grace," as a characteristic of self-appointed leaders who are found qualified to lead those in distress. He views such prophets, with their direct and personal relationships with others, as truly revolutionary forces in history. Subsequently, there occurs among the original participants a cooling-off of this extraordinary condition of faith and fervor that is followed by the routinization of activities. In this way, charisma is transformed into an impersonal bureaucracy. This institutionalization of power and authority is characterized by the elaboration and standardization of statuses and roles, the definition of well-defined rights, obligations, and duties, and the codification of procedures and processes.[54]

Park strikes off at a different angle. He conceives the city as the focal point for commerce, which encourages people of diverse talents and skills to migrate there. This agglomeration of individual talents modifies the earlier society, which was based on culture, caste, and status, and substitutes a new order exemplified by such economic characteristics as occupation and vocation. Guilds or labor unions, which are then established on the basis of common work or trade interests, differ from the earlier associations that were based on kinship or neighborhood. The solidarity of industrial organizations depends upon a community of economic interests rather than sentiment and habit. Changes in the nature of organization and in the distribution of population result in changes in the nature and character of urban population, as evidenced by the substitution of indirect for direct social relations in the associations of individuals in the community. "... [W]here thousands of people live side by side for years without so much as a bowing acquaintance, these intimate relationships of the primary group are weakened and the moral order which rested upon them is gradually dissolved."[55] Under such circumstances, social control among diverse populations becomes exceedingly difficult. Restraints previously based on mores must be replaced by laws as primary relationships are replaced by secondary relationships in an urban environment.[56]

Wirth suggests that ever since Aristotle's time there has been some understanding of interrelationships based upon the number of people and the nature of their civilization; the larger the number, the greater the *potential* differences between them. A diverse urban community, therefore, can be expected to show more extremes in culture, behavior, and economic life than a rural community. As a result, primary bonds of kinship and neighborliness, as well as sentiments resulting from generations of common traditions, are either very weak or missing. Under urban conditions of impersonality and superficiality in interpersonal relationships, formal controls are substituted for the emotional controls of primary intimate groups, which leads to a need for the urban individual to find a mode of self-expression through organizational activities.[57] In this manner he achieves status and develops his personality. Under these conditions, self-government is a fiction since social control is achieved through formally organized groups.[58] While some see hope for social order in a return to the concept of neighborhood, the trend of civilization seems to be leading in another direction according to Wirth. "There can be no return to the local, self-contained neighborly community except by giving up the technological and cultural advantages of this shifting, insecure, and interdependent, though intensely interesting and far-flung community life, which few would be willing to do."[59]

Greer finds the increase in societal scale is accompanied by the growth of large-scale organizational control systems like the army and civilian public and private bureaucracies. This is a by-product of technological advances such as the development of nonhuman energy sources, the growing complexity of organizations exemplified by the integration of men and machines, and rise in productivity per person. A decrease in travel time results in an increase in distance, which leads to the geographic specialization of service functions; Florida is a recreation area while Texas is the nation's major source for natural gas. This geographic and functional differentiation brings forth giant organizations capable of operating on a national basis. As the machine takes over, there is a diminished demand for unskilled labor. In place of brute power, there is a need for brain power that requires greater individual educational attainment. "Thus, as the society increases in scale, only a small and dwindling proportion remain rural, and there is a general upward movement of the entire population with respect to occupational level, educational level, and income level."[60] Society, or the "bounded network of interdependence resulting in mutual control of behavior . . ."[61] and organizations increase in scale jointly. This is reflected in the extension of the society and a transformation of the internal order. Government or the economic system may be initially dominant, but they eventually coincide in scale as they are complementary. Greer observes that the critical effect of the transformation of the internal order is the extension of the control system.

The common conceptual cord tying together Tönnies, Weber, Park, Wirth, and Greer is their view that a change in the nature of man's relationships results from changes in societal scale. His early interpersonal relationships are direct, "primary" interchanges that later become modified to indirect, "secondary" relationships. As societies grow from rural folk villages into urban places, the original, close personal kinships are replaced by an impersonal bureaucracy. In this milieu, the changing role of the state is reflected in its assumption of greater responsibility (e.g., the institutionalization of authority and the growth and development of planned social processes) as part of the increase in societal scale. In sum, a national, impersonal, administrative and political system emerges to replace the local personal, communal system.

Summary

We have observed that natural relocation processes have been under way since the beginning of recorded history. These activities reflect the changing nature of society over time. The evolution of cities from prehistoric through post-industrial civilizations apparently has had the effect of encouraging and hastening the voluntary relocation of peoples in response to such natural or manmade phenomena as floods and famines or wars and industrialization. Consideration of the evolution, growth, and changing functions of the city lends support to this interpretation of urban places as areas of growth and change. Some view the city in ecological terms as a growing, living organism while others record the physical and social mobility of its occupants. Several contemporary approaches go beyond physical and spatial concerns to consider those communications processes that are unique to urban places. All of these varying approaches, however, interpret society as a changing and mobile entity.

Another important factor is the growth of state intervention in societal processes as an outcome of an ever-increasing complex physical and social environment. As man's interpersonal relationships move from the collective to the individual, from charismatic to bureaucratic, from personal to impersonal, and from primary to secondary, there is an increased need for the state to order the affairs of society. This enhanced interest and need is exemplified by the growing involvement of the state in specific relocation processes, such as the present relocation programs in the United States.

The development of various relocation programs will be considered next within the rubric of continuing and enlarging state involvement in the planned movement of peoples. Federally induced relocation programs of other periods will also be reviewed to see how they fit within another rubric, our professed democratic institutions, goals, and aspirations. Our purpose is to determine whether and to what degree state involvement in relocation activities has served to enhance or diminish one of the primary goals of American society: the enlargement of social democracy through individual growth and development.

Part II:
Metamorphosis of Federal Relocation Policies

3

Democratic and Authoritarian Models of Relocation

Early Land Disposition Policies

The seeming unending supply of land in frontier America provided substance for a vision of this country as one of opportunity, growth, and social progress. Tocqueville in 1832 considered this image of a new nation, free of tyranny and open for settlement, as one reason for the success of the American experiment in democracy.[1] To those men who were members of the Articles of Confederation, the land represented a form of wealth, to be sold as needed for revenue. Only later was it considered primarily as a resource for settlement.

The revenue resource approach is reflected in the Land Ordinance Act of 1785, which set the land disposition policies of the United States for almost one hundred years. The Act provided for the sale of one square mile lots in the Ohio Territory at public auction for an upset price of one dollar an acre.[2] The law, however, had limited appeal since settlers could purchase equivalent property in western New York on credit for as low as twenty cents an acre.[3]

Frontiersmen wanted free land, but this was contrary to the views of the Continental Congress, which hoped to derive enough income from land sales to pay off the debts incurred during the Revolutionary War since there was no other way to raise money at that time. Several states adopted a more realistic attitude towards the question of free land. They passed laws recognizing squatter's rights or preemption, whereby an individual could acquire title to a piece of the public domain at a fixed price after having settled on it for a given period. This pragmatic approach was geared to meet the needs and realities of the emerging frontier since the enforcement of laws prohibiting illegal occupancy was exceedingly difficult.[4]

Political democracy was strengthened in 1787 by the adoption of the Northwest Ordinance, which provided a bill of rights for new territories and set up an administrative process for admitting them into the nation as states. But the revenue approach towards land was maintained by the Continental Congress, which sold some seven million acres under this Act to three syndicates of speculators as a means for raising ready cash.[5]

The close of the War of 1812, new treaties with Indians, the completion of new roads, and the demand for still more land unleashed a flood of migration into the territories west of the Appalachians. Pressures were building for more liberal land laws. One historian writes: "The United States in general was on the move, and much of this movement was to the West; and a now peaceful Atlantic Ocean facilitated migration from Europe, especially from the British Isles."[6]

29

From 1787 to 1825, some nineteen million acres of the public domain were sold despite clouded titles, speculation, squatters, and conflicts of interest by members of Congress.[7] The effects of federal land disposition policies is revealed by the tremendous population increases in the frontier from 1810 to 1820. In Ohio, the increase was from 230,000 to 582,000, while in Indiana the growth was even more impressive—from 24,000 to 147,000. Illinois registered an increase of 350 percent; Missouri, 215 percent; Mississippi, 89 percent; Tennessee, 68 percent; and Kentucky, 39 percent.[8] By 1830, fully one-third of the country's population had settled in an area beyond the original thirteen states, which, in turn, had forced the Indians to move increasingly further west. At that time, Pittsburgh had some 15,000 residents; Cincinnati, 25,000; Louisville, 10,000; and Lexington, 6,000. Across the Mississippi, St. Louis grew to 5,000, while New Orleans counted 46,000 people. As these cities grew, so did their commercial activities, reflecting their growing roles as distribution centers in the new territories.[9]

The spreading settlers demanded that Indian territories be ceded to the federal government even as they swarmed into these areas from all sides. The conflict over land between the settlers and the Indians resulted in two key actions in 1830 by Andrew Jackson, a frontier-oriented president. The first (which will be discussed in more detail later) was the forced removal of Indian tribes from Alabama, North Carolina, South Carolina, Florida, Tennessee, Georgia, and Mississippi to Oklahoma Territory, west of the Mississippi. The second was the passage of a temporary Preemption Act, which authorized the sale of up to 160 acres of land at $1.25 per acre to any squatter who had a tract in cultivation in 1829. Both steps were important harbingers of new trends in the westward movement: the forced removal of the Indians set a pattern for more and similar authoritarian programs of Indian removals, while the Preemption Act encouraged squatting as a form of land settlement rather than the purchase of land at an auction.[10] Andrew Jackson, Indian fighter and frontier man, was the embodiment of the authoritarian-democratic political dichotomy that may be said to be characteristic of this nation from its founding to date. His activist, interventionist policies characterize the increasing role of the federal government in response to the political, economic, and social concerns of that period.

By 1841, the federal government formally established the priority of land settlement ahead of its original concern for revenue raising. Congress passed an omnibus land-distribution-preemption bill whereby settlement on land prior to purchase was no longer illegal per se. A claim could be staked out for 160 acres at $1.25 per acre, payable in four installments. Jefferson's prophecy in 1776 that the frontiersmen would settle the land in spite of everyone had been at last recognized by a law, which, according to Roy Robbins, "was the capstone in the democratization of the public land system."[11]

From 1854 onward, the South sensed its danger from a growing nonslave-owning, western agrarian economy allied to the manufacturing east. It opposed preemption and cheap land and fought further legislative attempts of this type in the new territories west of the Mississippi.[12] In this hostile atmosphere, President Buchanan, a Democrat, vetoed in 1860 a free land, homestead bill. But with the advent of the Civil War and the secession of the South, President Lincoln, in 1862, easily secured its passage. The rights formerly granted only to squatters under the Preemption Act of 1841 now devolved upon anyone interested in settling on up to 160 acres of land in the surveyed public domain. Title vested to the settler at no cost after five years of occupancy or after six months at the price of $1.25 per acre. The passage of the Homestead Act was hailed by some as the greatest democratic measure in recorded history and a fitting climax to the populist land movement in America.[13]

The Homestead Act was a watershed in the attitude of Congress toward the disposition of the remaining public domain since subsequent laws favored the exploitation of public lands by private interests. In addition to establishing nearly one and a half million homesteads, the Republican-dominated federal government in the post-Civil War era actively encouraged the growth of the railroads and the development of agricultural colleges by the passage of land grant legislation. Under the Pacific Railway Act, some forty-five million acres was granted to the Union and Central Pacific Railroads along with sixty million dollars in loans to build a transcontinental railroad. The railroads sold the lands to the settlers as a means of raising revenue and to encourage settlement so as to create the trade necessary to support the new railroads. Under the Morrill Act, some thirteen million acres of public land were donated to the states to support the establishment of agricultural and mechanical colleges.[14] By 1870, it was becoming evident that federal policies originally designed to promote the settlement of land, were no longer effective nor applicable as the American frontier had all but disappeared.

The governmental role in the disposition of land, initially to raise revenue and later to encourage its settlement by a process of voluntary relocation, reveals the interplay of conflicting economic, social, and political forces. Although the enhancement of the democratic process through the relocation of white settlers was achieved, it was at the cost of depriving the Indian tribal societies of their culture, their lands, and, for many, their lives. This problem exemplifies the erratic and sometimes schitzoid application of the professed American democratic credo and actions undertaken under the guise of this credo. It symbolizes the dichotomy in American history between the espousal of social equity and the pragmatic nature of our politics.

Another theme here is the growing role of government as an intervenor in society. A government conceived by Jefferson and his followers in terms of a "limited involvement in the affairs of men" could not be maintained. The physical growth of American society, which resulted from revolutionary changes in the nature and locale of work, communication, and transportation, required a role for government far different than the Jeffersonian model of aloofness. Social equity and individual enhancement had been served by the intervention of the federal government in the disposition of the public lands to white settlers, but this was achieved only by denying to the Indians the rights guaranteed to all peoples in the Northwest Ordinance, the Declaration of Independence, and the Bill of Rights. A prototype case study of Indian removal reveals the disparity between the ideal and the real, thereby underscoring democracy's dilemma: the irregular and at times inequitable nature of the progression towards the model of social growth and equality envisioned in 1776.

Indian Removal: A Case Study

Article Three of the Northwest Ordinance declares:

the utmost good faith shall always be observed towards the Indians; their lands and property shall never be taken from them without their consent; and in their property, rights and liberty, they shall never be invaded or disturbed, unless in just and lawful wars authorized by Congress; but laws founded in justice and humanity, shall from time to time be made for preventing wrongs being done to them, and for preserving peace and friendship with them.[15]

Unfortunately, this expression of good faith by the Continental Congress and its successor soon conflicted with the demands and needs of a growing American civilization; if the expansion of the nation was to be achieved, it required the removal of the Indians from much of the lands they held.[16]

One of the earliest declarations of Indian policy was outlined by Henry Knox, a former Revolutionary War general who was in charge of Indian Affairs in the War Department during George Washington's administration. In a letter to Washington and Congress in 1789, he advocated the following policies:

1. Passage of a law stating the Indians own the lands they occupy and that they can be divested of them only by purchase of the United States or with the approval of the United States;
2. In keeping with the practice of European countries, the different tribes should be considered as sovereign nations and not as subjects of any state;
3. White emigration should be restrained and regulated into Indian territory, and if need be, armed force should be used to enforce such authority;
4. The native population of Indians must be preserved and not allowed to become extinct;
5. The Indians should be taught to adopt the civilization of America, including a desire for exclusive property ownership rather than tribal ownership;
6. Missionaries should be appointed to live among the Indians to teach them farming and other domestic pursuits.[17]

These concepts along with the Northwest Ordinance provided the underlying theory that governed federal actions towards the Indians for some forty years in what might be considered a guardian-child relationship. However, the gap in theory and practice was revealed not only by the War of 1812 in which the Indians supported the British, but also by the subsequent skirmishes between settlers and Indians. By 1840, the Indians had ceded some 443 million acres and received in exchange approximately 49 million acres worth $1.25 per acre plus cash and goods valued at $31 million. The aggregate sum of $85 million paid to the Indians represents approximately one-sixth the value of the lands secured by the United States.[18] The direction of federal Indian policy can also be demonstrated by the amount spent on wars with the Indians as compared with programs for their pacification. It is estimated that the Indian wars cost some $200 million against $60 million spent on peaceful pursuits. Thus, for every dollar devoted to education, missionary endeavors, and the like, the United States spent about three and a half dollars on war.[19]

Although the dollars and cents issues of Indian policy are important, of greater moment here are the means used by the federal government to acquire Indian lands. The case study below of the forced removal of the Choctaw Indians from Mississippi to the Arkansas Territory in 1830 set a pattern for later programs of a similar nature. During the 1820s, Secretary of War John C. Calhoun tried to enforce President Monroe's Indian policy of liquidating Indian lands by peaceful means whenever they blocked the advance of settlers. The Choctaws, located in Mississippi, fought on the American side of the War of 1812, along with Andrew Jackson, at the Battle of New Orleans. They were primarily a stable, peaceful, agricultural group, and their relationships with the United States were good. Some land cessions, which had been negotiated at various times, were generally to the satisfaction of both sides. But in 1817, the admission of Mississippi into the Union shattered any hopes for continued peaceful coexistence since that state insisted on the removal of the Indians.[20]

In order to save the Indians from the threat of extinction, Calhoun advocated a policy of their peaceful removal to west of the Mississippi River. This approach yielded him little except first to antagonize the Mississippi settlers and then Andrew Jackson, who after succeeding Monroe as president appointed Calhoun as a commissioner to negotiate a removal treaty with the Choctaws. Jackson's approach was to use force if the Indians refused to capitulate.[21]

Jackson himself had earlier succeeded in negotiating the Treaty of Doak's Stand with the Choctaws, which Congress ratified in 1821 and which was the first treaty incorporating Indian removal to western lands with an assignment to them of lands designated as Indian territory. Under its terms, the Choctaws were to vacate five million acres in exchange for thirteen million acres in Arkansas Territory. However, the Choctaws refused to move after the one-year grace period permitted by the Treaty and instead went to Washington to negotiate a new agreement. The federal government called the Indians into councils and gorged them with food and drink. The chiefs, warriors, and other influential men of the tribes were induced by argument, persuasion, cajolery, bribes, and threats to agree to terms designated in the treaties. In this way, through bluff and bluster, the federal government formally inaugurated the removal of the Indians.[22] In 1825, another treaty was finally negotiated but the Choctaws still refused to relocate, resulting in a stalemate.

Jackson's election as president in 1828 signalled an end to Calhoun's policy of moderation and the substitution of force whenever necessary. Jackson initiated his program: either voluntary Indian removal westward or the eventual loss of their tribal identity and lands, and the recognition of state jurisdiction over them. On June 30, 1830, Congress passed the Indian Removal Act mandating the removal of the Choctaw Indians to a territory west of the Mississippi.[23]

Recognizing the futility of further resistance, on September 26, 1830, the Choctaws signed the Treaty of Dancing Rabbit Creek, which contained four major provisions:

1. The entire tribe would relocate within a three year period, approximately one-third each year; the federal government would pay the cost of relocating personal possessions and livestock and would furnish necessary transportation and full subsistence for one year after arrival in Indian territory.
2. The federal government would guarantee peace and security from white encroachments on Indian lands.
3. Gifts of cash and goods were to include the continuance of all annuities in effect before the new Treaty was signed, payment of all educational costs for forty Choctaw children for twenty years, a tribal annuity of $20,000 for twenty years, annual payments of $2,500 to employ three teachers, a $10,000 donation to build a council house, church, and schools, and a gift after relocation of 2,100 blankets, 1,000 axes, 400 looms, and rifles, ammunitions, hoes, and personal articles.
4. Individual land grants would be made to Choctaw chiefs along with the right to maintain reservations in Mississippi for those members of the tribe wishing to remain, provided they registered with the Indian agent in Mississippi by a specific date.[24]

Indian agents were to assume the responsibility for the ensuing relocation of some 18,000 Choctaws, as well as 151 whites and 521 slaves, to the Arkansas Territory, some 550 miles beyond their ancestral home. The agents were to be stationed at the places of departure and arrival. Corncribs and smokehouses were to be posted on the route so as to minimize any hardships. The Choctaws would leave home—by wagons, by horseback, by foot—headed toward the Mississippi River only with their essentials.

Thus, the relocation program was launched without compass or rudder into the uncharted sea of Indian removal; for the first time, the federal government was about to engage on a large scale in the removal of the Indians from their homes. It obligated itself to assemble and feed them, transport them across the Mississippi River by steamboats and then overland through swamps and across streams; to build roads and bridges, and finally to settle these harassed men and women including the aged and decrepit, children, babies and livestock in their new home.[25]

By the end of October 1831, the first contingent of approximately 4,000 Indians started out. They soon encountered severe winter storms; during one of which some walked barefoot for twenty-four hours before reaching Vicksburg. In December and January, when their need was greatest, there were few shoes or blankets available. These had been shipped in error to another point, as the logistics of removal went awry. In March 1832, some five months later, 3,749 sick, exhausted, discouraged Choctaws reached their new homeland; the remainder had died along the way. The Indian agents were dismissed after this debacle, and the War Department thenceforth took over the relocation task.[26]

Not all the Indians left by escorted conveys. The federal government provided a bonus of ten dollars to each person who removed to Arkansas by his own resources. Few Indians had any money, and that some were willing to live on the precarious fare gained by hunting on a journey of weeks indicates how highly they valued it. It is estimated that starting in November 1832, a total of 3,215 Indians eventually self-relocated to be eligible for the cash bonus.[27]

The second escorted relocation exodus in 1832 was hit by cholera, and more Indians died, not only from this dread disease but from the forced relocation marches, the last of which began in 1833. The terms of the Treaty of Dancing Rabbit Creek had called for approximately 12,500 Choctaws to be relocated and some 5,000 to remain in Mississippi. However, many of those who stayed behind were later forced into Indian territory; they had been deceived by the Indian agents regarding the necessity for promptly registering their intention to remain behind and therefore lost their Treaty rights to retain possession of their Mississippi lands. Subsequent removal programs were undertaken from 1836 to 1849 to clear Mississippi of these remaining Indians, and a final effort was made around 1900.[28] Today, only about 1,500 Choctaws live in Mississippi, the descendents of those permitted to remain under the terms of Article 14 of the Treaty.

This first forced relocation program in American history was achieved at a total cost of approximately $5,000,000, or $277 per person, including the direct costs of transportation that amounted to $25 each. The federal government realized approximately $8,000,000 from land sales. Under the Treaty provisions, the government had pledged not to profit from land sales, and in a later lawsuit brought by the Choctaws, the tribe was awarded close to $3,000,000—most of which went toward legal costs. In effect, the Choctaws paid for their own removal program.[29] This process was later repeated for other Southern tribes, including the Creeks, Cherokees, Chickasaws, and Seminoles, who with the Choctaws comprised the Five Civilized Tribes. One historian states: "The policy of the United States in liquidating the institutions of the Five Tribes was a gigantic blunder that ended a hopeful experiment in Indian development, destroyed a unique civilization, and degraded thousands of individuals."[30]

As recounted above, the Indians were forced to bear the financial and social burden of the removal programs, while the white settlers were the beneficiaries of these federal interventions. Although the processes of land disposal to white settlers became more democratic, especially with the passage of the Homestead Act, the land acquisition program was achieved at the expense of the Indians. While the esoteric national political goal of "manifest destiny"—by which the country's coasts were to be washed by the waters of two oceans—combined with the land hunger of the citizenry to provide a philosophic justification for the programs of Indian removal, the result was nevertheless a shredding of the sanctity of the Constitution, contracts, treaties, and pledges and a deprivation of the Indians' human and legal rights and, in many cases, their very lives.

This deprivation of rights is not limited to the nineteenth century with its nationalistic political philosophy and its economic attitude of unfettered individual enterprise. As recently as 1942 the United States engaged in another mass evacuation program that denied an entire ethnic group its civil rights merely on the basis of ethnicity. The forced evacuation of Americans of Japanese descent early in World War II demonstrates the fragility of the libertarian framework that encapsulates our nation.

Japanese Removal: A Case Study

The forced relocation of some 110,000 West Coast Japanese early in 1942 represents another extremely negative consequence of state intervention, this time under the guise of a wartime emergency. Constitutional guarantees of liberty yielded to subjection; tolerance, to prejudice; and freedom of movement, to internment behind barbed wire.[31] Approximately 70,000 *Nisei*, or American-born Japanese, and 40,000 *Issei*, resident aliens born in Japan and denied citizenship rights in this country, were removed from their homes along the coasts of Washington, Oregon, and California during March through May of 1942 and were relocated to internment camps in the interior of California, Idaho, Wyoming, Utah, Colorado, Arizona, and Arkansas.[32]

The surprise Japanese attack on Pearl Harbor on December 7, 1941, was the precipitating cause for this largest, single, forced migration in American history. Nevertheless, the treatment of some 160,000 people of Japanese origin in the Hawaiian Islands stands in sharp contrast to the cavalier military acts of the Western Defense Command on the United States mainland, for in Hawaii, General Delos Emmons recognized the futility and immorality of arresting one-third of the Island's population under martial law and reassured the Japanese residents that they would be safe if they did not violate regulations and civil laws.[33]

On the mainland and especially in California, there were economic, social, cultural, and political antecedents for demanding the unprecedented removal of the Japanese from that area after the attack on Pearl Harbor. The well-springs of anti-Oriental feeling go deep in that part of the country. These were originally based upon the economic competition from immigrant Japanese farmers who, at the beginning of the twentieth century, challenged the native whites for low-paying laborer's jobs in the fertile California valley farms and towns.[34]

Alexander Leighton in the *Governing of Men* draws the following profile of the Japanese born *Issei*: they came to the United States around 1900—mostly young men from poor homes—very often as farmers. Since they were willing to work for lower wages, labor groups objected to the competition for jobs. After several years of labor these immigrants would offer to purchase farmlands through American intermediaries for a price higher than the whites. The white farmers reacted negatively to this situation by forming anti-Japanese organizations. Denied the rights of citizenship and with folkways and religion different from western society, the rejected *Isseis* tended to cling together as a tightly knit ethnic, social, and cultural community and displayed little need or desire to learn English or adopt American customs. Although their early dreams of returning to Japan were fading, their outlook and traditions were still largely Japanese with an almost puritanical emphasis on hard work, personal integrity, self-sacrifice, filial piety, and education.[35]

In contrast, the *Niseis*, the first American-born generation, wanted to be modern and accepted by society. Rejecting the goals of their parents, they turned to the larger society for their models of emulation and growth as they opted for the American culture. Although a long way on the road to assimilation into American life and society, by 1942 they still were not completely accepted.[36]

Social and cultural antipathies were manifested early by the adoption of an anti-miscegenation law in California. Support for restrictive economic, political, and social legislation came from, among others, The Native Sons of the Golden West, the Hearst Press, The American Legion, the California Real Estate Association, and the Joint Immigration Committee of the California State Legislature. Their opposition to the Japanese, based on racial and economic factors, was vocal, strident and continual.[37] Arrayed on the side of the Japanese were various religious groups, such as the YMCA and the Protestant churches that were earlier engaged in missionary activities in Japan, several leading West Coast educators, and the Japanese American Citizens League; but all were generally too weak to offset the power of the press and the other well-organized groups.[38] This was the atmosphere that enveloped the West Coast at the time of the Japanese attack on Pearl Harbor.

Immediately after the attack, the Justice Department arrested Japanese, German, and Italian aliens. Some 500 *Issei* fishermen on Terminal Island and farmers in Guadalupe, California, were interned on December 7, 1941. In this early period, 6,000 *Issei* were locked up. A little later, the number of aliens arrested totalled 16,000 and included 1,200 German and Italian seamen. One-third were interned, nearly 50 percent of which were Germans; the rest were paroled. All the detained aliens were moved to midwest internment camps, although there were no verified instances of sabotage or espionage by any West Coast Japanese at any time. The Treasury Department also impounded $131 million of *Issei* funds.[39]

In January 1942, civilian control over aliens yielded to the military who assumed this responsibility. Morton Grodzins in his book, *Americans Betrayed*, identifies January 25 as the week of a change in public sentiment towards the Japanese as the entire group came to be identified with the enemy.[40] "Many traditionally anti-Japanese individuals and organizations realized that the war with Japan presented them with a natural opportunity to further their long-term aims."[41] Aided and abetted by the old-time proponents of Japanese exclusion, more and more community organizations passed resolutions demanding the evacuation of the Japanese. Eventually, every West Coast mayor—with the exception of the mayor of Tacoma—favored the forced relocation of all Japanese. Voices of restraint raised by the American Civil Liberties Union, the American Friends Service Committee, and the Northern California Committee on Fair Play for Citizens and Aliens of Japanese Ancestry were drowned by the cascading voices of fear and prejudice demanding the forced immediate relocation of the Japanese.[42]

The build-up of public pressures pushed President Franklin D. Roosevelt to issue Executive Order 9066 on February 19, 1942, which authorized the Army to establish military areas and to exclude any and all persons from them. Roosevelt's point of view, expressed later by Attorney General Francis Biddle, was that whatever was necessary to defend the country must be done.[43] "The necessity for protecting coastal areas, the widespread hostility toward resident Japanese, racial animus, economic cupidity, fears of attack and apprehension over the growing victories of the enemy—these factors became so intertwined that their separation was impossible," states Grodzins. "Yet they all had the common feature of pushing in the direction of evacuation."[44]

On March 24, 1942, Bainbridge Island across Puget Sound from Seattle, was chosen by the Army as the first area requiring the removal of the Japanese by March 30, only six days later. The eviction day was raw and overcast, not unusual for the locale at that time of year. Bill Hosokawa describes the removal scene:

... they began to gather at the assembly point long before the designated hour, each of the fifty-four families carrying only the meager items authorized by the

Army—bedding, linens, toilet articles, extra clothing, enamel plates, and eating utensils, as all else, the possessions collected over a lifetime, had to be stored with friends, delivered to a government warehouse, sold, or abandoned.

... the ferryboat hooted and eased out of its slip and some of the *Nisei* looked back for the last time on the island that had been their only home. ... [those who arrived on the mainland] were transferred to dilapidated railroad coaches for the long, miserable ride to Manzanar [an internment camp in Southwestern California].[45]

The Wartime Civil Control Administration (WCCA) was given the responsibility for administering the first phase of the relocation evacuation program. They divided the West Coast into 108 exclusion areas with roughly 1,000 people in each. The process went as follows: a notice of exclusion was posted to announce the requirement that each family head or single person must register at the local WCCA control station in a public hall or school gym. Borrowed staff from federal agencies and *Nisei* interpreters helped in filling out forms, assigning family numbers, issuing identification tags, and the like, for evacuation one week later. Families with their limited possessions were then removed by bus to local Assembly Centers—such as fairgrounds and racetracks—where they occupied hastily-painted, ill-smelling barns or crude shelters until the relocation camps could be built. Fifteen Assembly Centers plus relocation camps at Manzanar and Poston in Arizona were utilized in this fashion.[46]

The next phase, removal to the relocation centers, came under the jurisdiction of the War Relocation Authority (WRA), which ran the camps but utilized Army patrols for security. "One day these Japanese-Americans were free citizens and residents of communities, law-abiding, productive, proud. The next, they were inmates of cramped, crowded American-style concentration camps, under armed guard, fed like prisoners in mess hall lines, deprived of privacy and dignity, shorn of their rights."[47] By the end of the summer of 1942, a total of 110,723 people had passed through the Assembly Centers on their way to the relocation camps.[48]

Executive Order No. 9102, dated March 18, 1942, created the WRA, as a unit of the Office of Emergency Management, to be responsible for housing and caring for the internees. Milton Eisenhower was chosen as its first director, to be followed shortly thereafter by Dillon S. Meyer. By mid-June 1942, Eisenhower had ten camp sites constructed into which the Japanese were required to move. Obsolete trains guarded by soldiers carried the internees eastward. At the internment camp, each family was given one of six "rooms" in a barracks, the largest space being twenty-four feet by twenty feet. A stove, a droplight, cots and mattresses were provided in each room.[49]

Around November 1942, even as the final evacuation was completed, the military necessity for relocation and internment ceased to exist; for the tide of the war in the Pacific had turned in favor of the United States. By then the Assembly Centers cost $10,700,000 to build; transportation costs were

$2,281,000; food costs $500,000; and the relocation camps cost $56,482,000. The internment program totalled $88,679,716 or about $800 per person relocated.[50]

While life in the relocation centers is replete with human interest stories, the focus that follows is limited to the interplay of the themes mentioned previously: the intervening nature of the state especially when national security appears in jeopardy, and the authoritarian deviations from our democratic credo. Edward S. Corwin, in discussing the elasticity of presidential power in time of war, writes about World War II: "all resources of constitutional power ever previously uncovered were brought into requisition on a scale hitherto unparalleled."[51] Presidents Lincoln, Wilson, and Franklin D. Roosevelt interpreted Article I, Section 2 of the Constitution, the clause that makes the president the Commander-in-Chief of the Army and Navy, as an absolute mandate required to guarantee the existence of the state. Lincoln grafted this powerful interpretation to the Constitutional clause requiring the president to see that the laws are faithfully executed, thereby creating the legal justification for the almost unlimited authority of the executive office in time of war.[52]

Corwin observes that "these two [constitutional] categories, taken together, assert for the President, for the first time in our history, an initiative of indefinite scope and legislative in effect in meeting the domestic aspects of a war emergency."[53] For the interpretation of the "due process" clause as a restraining element on excessive legislative or executive power in time of war is "highly malleable" and even the Bill of Rights can assume an "unaccustomed flexibility."[54]

This absolute power of the president in time of war was subject to legal challenge in the Supreme Court. In *Korematsu v. United States*, decided in December 1944, the validity of the Executive Order interning the Japanese and supporting legislation authorized by Congress was argued. The issue was the government's right to detain a citizen of Japanese ancestry who had violated orders to report for evacuation. Korematsu claimed that the Army and the WRA had exceeded their authority, due process had been ignored, and the evacuation was racially inspired. The Army argued the primacy of "military necessity." The majority of the court upheld the Army's line of reasoning, thereby neglecting to deal with the important constitutional issues raised in the case. In his analysis of the decision of the court in the Korematsu case, Eugene V. Rostow concludes the Executive Order was "calculated to produce individual injustice and deep-seated social maladjustments of a cumulative and sinister kind,"[55] since the Supreme Court accepted the doctrine of ethnic differences as a criterion for discrimination. The issue of "military necessity" thus appeared not to be based on military need but on prejudice.

This case vividly illumines the absolute, authoritarian nature of state involvement under the guise of military necessity or in instances of presumed emergency. An absolutism based on ethnic considerations was declared justified during the War, thereby weakening the basic democratic foundations of the nation. The case history of the forced relocation of Americans of Japanese descent during World War II has been castigated "as one of the most spectacular breakdowns of government responsibility in our history."[56]

The final administrative cost for relocation and internment totalled $248,716,746 for an average of $2,261 per person. This excludes the economic losses suffered by the relocatees—a figure estimated by the Federal Reserve Bank at $400,000,000. By way of later federal contrition, on July 2, 1948, President Harry S. Truman signed the Japanese American Evacuation Claims Act. Some $38,000,000 in indemnification was paid to the Japanese, or about ten cents for each dollar they lost.[57]

Summary

In the case studies of the involuntary Indian and Japanese relocation programs, the state, under the guise of national destiny and national defense, forced the removal of the then-considered alien populations. Faced with the threat of racial extinction, both groups moved with relative acquiescence. Despite our basic manifestos of freedom and democracy, the state exercised absolute penultimate power; in one instance, just short of racial extinction, in the other, racial deportation. These two involuntary relocation programs reflect a total derogation of individual and group civil liberties.

The disposition of the public domain was in the nature of a zero-sum game in which the benefits to one group, the white settlers, were achieved at the cost to another group, the Indians. In one respect the role of the federal government in the nineteenth-century program of land disposition was essentially passive, insofar as there was no compulsion on the part of the white settlers to move. On the contrary, it was they who forced the government to pursue liberal financial policies for the disposition of the public domain. Although the earliest federal objectives were fiscally oriented—to raise enough money through the sale of land to pay off the Revolutionary War debts—the adoption of the Homestead Act some one hundred years afterward indicates a transformed objective. This was an economic redistribution program aimed at developing the remainder of the nation. Unfortunately, this revolutionary policy change forced the Indians to yield their ancestral homelands and much of their communal, tribal lifestyles if they were to survive. Both the Indian and Japanese case histories exemplify the nadir of federal relocation programs as instruments of positive state involvement and democratic public policy.

The earliest federal relocation policies were relatively amorphous, befitting a young pre-industrial and mainly agricultural country. They finally resulted in the disposition of the public lands as part of a broad, national policy. But in order to make this transition, a transformation was required in the depth and nature of the involvement of the federal interest. This was accomplished by the federal government's repudiation of its initial relationships with the Indians. The early co-existence model developed by Henry Knox under Washington, yielded to the forced relocation and removal model of Jackson. The white man's benefits, achieved at the red man's cost, has saddled the United States with an economic and social due bill that is still largely unpaid—more than one hundred years after the disposition of the public lands. Indian removal is a classic illustration of the interrelatedness of our two themes: the expanding role of the federal government growing out of a change in societal scale, and the mixed model of social justice and individual growth resulting from this public program.

The forced removal of the Japanese during World War II demonstrates an abuse of power by a democratic state. The United States, in moving to protect what it perceived as a threat to its national security, did so at the cost of abrogating the political, economic, and social rights of an entire ethnic minority group. This model of state absolutism is far removed from the democratic ideal. It indicates that state intervention has a democratic or authoritarian potential that serves to enlarge man's social choices and growth or diminish them. In the Japanese model, the state diminished them.

These three models of relocation exhibit an interventionist spectrum ranging from the democratic, egalitarian heights of federal land disposition policies to the authoritarian depths of Indian and Japanese removal programs. But such predominantly negative relocation portraits are not the only ones that may be drawn.

More recent history demonstrates the development of other patterns in relocation. The intervention of the state in the national economic emergency during the 1930s and the resettlement programs of President Franklin D. Roosevelt, provide another scenario in contrast to those already discussed. We next consider the nature and extent of the rural resettlement programs of the New Deal and how these served as instruments for advancing social and economic equity and enhancing individual growth.

4 The New Deal and Rural Relocation

Subsistence Homesteads and Rural Resettlement

In 1928 President Herbert C. Hoover and the nation were firmly committed to a free market economy, one in which major private choices serve to regulate investment, production, prices, and wages.[1] Despite warnings of a possible economic crisis, Hoover viewed the role of the state as an acquiescent player in the "private economy game." Since he conceived the federal responsibility as basically passive, his approach to the nation's economic problems reflected his failure to exercise presidential initiative and power.[2] To him, the state was an instrument to "discipline the sinful, and the righteous, provide the mechanisms of a fair and stable market, and broaden the opportunities for all; but government, a tool of private choice, should not make the crucial choices."[3] His great fear of governmental restriction and regulation as a means for regulating the economy immobilized him during the crisis of the depression.[4] Hoover's interpretation of the role of government as a "weak player" resulted in his replacement by the redoubtable rookie, Franklin Delano Roosevelt, who refused to strike out in the face of depression, doubt, or disaster.

F.D.R., in his first inaugural addresss, declared he was prepared to recommend legislation required to restore prosperity. If Congress failed to act under these conditions of national emergency, then "I shall ask the Congress for the one remaining instrument to meet the crisis—broad executive power to wage a war against the emergency as great as the power that would be given me if in fact invaded by a foreign foe."[5]

The Depression helped crystallize different conceptions of the role of the state as the economic issues of the 1932 election were honed to razor sharpness. Roosevelt's analogy to war and a great national emergency served as his justification for enlarging the interest of the federal government in the affairs of men and more truly reflected the wants of the nation than Hoover's approach of relative noninvolvement.[a]

The early New Deal was characterized by innovative, interventionist legislation. It was essentially a program towards spreading economic democracy through economic planning and collectivism. During the first "hundred days," one of the key pieces of legislation was the Agricultural Adjustment Act, designed to raise the general level of prices paid to the farmer for the voluntary

---

[a]Roosevelt received 88.89 percent of the electoral votes with 11.11 percent going to Hoover; see Joseph Nathan Kane, *Facts About the Presidents* (New York: Pocket Books, Fifth Printing, 1968), p. 291.

43

reduction of his output. This was to be achieved through the retirement of submarginal farm lands.[6] F.D.R. appointed Henry Wallace, editor and owner of an Iowa farm journal, as Secretary of Agriculture to administer this unique approach to agricultural reform. Rexford Tugwell, economics professor and social reformer, was chosen by F.D.R. to be Wallace's Assistant Secretary. Tugwell was a strong advocate of economic planning and government controls. He believed that uncontrolled agricultural production led to the destructive use of land, and agriculture required reorganization and consolidation similar to that produced by the industrial revolution. Factories and cities should be able to absorb any excess farm labor created by a major land reorganization scheme. Henry Wallace was also committed to a policy of greater social controls. With appointees of similar persuasion such as Mordecai Ezekial, M.L. Wilson, W.W. Alexander, and Lewis C. Gray, it was evident there would be a transformation in the nature of the usual activities of a conservative Department of Agriculture.[7]

The beginnings of the New Deal rural relocation activities were germinated by the subsistence homesteads program run by M.L. Wilson, Director of the Division of Subsistence Homesteads. This agency was located within the Civil Works Administration of the Department of Interior and was under the overall aegis of Harold Ickes. Wilson estimated that two million people would eventually be displaced by federal land use planning activities. His viewpoint differed somewhat from Tugwell's since he felt these farmers, miners, and migrant workers would not be able to get jobs in the cities. His approach was the leased subsistence homestead of a few acres located near a city. Under this plan, a family could grow its own food and work in a nearby industry if employment was available. In this way displaced farmers, miners, or factory workers could subsist side by side on leased homesites, thereby creating a new balance between agriculture and industry.[8] Wilson viewed the lack of social pressure and neighborliness of a rural community as a natural way of life compared to the restrictions and tensions of city living. To him there were great moral and spiritual values arising from contact with the soil and these transcended the urban dweller's concern for things and money.[9] F.D.R. was also a staunch supporter of this approach and earlier had advocated planning the use of land jointly for industry and agriculture in New York State by declaring that "a problem arises out of [the failure of] the proper balance between urban and rural life."[10]

The fiscal seed for the subsistence homesteads program was contained within the womb of the National Industrial Recovery Act of 1933. Title II, Section 208, provided $25,000,000 for making loans and for otherwise aiding in the purchase of land and the construction of subsistence homesteads. There was no further definition of Congressional intent; the details of the program were left to its administrators.[11] Wilson, in his desire to achieve a better life for all, believed that democratic participation in community planning at the local level had to be a core characteristic of the subsistence homesteads program. His "community idea" included a new style of village life modelled along the lines of the earlier religious communes and was dependent upon handicraft industries, community activities, closer family relationships, and cooperative enterprises. These idealistic goals were to be achieved through a program of educating the generally skeptical miners, city-dwellers, and now landless farmers.[12]

The federal program included four types of subsistence communities: (1) part-time farming combined with industrial employment near cities, (2) colonies for stranded jobless miners, (3) colonies for relocated farmers removed from submarginal lands, and (4) villages built around decentralized industries. A typical colony was to contain twenty-five to one hundred families on one to five acres of land. A cinder block house and the land it stood upon were to be leased to the families with a promise of eventual sale to them. Each house was to contain at least four rooms, a bath, and electricity.[13]

On December 2, 1933, the Federal Subsistence Homesteads Corporation was organized to lend construction money to local development corporations at four percent interest for twenty years. This approach would permit local taxation and local political jurisdiction. Six months later, 32 communities had their plans approved for construction. The first site to be developed, Arthurdale in West Virginia, was designed for unemployed miners. Three other similar projects, one in Tennessee, one in Pennsylvania, and another in West Virginia, were also under way, each with 250 to 300 units. Planned as part rural and part industrial communities, an influx of industry was essential for their survival since all of the miners were relief recipients. This economic problem was never solved completely during the life of this conceptual chimera. Tenant selection policies were left to the local corporations but the federal agency suggested the use of home investigators, training programs for prospective tenants, and certain minimum financial, health, and farming requirements in addition to a requirement for a stable family life. In order to minimize the possibility of choosing unfit occupants, all applications for dwellings had to be approved in Washington.[14]

When Wilson left the Division of Subsistence Homesteads in June 1934, 31 industrial-based developments were announced although only 23 were completed. These proved to be more successful than the other communes; since they were located closer to cities, they provided for part-time industrial employment along with their limited farming facilities. They averaged from 25 to 125 units and were located primarily throughout the South. Two years later, in 1935, the subsistence program had planned 3,300 units and completed 700, with 1,369 under construction. The remaining 1,300 or so units were just in the preliminary land purchase stage. Only $8,000,000 of the original appropriation of $25,000,000 had been spent.[15]

The program was under sharp legislative attack for its lackluster performance: under fiscal attack from the Comptroller General who succeeded in forcing the agency's records to conform to standard accounting practices; under legal attack from the Solicitor-General who claimed that the law only provided aid for the redistribution of population in industrial centers and not for the resettlement of farmers; and under social attack from farmers and the general public who questioned a leased land program in place of the more traditional concept of ownership of private property. It was evident the program was to have a short life. Since the subsistence homesteads program was rooted in the soil, Henry Wallace and Rexford Tugwell had some interest in it. Both felt it was a mistake to try to combine land acquisition and resettlement with rural housing and industrial relocation for destitute city dwellers, farmers, and miners. Tugwell described the program as an adventure in escapism and while he thought some sort of resettlement program was desirable, he felt it should be administered by the Department of Agriculture rather than by the Department of Interior. The program, hatched in the broadened democratic and utopian depression atmosphere of 1933, had become a political ugly duckling in 1935.[16]

On May 15, 1935, Roosevelt transferred the Division of Subsistence Homesteads to the newly formed Resettlement Administration under Tugwell. Although the subsistence program was originally intended as a significant experiment in land use planning, the relocation of low-income households, and the enlargement of communal life, it did not materially attack or eliminate poverty, it did not relocate many families, nor did it serve to join agrarian to urban interests.[17] One of its original goals, the development of collective communities, made the program increasingly vulnerable to political criticism. One commentator observed that the basic law had been drafted with little understanding of the obstacles its administration would face in the competitive world of politics, law, economics, and conflicting social theories.[18]

Along with the Division of Subsistence Homesteads of the Department of Interior, another agency was established to resettle farmers from depressed lands. The Rural Rehabilitation Administration (RRA) was created as part of the independent Emergency Relief Administration. Formed in 1933, it worked through local rural rehabilitation corporations similar to those under the Subsistence Homesteads program. The RRA hoped to develop 100 to 150 communities with up to 1,000 families, each of whom would derive their sustenance from a rural and industrial base. This program, which required the residents to build their own dwellings and then purchase them and thereby repay the government for its investment, thus conformed to the traditional self-help and home ownership ethic of the country. The emphasis was to be placed on such economically useful activities geared to farming as processing specialized food products or craft production.[19]

Even this more realistic resettlement program was to founder in the interstice between articulation and achievement. The RRA completed only two projects and had about 23 more in planning when it was absorbed by the Resettlement Administration in 1935. They contained 1,814 dwelling units as compared with the 3,304 units planned by the Subsistence Homesteads program. Like the latter, communities were designed to supply economic and social rehabilitation programs, as well as shelter, for the family. After a one-year tenancy, a house could be purchased at terms of 3 percent interest and twenty-year payments. This home purchase proviso was one of the major distinctions between the programs of the Subsistence Homesteads Division and the Rural Rehabilitation Administration.[20]

Although the first New Deal attempts at providing relocation housing under the Subsistence Homesteads Division and the RRA were failures in an economic and social sense, they had great significance, for they represented the first positive steps taken by the federal government to relocate and supply shelter to the rural poor. As such, they were the forerunners of the later slum clearance and public housing programs designed to aid the urban poor. Furthermore, these programs were illustrative of a new attitude on the part of the federal government: a willingness to step into the economic void created by uncontrolled market forces and to undertake social experiments to change the lifestyles of the rural underclass. Though these attempts to redress fundamental economic and social imbalances failed, most importantly, the federal government took the initiative to intervene on behalf of the poor in an attempt to extend to them a measure of social equity during a time one historian calls "The Third American Revolution."[21]

The Resettlement Administration

The original mandate of the Resettlement Administration that F.D.R. placed under Tugwell in 1935 included the following objectives:

1. Resettlement of low-income or destitute families from urban and rural areas by providing for the development of communities in such areas;
2. Continuation of the program of marginal land retirement including emphasis on positive re-use of such areas through reforestation, flood and erosion control, and recreational use;
3. Maintenance of the rural rehabilitation program by granting to the agency the power of eminent domain and the right to purchase, sell, or lease properties thus acquired;
4. Any other useful projects designed to relieve unemployment.[22]

"The Resettlement Administration had the clearest mandate yet given for the initiation of new communities," states Paul Conkin, and, "in mid-1935 it seemed as if the community-building program of the New Deal had only begun."[23] But the appointment of the stormy and controversial Tugwell to head the new Agency guaranteed only its temporary existence and a certain liquidation, which in fact occurred a year and a half later.[24] Tugwell favored the development of suburban resettlements nourished and supported by nearby cities. This contravened the earlier notion of rural subsistence homesteads supported by attempts to recruit industry to underdeveloped environments.[25] His concept of an organic society, reminiscent of the Chicago school of urban sociologists, visualized a cooperative, collective economy with its own purposeful, functioning government. This meant that such communities had to be writ large, for diminutive plans could not produce the utopian physical and social milieus he conceived.

To Tugwell, the ideal form for urban and rural resettlement was the greenbelt city derived from Ebenezer Howard's concept of a greensward surrounding a suburban town. Land was to be leased by the government and individual purchase was to be achieved only after a long rental term (which is a contradiction of the American experience in land disposition noted earlier). This collectivist policy was considered radical and dangerous by congressional American traditionalists who were cast either in the Jeffersonian agrarian mold or the Hamilton urban-industrial form. Almost $50,000,000 was to be spent for rural resettlement programs as compared to an actual $8,000,000 spent by the Division of Subsistence Homesteads.[26] About one hundred rural projects, located primarily in the South, were initiated. These called for a complete dependence upon agriculture as the economic backbone. The typical rural project contained about one hundred farm units with from forty to one hundred acres. A frame house of three to five rooms without plumbing comprised the basic shelter. Tenure was by lease with rents geared to a percentage of the annual value of the crop produced. Community facilities such as a school, a meeting room, a cooperative, a cotton gin or a warehouse were usually provided.[27]

The rural projects program was strongly criticized because of the construction costs it engendered. Tugwell built 2,267 dwelling units at $36,000,000 for a unit cost of almost $16,000, as compared to an average unit cost of $9,000 under the first subsistence homesteads program and $8,800 under the rehabilitation program.[28] Conkin views Tugwell as a tragic figure unable to communicate with the less conceptual minded and more concretely oriented majority of the people. Furthermore, his interests were different from those of the rigidified Department of Agriculture, which was less concerned with the poor farmer and viewed the middle- and upper-income farmer as its constituency. Tugwell, however, was interested in the welfare of the submarginal farmer working land that was similarly submarginal. Consequently, his Resettlement Administration became the ideological home for more than a million rural families on relief.[29]

Tugwell's greenbelt towns were soon subject to legal problems that forced him to give up one of these four proposed communities. A planned Greenbrook development near Bound Brook, New Jersey, was opposed by the town because of possible tax drains, architectural styles inappropriate to the area, and a fear that it would attract a low-class group. On May 18, 1936, the District Court of Appeals in Washington ruled that the Emergency Relief Appropriation Act of 1935, the financial source for the Resettlement Administration, was unconstitutional. The failure of Congress to specify the use of funds for particular projects was deemed an excessive delegation of legislative powers to the president. In addition, on May 29, the U.S. Supreme Court declared unconstitutional the National Recovery Act. In the face of these negative decisions, Tugwell and his staff chose not to appeal the verdict in the New Jersey case but instead to continue with three remaining greenbelt towns not subject to the court decision.[30]

The original greenbelt scheme that called for 5,000 housing units was later reduced to 3,500 because of cost factors. Towns were planned outside of Washington, D.C., to be known as Greenbelt, Maryland, with 1,000 units; Greenhills, outside Cincinnati, Ohio, also with 1,000 units; Greendale, on the outskirts of Milwaukee, Wisconsin, planned for 750 units; and the legally killed Greenbrook, near Bound Brook, New Jersey, to contain 750 units. The goal was to construct the highest quality facilities consistent with reasonable initial costs to serve as a yardstick for planners, architects, builders, and the public. Physical planning for the towns was outstanding. Separation of pedestrian from auto traffic, densities of approximately five families per acre, land reserves for future use in the surrounding greenbelt, the bunching of communal and commercial facilities, superblocks and cul-de-sacs—all commonplace today—were at that time innovative and well received by critics.[31]

So as to insure the positive acceptance of the greenbelt towns in their areas, Tugwell's staff "skimmed the cream" in choosing the tenants. Initially only low-income families, defined as those earning between $1,000 to $1,999 annually, were to be eligible. This was later raised to $1,200 to $2,000—a range defined as moderate income. Rents were geared to 25 percent of income, which resulted in rents from $21 for one and a half rooms in an apartment to $45 for four and a half rooms in a detached house. Families were chosen from among low-income workers to insure long-term stability and low-cost maintenance. Home visits, credit checks, physical examinations, and an evaluation of the family's communal integration as a normal, home-loving group were other prerequisites for occupancy. Efforts were made to retain a religious ratio similar to that existing in the nearby city, but blacks of any denomination were excluded.[32]

"The Resettlement Administration sought to insure the general success of the greenbelt towns, both as physical and social experiments, by rigorously excluding those whose backgrounds might create problems and inevitable bad publicity." But, as Joseph Arnold points out, "the boldness of the R.A.'s physical planning is hardly matched by the boldness or even the basic equity of the social planning."[33]

Another interesting aspect of the greenbelt towns was their early attempts at enlarging participatory democracy by sponsoring cooperative ventures of all types. In keeping with the philosophy of Tugwell and the Resettlement Administration, people who were organizational-minded were among those admitted to initial residence. This led to a plethora of clubs, cooperative health associations, marketing groups, and consumer services organizations. With the exception of Greenbelt, Maryland, all the early enthusiasm over cooperative living soon eroded due to the unusual time and energy required for successful cooperative ventures. Turnover in occupancy also led to tenant and group instability, thereby vitiating communal efforts that demand long-term commitments.[34] Tugwell resigned on December 31, 1936.

After World War II, the greenbelt homes, which cost approximately $16,000,000 to build, were sold to local community corporations comprising war veterans and to residents of the units at approximately half their original cost, thus closing the chapter on this social experiment in enlarging democracy.[35] To Arnold, "the history of the greenbelt towns is the story of a road not taken." The program was rejected by Congress and ignored by the private building and real estate industry. Its failure is traceable to its challenge of the conventional patterns of individual home ownership.[36] Despite their demise, the greenbelt towns generally represented the most innovative, original attempts in communal development under public aegis in this country.[37]

According to Sidney Baldwin: "The original creation of the Resettlement Administration and the initiation of its provocative programs were accomplished through the power of an embattled President, enjoying a large measure of popular support, struggling in a dark hour of national crisis to cope with a numbing economic and social emergency."[38] Once the "climate of crisis" began to cool, the programs, policies, and agency had to seek legitimacy through traditional channels via the political process. Its failure to participate in the legislative baptismal rites raised some serious questions about its legitimacy and origins of birth, a condition which seems equally true in political as in familial relationships.

An evaluation by social critics of the short-lived Resettlement Administration's relocation and housing activities would probably consider them to be failures. But this is only true if one judges the agency by conventional economic and political yardsticks. Its development costs exceeded those of its two predecessors, its social goals were utopian, running counter to the American ideal of home ownership, and the personality of Tugwell was too abrasive to smooth the rocky congressional road an agency must travel for its continued existence. In two other aspects, however, the Resettlement Administration's concepts and activities were forerunners for later programs.

The greenbelt town with its emphasis on creating a self-contained planned physical milieu that included housing, shopping, and commercial and recreational facilities, was the forerunner of the currently popular planned development communities scheme. In addition, Tugwell's interest in social organization came to bloom in the multitude of community groups and underscored the creativity and latent capabilities of the residents of the greenbelt towns. This social concept is again unfolding under the rubric of "community participation," where these early seedlings of the Resettlement Administration are sprouting again. The housing programs of the agency and its forebears were germinal sources for the later public housing program. They represent an enlargement of federal interest in providing for one of man's basic needs by constructing decent shelter for poor relocatees at affordable rentals.

The Farm Security Administration

Congress was not about to throw out both bath water and baby along with Tugwell even though it rejected any further resettlement programs similar to those that had provided shelter to 10,000 families since 1933. In July 1937, Congress passed the Bankhead-Jones Act, which established a Farmer's Home Corporation under the Department of Agriculture. This new unit was authorized to lend tenant farmers $10,000,000 during its first year, $25,000,000 in its second year, and $50,000,000 thereafter to purchase land. Following this new congressional mandate, Henry Wallace set up the Farm Security Administration (FSA) as the new action arm for his Department. It absorbed the functions and staff of the Resettlement Administration and undertook the administration of the new farm tenant land purchase program.[39]

Although Congress permitted the completion of the rehabilitation activities undertaken by the Resettlement Administration, it tried to restrict the activities of the new agency to money lending and the disposal of the communities built by its predecessors. But the FSA, by inheriting the same personnel, merely shifted its approach from direct construction of communal towns to encouraging groups of farmers to do the same with funds loaned to them by the Agency. The farmer associations became the new instruments for continuing these and other activities expressly forbidden by Congress.

Illustrative of the vacuum filled by the FSA in the field of rural relocation was its program for some 18,000 farm families made homeless as a result of the acquisition of their properties for military installations in World War II. The FSA established nonprofit defense relocation corporations financed with unspent rural rehabilitation funds borrowed from the Reconstruction Finance Corporation. For example, the Missouri Defense Association, Inc., bought 45,000 acres of land for $25 an acre to provide new farms for 255 families at an average land cost of $4,000. Houses and farms were estimated to cost an additional $3,000. Loans were granted where necessary with opportunities to purchase the land over a 99-year period. Between December 27, 1940, and February 6, 1942, eighteen relocation corporations, located in the Midwest and South, acquired 256,000 acres at a cost of close to $10,000,000 for approximately 2,500 farms. This activity was soon curtailed by the Comptroller General who questioned the legality of the expenditure of funds to buy land for this purpose.

Early in 1942, the FSA was given the job of finding farm operators for some

6,000 small farms vacated by their Japanese owners who were interned during World War II. The agency granted $3,500,000 in loans to operators who purchased 232,000 acres. Under the Lanham Housing Act of 1940, it also initiated construction of 1,350 dwelling units, located near industrial installations, during the period just prior to World War II until Congress created the National Housing Agency.[40] But the demise of this agency was soon forthcoming since it failed to sell off the federally owned rural projects.

In 1946, Congress passed the Farmer's Home Corporation bill, which was given a mandate to dispose of the resettlement projects.[41] This resulted in a tremendous fiscal loss to the government, which realized only from one-fourth to one-half the cost of the 15,000 or so units sold between 1944 and 1946. The greenbelt towns and the subsistence homesteads that were earlier transferred to the newly created Federal Public Housing Authority were also to be sold. By the end of 1945, only thirty homestead units along with the three greenbelt towns remained unsold.[42]

In sum, these rural rehousing and relocation programs reveal the threads of an increasing federal interest in relocation processes as well as the erratic nature of the movement to encourage individual social growth. The three years of intense depression from 1930 to 1933 created a new mood and a demand for economic and social reform as never before. The programs of the Subsistence Homesteads Division, the Resettlement Administration, and the Farm Security Administration were major instruments in an attempt to fight rural poverty by resettling farmers elsewhere on more productive lands, in more productive ventures, and in decent shelter. Land retirement programs, farmer resettlement, leased lands, and mutual construction activities were among the most progressive components of individual and group rural democracy ever espoused by the federal administration. During the depths of the depression these action-oriented programs were capable of attracting the support of people with very diverse political creeds. Their ultimate failure represents in part the shift towards conservatism after 1936.

Agency advocacy of leased homes and farms, which contradicted the American credo of personal, private ownership of land and house; the hasty accretion of overlapping programs, which were incapable of quick, easy enactment; a growing anti-New Deal sentiment and the personal antagonisms aroused by key program administrators all resulted in the demise of these daring, rural, economic and social experiments.[43] Nevertheless, another great rural experiment involving the use of relocation processes was under way. While the Tennessee Valley Authority, in an economic sense, was perhaps the most successful of all the rural ventures of the New Deal, we shall consider only its social program in the next section as illustrated by its early relocation activities.

The Tennessee Valley Authority

From 1824 to 1918, the use of the Tennessee River for navigational purposes, especially around Muscle Shoals in Alabama, had been a recurrent congressional issue. The improvement of this internal waterway was first suggested by President James Monroe and his Secretary of War, Calhoun, but the development of the railway system made this issue irrelevant then. Not until the first World War did Muscle Shoals regain some prominence, and then in another context.[44]

In 1916, President Woodrow Wilson secured the passage of the National Defense Act, which authorized the construction of plants to manufacture nitrate for munitions and fertilizers. In 1918, $20 million was appropriated to build a plant at Muscle Shoals. This plant was only partially constructed—at a cost of $127,000,000—by the war's end, when its completion became unnecessary. Its disposition raised bitter controversy as Henry Ford and other private individuals and groups offered to purchase the facilities. But Senator George Norris of Nebraska, a progressive, insisted upon retaining public ownership.[45] This issue remained unresolved until the passage of the Tennessee Valley Act fifteen years later.[46]

On April 10, 1933, F.D.R. in a message to both the House and Senate urging passage of the Act said: "this power development of war days leads logically to national planning for a complete river watershed involving many states and the future lives and welfare of millions. It touches and gives life to all forms of human concerns."[47]

The preamble to the Act includes several rather broad objectives:

1. An interest in furthering national defense;
2. Agricultural and industrial development;
3. Improvement of navigation;
4. Reforestation;
5. The removal of marginal lands;
6. Control of flood waters in the Tennessee and Mississippi River basins.

To further these goals, a public corporation, the TVA, was established with the federal government as the sole stockholder.[48]

Philip Selznick, in *TVA and the Grass Roots*, states: "If this had been all, the project would still have represented an important extension of government activity and responsibility."[49] But the dreams of its supporters were far greater than the objectives of the Act. They visualized the public corporate organizational form encompassing a specific geographic region of several states as a new style of federalism. Furthermore, social and economic planning, an issue transcending mere power development, was also contemplated. Specific economic tasks mentioned in the Act were to be clothed with a sense of social responsibility that envisioned the cooperation of the people of the region.[50]

According to David Lillienthal, the first chairman of the TVA, its methods for encouraging democratic participation in effectuating its programs were contained within roots found deep in the soil of American tradition and common experience. He states the TVA effectuated change within the framework of American life while property rights and social institutions remained unscathed.[51] The TVA philosophy also envisaged the development of the social capital of the area, namely its people, which could best be achieved through the doctrine of "grass roots," or participatory democracy. "The story of the TVA at the grass roots . . . is an account of how through a modern expression of ancient democratic principles human energies have been released in furtherance of a common purpose," states Lillienthal.[52] If this is so, an examination of several TVA relocation programs resulting from its building programs should support and enhance the Lillienthal hypothesis of "grass roots" democracy.

The Tennessee Valley Act gives the Authority the power to lease real and personal property and dispose of same, to exercise the right of condemnation or eminent domain, and to acquire real estate for dams, power stations and other facilities along the Tennessee River and its tributaries. It also authorizes the president to recommend legislation for the proper use of marginal lands and for the economic and social well-being of the people living in the region.[53] These sections provide the substantive, legal authority for carrying out relocation programs in conjunction with the construction of dams and power stations.

During a thirty-year period, from 1934 to 1963, the TVA relocated some 15,000 households at an average cost of $110 per family. Until 1963, it did not make any direct relocation payments but provided for additional compensation to property owners in the land prices to cover such expenses. Tenants, however, received no such benefits.[54] According to Selznick, 11,412 households relocated from TVA reservoir areas to March 1943. Of these, 4,036 were property owners and 7,376 were tenants.[55] During its first ten years, almost 70 percent of TVA's relocatees were tenants who were ineligible to receive any type of financial assistance for relocation.

In a final report in 1937 on its activities at the Wheeler Reservoir Site, the TVA notes the relocation problem became more acute especially since it had no legislative authority to provide direct benefits to reservoir families. The Removal Section served strictly as a referral agency and attempted to persuade other units of government to assume responsibility for rehousing its site occupants. Of 835 Wheeler Dam families, only 52 were landowners, which reflects the depressed economic and social conditions then extant in that region and throughout the country. "The TVA program," states the report, "though it aimed to relieve over a long-time period some of the conditions which prevailed, temporarily added to the maladjustment by taking thousands of acres of fertile land out of production, thereby causing 835 families to relocate in an already crowded area."[56]

The Family Removal Section pinned its hopes for securing necessary housing resources on the availability of such units from the Resettlement Administration, but this proved to be illusory since that organization's housing activities had no major bearing on TVA's needs. A casework approach was adopted for dealing with the problems of the tenants and owners, with special attention directed towards families with social and economic difficulties. Only 74 families, or 9 percent of the total workload, received any help from other agencies. The total interim administrative cost to the TVA for this counselling program was $26,402.26 for an average cost per family of $32.16. Final costs were $62,325.92 averaging $74.20 per family.[57] In concluding, the study acknowledges the need for further work towards the goal of equitable population readjustment. Table 4-1 summarizes the social effects of relocation based upon a sampling of 100 families. This report is believed to be among the earliest of its kind, and is unique for its examination of the social implications of relocation.

The report goes on to say that the principal reason for unfavorable relocatee attitudes towards the TVA is the fact that only 31 percent relocated on land as good or better and with general conditions improved. Given this consequence and the fact that no less than 34 of the 100 families moved to unsatisfactory accommodations, there seems to be sufficient reason for questioning the report's conclusion that 67 percent of the households relocated were "favorably disposed" to their new location and the TVA.

A 1940 summary evaluation of 2,899 families forced to move for the Norris Dam between 1935 and 1937 reveals that in this case, aid from other TVA divisions or outside agency assistance was provided to 11 percent of the households. The nature of the help and the number of families assisted were:

1. Aid from the Resettlement Administration, 39 families;
2. Temporary loan of tents from TVA, 45 families;
3. Receipt of salvaged building items from TVA, 72 families;
4. Trucking service for moving from TVA, 156 families.

Table 4-1
Effects of Relocation on Wheeler Area Residents, by Percentage, 1937

Criteria	Better than Before	Similar	Worse than Before	Percent Total
Location (relative to market, schools, work, etc.)	39	54	7	100
Housing[a]	37[b]	29	39	105
Health and Sanitation	50	41	9	100
Land	8	23	69	100
Attitudes	67	–	33	100

[a]Percentages in this category total 105 as presented in the Wheeler Area Report. To compensate for this presumed arithmetic error, the "worse than before" percentage has been arbitrarily reduced by 5 in the text of this volume.

[b]Includes 10 that, while improved, were still inadequate.

Source: Tennessee Valley Authority, *Population Readjustment, Wheeler Area*, February 1, 1937, pp. 12-13.

TVA administrative costs here ran to $83 per family. "The service rendered the majority of the families consisted chiefly of guidance and cooperation rather than material assistance."[58] This service was provided initially by the University of Tennessee Agricultural Extension Division and later by a TVA staff of ten to fifteen caseworkers.[59]

The full relocation report, prepared three years earlier in September 1937 states in a frank and poignant introduction, "A bewildered people—approximately 2,900 rural families—the greater number of whom had lived their entire lives in the same community, were faced with the problem of seeking new homes in 'foreign' lands."[60] Tenant families such as sharecroppers and squatters comprised 41 percent of those relocated. The average cost of moving was about $75, an amount each tenant had to bear despite an estimated annual spendable income of only $400 per family. Tenant families complained that in addition to paying their own moving costs, collateral but noncompensable values such as markets for their farm products, their credit, and their good will were being destroyed.[61]

The *modus operandi* of the TVA in this case study was similar to that in the earlier Wheeler Dam relocation program. Staff encouragement, use of meager material and financial resources, and agency referrals were the major instruments for effectuating relocation. Heavy emphasis is placed in this study on cooperation—that is, the cooperation of the Family Removal Section with other TVA divisions and with public and private agencies. But the presumed depth and efficacy of the various forms of assistance is belied by the data. The report observes that without the help of relatives, neighbors, and friends, the relocation of the reservoir families would have been impossible. It concludes with the guarded observation that on the whole, living conditions seem to be improved for the families displaced for the Norris Dam.[62]

In September 1970, a relocation analysis was undertaken by a summer student intern for an area known as the Land Between the Lakes. Approximately 1,000 families were involved, including some 25 percent who were owners of seasonal, vacation homes. This was the first case in TVA experience in which the land use was for recreational purposes rather than for a dam.[63] This report deals primarily with land purchase policies, and by design, does not deal with the demographic characteristics, social problems, and housing needs of the relocatees. Its recommendations are essentially procedural but among its most salient observations is that the housing needs of the population and the availability of housing resources apparently were not an important input in establishing the feasibility of the project, nor were there any attempts to see that such needs were provided for in the operational phase of the program. A more responsible approach in this respect, according to the report, would ". . . refute those who maintain the TVA is heartless in its efficiency."[64]

On the basis of the above reports, it is fair to state that as late as 1970, the TVA was not among the leading agencies in terms of providing significant financial assistance or effective social help to its relocation households; nor did the TVA reports indicate the nature of aid, if any, for the single-person household or commercial enterprise. Within the framework of general relocation practices up to 1970, the TVA relocation programs are probably representative of most other federal agency activities in this field—that is to say, many relocation assistance programs up to 1970 were at best empathetic; many lacked material resources such as money, housing, land, or social service aids to be of real assistance. If one utilizes the Lillienthal yardstick of "grass roots" participatory democracy to measure relocation effectiveness, in these cases there appears to be a significant gap between rhetoric and reality. Seemingly, the TVA studies fail to show an understanding of the crucial difference between consulting with outside organizations for help in relocating families and its responsibility for providing direct financial or housing assistance or counselling services. A registry of sections of the TVA and outside organizations, which could be called upon to play some role in helping families move, may be necessary, but it is not a sufficient condition to support Lillienthal's proposition regarding the application of "grass roots" democracy. Selznick states: "The tendency of democratic participation to break down into *administrative involvement* requires continual attention" [italics added].[65] The early TVA studies appear to indicate that the shadow of "grass roots" democracy was substituted for the substance of creative and meaningful forms of direct relocation assistance and community participation in the relocation process.

The TVA may have neglected an opportunity for promoting social growth and democracy at the "micro" level through individually designed relocation programs in favor of broad "macro" economic and social policies for improving the general condition of the region. The TVA concept is probably the most daring extension of federal interest and involvement on the regional level and serves as a prototype for many foreign regional planning models. Notwithstanding, it appears to have made little use of the social potential of planned relocation processes as a means for enhancing individual growth at the "grass-roots" level.

Summary

The Great Depression provided the economic and social climate for extending federal intervention through social programs involving rural housing and relocation to a degree heretofore unknown in American history. This economic tragedy, which befell all social classes in America, generated the demand for a transformation in the role of the state. Franklin D. Roosevelt was sagacious enough to grasp this challenge. The responsibility for monitoring the heretofore largely uncontrolled economic milieu and providing for individual security shifted from the private to the public domain.

Attempts to demonstrate the feasibility of state intervention in rural America by restructuring individual patterns of living among farmers to a more communal way of life were unsuccessful, but several other New Deal social experiments succeeded far beyond anyone's imagination. No one today questions the role of the state in providing social security insurance benefits, unemployment insurance, and insurance for home mortgage loans.

Within the first thirty years of this century, the nation had grown and increased in complexity at a rate far greater than any other comparable period in its history. In recognition of this changing economic and social scene, the American people, in 1932, elected to move from orthodoxy to reform—from laissez-faire economics to welfare economics. The economic crisis that faced F.D.R. required an active, participating interest by government sufficient to cope with the changes and increases in the scale and complexity of life. F.D.R. brought the full machinery of government into play in what may be said to be a self-fulfilling relationship between the complexities and needs of advancing technology and the increasing intercession of the state.

One expression of this enhanced federal interest was the provision of housing for the nation's farmers in a new physical and social milieu designed to break their cycle of poverty. These rural rehousing and relocation programs were among the first attempts at extending social democracy through individual enhancement under the relocation process. While this attempted transformation of much of rural America was under way, in the same physical environment a more traditional pattern of agency behavior in relocation was developing. In enhancing that region's physical assets, the TVA was doing so at the expense of the relocatees who were required to move in the face of the physical advances of the agency. The TVA relocation model was less than satisfactory in terms of extending social equity, especially in light of the agency's professed policy of "grass roots" participation. Once again, the erratic nature of relocation programs is dramatically demonstrated; on the one hand there are the utopian attempts at developing model rural communities and Greenbelt towns; on the other, there are the TVA relocation programs with their limited social and economic resources.

Despite the inability of the rural housing programs to produce a significant volume of low-cost housing for the poor or to relieve poverty, these programs and the public housing program that came later, demonstrated the direct and immediate interest of the federal government in the economic and social betterment of the people. This was true not only in the rural regions but also in the urban areas as well. Such similar concern was evinced in part through the housing built by the Public Works Administration (PWA) and under the Wagner Act of 1937, which provided the first public housing resources for the urban poor and near-poor. In the following pages we shall examine the scale of federal interest in public housing, slum clearance, and relocation programs in the nation's beleaguered cities.

5

Urban Relocation, Phase I: 1918 to 1945

Relocation Housing during World War I

The federal government's housing construction programs during World War I are probably the first such direct activity to provide shelter for relocated war workers. Families and single men streamed to urban centers to work in war plants and in search of jobs. All needed places to live. With labor turnover as high as 700 percent, war production was jeopardized for want of accommodations, as rents for even slum units soared to new highs.[1]

By the summer of 1917 the issue of federal intervention was no longer questioned except for the nature of the dwelling units to be provided. The Council of National Defense, a citizens group set up by President Wilson to insure an efficient system of war materials production, recommended that permanent housing of good quality be built for transient war workers.[2] Despite some early congressional division over temporary barracks versus permanent housing, the latter approach was voted by Congress and was to be achieved by organizing two separate corporations to provide permanent housing facilities.[3]

The United States Housing Corporation (USHC) was chartered in New York in 1918 as a subsidiary of the Bureau of Industrial Transportation and Housing of the Department of Labor. The same year the Emergency Fleet Corporation (EFC) was also incorporated as a component of the United States Shipping Board. The USHC ultimately received $100,000,000 for construction while the EFC got $125,000,000.

The development processes of each corporation varied widely. The USHC built and administered its housing program directly. The EFC made loans to real estate subsidiaries of ship-building corporations, which in turn built the housing units. In addition to the two corporations, the Ordinance Department of the Army also built some temporary housing including dormitories, churches, schools, and shopping facilities in isolated areas close to munitions factories. Eventually their accommodations housed some 45,000 persons.[4]

The USHC had plans under way for 128 sites in 71 communities, 40 of which were under construction when the war ended. This program was to provide accommodations for approximately 25,000 families and 33,000 single workers at a cost not to exceed $45,000,000. Despite a favorable rate of construction progress, this work was halted by the tradition-minded, private enterprise-oriented Congress. They permitted only 24 or so projects that contained 6,148 family units to be completed. Greater encouragement was shown toward the

EFC whose plans were designed to house 55,000 persons (or about 16,000 families) at a cost of $67,000,000. Of the EFC projects, 81 percent were allowed to be completed.[5]

Edith E. Wood speculates that the difference in attitudes displayed by Congress toward these agencies mirrored the means they used for achieving their desired goals. The dwellings built by the USHC were government owned and government managed. Those of the EFC were a war-borne version of company housing for employees—that is, the ship-building corporations owned the land and managed the buildings. The latter approach was more in keeping with acceptable and conventional practices for providing housing facilities through private enterprise. Regardless, both agencies built housing units for some 16,000 families in new urban areas. Many of their original renter occupants were later able to buy their houses or continue renting them as they desired. The program's significance, as Wood states, is that "it proved that government housing could be produced and administered in the United States without scandal, without extravagance, without the sky falling, or the constitution going on the scrap heap."[6]

The Depression and Public Housing Legislation

The next forward step occurred during the depression. Title II of the National Industrial Recovery Act of 1933 authorized the creation of the Federal Emergency Administration of Public Works. It was to develop a comprehensive program of public construction such as low-cost housing and slum clearance projects with a view toward increasing employment quickly. Of great significance later, the Act provided for the power of eminent domain, which vested in an agency the authority to acquire privately held property to meet the needs of the state.[7] Another provision of that Act allocated a $25,000,000 revolving fund "for aiding the redistribution of the overbalance of population in industrial centers . . . for making loans for and otherwise aiding in the purchase of subsistence homesteads."[8] The primary purpose of the Act was to revitalize the economy by stimulating production as a means for increasing employment. Housing construction, a heavy utilizer of all types of labor, was a "chosen instrument" for achieving this goal through the use of local public building corporations.

From July 1933 to February 1934, over 500 applications for projects were received from various localities by the agency administrator, Harold L. Ickes. These totalled more than $1,000,000,000, but only 7 projects, valued at $11,000,000, were ever completed. The reason for the high death rate of submitted applications was the Agency's requirement of an investment of 30 percent of the equity by the borrower. Dissatisfied with this slow construction progress, Ickes and Roosevelt decided to establish a Public Works Emergency Corporation (PWA) as the direct planning and building arm of the federal government. Although Roosevelt designated the PWA as a building agency, the federal courts in a basic case decided otherwise by declaring the federal government had no power to condemn private property for low-cost housing and slum clearance projects and for the purposes of reducing unemployment.[9] The decision in effect mandated the use of state authorized local agencies or housing authorities financed under the federal spending power, not subject to challenge by taxpayer's action. The state courts then upheld state and local power to condemn property for low-income housing and slum clearance as public uses within the scope of their power of eminent domain.[10] Up to 1937, the PWA provided funds for 51 projects at a total cost of $136,182,000, creating 22,000 apartments at $6,200 per unit.[11]

In 1934, federal interest in providing housing was secondary to its concerns for reducing unemployment. Nevertheless the PWA program established a legislative beachhead that recognized low-cost housing and slum clearance programs as a federal responsibility.[12] Interestingly, the slum clearance laws during the New Deal made little or no public reference to the relocation needs of the people displaced by such programs. Langdon W. Post, the first Chairman of the New York City Housing Authority, in describing the effect of the earliest completed PWA project, Williamsburg Houses in Brooklyn, practically ignores family relocation activities in writing: "Where formerly 90 percent of the land on which it stands was covered with old, dirty, unsanitary firetraps there now exist new, fireproof, clean and healthful buildings covering but 33 percent of the land and offering a home to thousands of persons; where 5,000 formerly lived, or rather existed, in fear and dirt, 6,000 will live in security and cleanliness."[13]

Public Housing Battles

The federal housing program was slowly emerging but public understanding and interest in housing or relocation was virtually nonexistent during the early New Deal days. Edith Wood and her fellow pioneers at the National Conference on Slum Clearance, held in Cleveland on July 6 and 7, 1933, were among the first to associate slum clearance with relocation. Wood noted two basic reasons to support slum clearance programs: first, to improve the health, welfare and morals of people living under unwholesome conditions, and second, to increase real estate values in blighted areas for the benefit of the entire city. "But, if public money is to be spent or philanthropic cooperation invited for slum clearance, it should be with the *first* set of aims in view, for so long as we keep them in view, re-housing is an essential part of the process—not re-housing for a new set of tenants, but *re-housing for the same tenants on the original site or elsewhere*" [italics added].[14] Later at the Conference, she declared, "no large-scale slum clearance should ever be undertaken which does not provide improved housing at rents they can pay for the dispossessed tenants."[15] Her incisiveness and insight is further demonstrated by her observation that the word "demolition" in other countries implies an obligation to rehouse those displaced, on the original site or elsewhere. She then makes what is believed to be the earliest rationale for planned relocation by saying, "If we are to accomplish anything worthwhile, we must conceive slum clearance as *a constructive measure of social progress*" [emphasis by Wood].[16] The Conference adopted several resolutions that declared that slum clearance must consider the needs of those to be moved so that they may be properly rehoused during and after construction, and also noted that great care is required to see that slum clearance does not result in the creation of other slums elsewhere in the city.[17]

From 1933 to 1935, federal involvement in slum clearance and urban housing was limited, reflecting the lack of public understanding or support for such programs. The lobbying efforts of newly organized public interest groups like the National Public Housing Conference and the National Association of Housing Officials along with individual advocates including Edith Wood, Catherine Bauer, Nathan Straus, Ernest Bohn, Ira Robbins, Coleman Woodbury, and others, persuaded the American Federation of Labor (AFL) at its 1935 convention, to endorse slum clearance and low-rent housing programs as a way to encourage employment.[18]

In 1935, the National Public Housing Conference drafted a public housing and slum clearance bill and convinced Senator Robert Wagner of New York to act as its sponsor. Wagner, who had grown up in the slums of Manhattan's Yorkville, was personally sympathetic toward this type of legislation.[19] However, there was strong opposition to any public housing program since it challenged the established approach through the private housing sector, and various private interest groups coalesced to wage an unrelenting and bitter fight against such legislation. The National Association of Real Estate Boards, The United States Building and Loan League, the National Retail Lumber Dealers Association, and the United States Chamber of Commerce launched an effective campaign against the proposed public housing program. By early 1935, both sides in the housing battle had established their positions. On the left were liberal social reformers who were interested in uplifting the conditions of the poor through a program of bettering their housing conditions. They were allied with labor unions looking to create more jobs in the construction industry. On the right were those groups who believed the federal government should not challenge the private enterprise system by extending housing facilities to segments of poor people in a few cities.[20]

The fight to adopt the United States Housing Act took two years and had to overcome the hesitancy of President Roosevelt who finally agreed to support the proposed legislation. He did so because he viewed it as a means for combatting unemployment and securing the big city and labor vote in the upcoming election of 1936.[21] On January 20, 1937, in his inaugural address on the steps of the Capitol, F.D.R.'s resonant voice was heard by millions on radio as he put the challenge to democracy in this form, "—in this nation I see tens of millions of its citizens—a substantial part of its whole population—who at this very moment are denied the greater part of what the very lowest standards of today call the necessities of life.... I see one-third of a nation ill-housed, ill-clad, ill-nourished."[22]

The Housing Act Passes

On September 1, 1937, Roosevelt signed S. 1685, the United States Housing Act, "... to provide financial assistance to the States and political subdivisions thereof for the elimination of unsafe and unsanitary housing conditions, for the eradication of slums, for the provision of decent, safe, and sanitary dwellings for families of low income and for the reduction of unemployment and the stimulation of business activity...."[23] The preamble of the Act starts with an emphasis on slum clearance and then provides for the development of low-rent housing or slum clearance projects. It requires the building of dwelling units equal in number to those to be demolished except where there exists a shortage of decent, safe, and sanitary housing. But nowhere in the original Act is there any mention of some form of consideration for the families whose shelters would be demolished.[24] The awareness of this problem was still to come.[25]

The Housing Act and its subsequent amendments may be considered a landmark piece of legislation for several reasons: (1) as a major advance of federal interest in the housing welfare of the low-income strata of American society; (2) as an extension of general welfare and social justice; (3) as a forerunner of the more comprehensive Housing Act of 1949 and the Community Development Act of 1974; and (4) as a definitive statement for such emerging terms as low-income, displaced persons, low-rent housing, slum clearance, and development.[a]

The 1937 Act created the United States Housing Authority within the Department of the Interior as the administrative instrument for effectuating the new public housing policy. The agency went through several organizational convolutions until September 9, 1965, when it was superseded by the new Department of Housing and Urban Development. Under the 1937 Act, it built 194,000 dwelling units and eliminated a like number of slum units.[26] The Authority was authorized to issue loans equal to 90 percent of the total cost of

---

[a]The definition of some of these terms are contained within the amendments to the basic Act over varying periods of time; for example, in Public Law 89-117, August 10, 1965: "The term displaced 'families' means families displaced by urban renewal or other governmental action." See U.S. Congress, House of Representatives, Committee on Banking and Currency, *Basic Laws and Authorities on Housing and Urban Development*, Revised through January 31, 1969, 91st Congress, 1st Sess., January 31, 1969, footnote 2, p. 226.

the project and annual subsidies towards debt service and operations to enable local public housing authorities to build low-rent housing or slum clearance projects. As noted previously, the Act also provides for the elimination, by demolition or improvement, of substandard housing units equal in number to the public housing units to be constructed.[b] Admission priorities to vacant apartments are provided first for displaced families and then to veterans.[27]

Later Relocation Amendments

The Housing Act of 1949 subsequently qualifies the basis for federal assistance for low-rent housing by requiring that the local public housing agency demonstrate the feasibility of the temporary relocation of individuals and families to be displaced from a housing site to other areas that "... are not generally less desirable in regard to public utilities and public and commercial facilities and at rents and prices within the financial means of individuals and families into decent, safe, and sanitary dwellings available to such individuals and families and reasonably accessible to their places of employment."[28]

As of January 27, 1964, the Housing Act authorizes, as part of the development expense, the cost of relocation payments to individuals, families, business concerns, or nonprofit organizations displaced for a low-rent housing project.[29] Insofar as relocation responsibilities relating to *public housing* are concerned, not until the 1964 Act was there congressional acknowledgement of a financial obligation by housing authorities towards displaced individuals and families. It requires that these agencies, like urban renewal agencies earlier, must provide decent shelter at a reasonable cost for relocatees in generally accessible areas containing public and commercial facilities. Some fifteen years after passage of the 1937 Act, Congress finally acknowledged a direct federal financial responsibility to public housing-site relocatees by authorizing relocation payments to them.

The New York City and Chicago Experiences

Some may raise a reasonable question as to what happened in the intervening period to families required to move from public housing slum clearance sites. Although the experiences of New York City and Chicago may be representative only of large cities and therefore may not be typical, the scope of their relocation activities for public housing lends them importance and will be reviewed here.

[b]Exceptions to this requirement are rural nonfarm or Indian areas or any low-rent housing project built on the site of a slum cleared after the enactment of the Housing Act of 1949.

New York City

Prior to World War II, the New York City Housing Authority was landlord to 5,187 families on fourteen slum clearance sites.[30] That agency's relocation program during the prewar period included the collateral approaches of self-relocation and offers of apartments.

In 1936, the Authority sponsored and supervised the WPA Vacancy and Rehousing Project. This operation provided a list of suitable dwellings for relocatees from condemned buildings required to be demolished. Burned-out families, families forced to move for other city improvements, and Housing Authority relocatees were all offered listings of available apartments. By 1939, the Vacancy Listings Bureau (as its name was changed) was forced to reduce its services following the withdrawal of WPA funds. Nonetheless, in 1938, several branch offices throughout the city registered 168,607 vacant units that were distributed to 38,024 persons, 21,535 of whom were claimed to be rehoused.[31] This bureau is believed to be the precursor of this type of relocation assistance which was provided in subsequent New York City programs.

The value of this listings service as a relocation aid is attested to in a report of the Citizens Housing Council of New York, which states: "Now that New York has embarked on a housing program which has as its ultimate goal the eradication of the slums, the community must be prepared to meet the immediate needs of those who, without public help, would suffer sorely during the transition period . . . we recommend that a Rehousing Bureau shall be set up as a permanent unit in the city government or in the New York City Housing Authority."[32]

The importance of self-relocation in vacating the early sites should also be mentioned, especially for the period prior to and during World War II. A 1940 vacancy rate of 6.5 percent in New York is an indicator of the general looseness of the housing market at that time.[33] Many tenants succeeded in finding places for themselves or with the assistance of local real estate firms or brokers.[34] Another relocation highlight in New York City occurred between January and November 1945, on the site of Stuyvesant Town, a private development sponsored by the Metropolitan Life Insurance Company under the New York State Housing Redevelopment Companies Law of 1942. Some 2,800 households were relocated by a private real estate agency that established a listings service similar to the Vacancy Listings Bureau. Within the first month of operation, 6,000 vacant apartments were registered and 250 site families moved, which is indicative of the relative availability of apartments.[35] With the exception of those immediately affected by relocation, there was little knowledge then of the hardships and the economic and social problems unearthed by various types of slum clearance programs.

By the end of World War II, the impact of relocation as a concomitant of slum clearance activity was becoming more evident. Returning war veterans preempted much of the private housing stock that was already being utilized to capacity. The New York City Housing Authority was forced to establish its own Site Management Division to expedite the relocation of some 8,300 families on its newly acquired sites.[36] Relocation benefits at that time were authorized only by federal agency administrative interpretation since they were not mandated under the Housing Act of 1937. The Authority was permitted to pay moving expenses, to allow a month's rent forgiveness, and to offer eligible site tenants a priority for vacant apartments in housing projects. The minimal financial payments were included as part of project development costs subject to the approval of the regional office of the Public Housing Administration. The decision to allow such costs was justified on the grounds that the legal expenses incident to gaining possession of the apartments by a court order would exceed the cost of the direct cash payments and rent allowances to the relocatees.[37] This form of financial aid was the earliest means for providing such benefits to public housing-site occupants, and as noted earlier, ultimately led to the establishment of direct relocation payments in the public housing program.

Chicago

Chicago's approach for assuming responsibility for tenant relocation was outlined in a memo prepared by the Metropolitan Housing Council, on November 9, 1934. That quasi-public agency assumed a policy role in relocation and delegated the responsibility for housing assistance to the Illinois Emergency Relief Commission. It was felt that the Council's broad social and housing interests, when fused to the financial aid available through the Relief Commission, would provide a suitable administrative vehicle for relocating some 22,000 Chicago slum residents. The Council established a Housing Service Bureau to secure listings of vacant apartments in Chicago. While they were apparently successful in assisting white families, only 20 percent of the black families were helped. As a result, the Council called upon the PWA to expedite the construction of subsistence homesteads for minority groups and to undertake the rehabilitation of vacant buildings.[38]

In what may be the first national public agency statement of relocation problems caused by the Housing Act of 1937, the United States Housing Authority Bulletin #10, *Relocation of Site Occupants*, dated June 30, 1938, stresses the need for careful treatment of site occupants in their relocation into decent, safe, and sanitary dwellings well within their financial reach.[39] Despite high national vacancy rates in 1938, the Bulletin emphasizes a housing shortage for lower-income families as a result of the relationship between their income and inability to pay a market rent for a decent vacant unit. The Bulletin however places final relocation responsibility on the individual family to exert initiative in finding a proper home and outlines a five-point relocation process that includes:

1. Creating advisory committees of local groups to assure cooperation and to interpret the housing and slum clearance program to the community;
2. Developing a public relations program directed especially toward groups antagonistic to the program;
3. Preparing relocation schedules to be coordinated with demolition schedules to minimize needless vacancies prior to actual site clearance;
4. Establishing a listing of vacant units to be offered to families;
5. Financial planning for the families so as to insure the availability of funds for moving expenses and security deposits.[40]

Jack Meltzer observes that in Chicago in the 1930s, excluding Bulletin #10 and the Emergency Relief Commission activity, there was slight consideration for formulating effective relocation programs although the idea of a public responsibility was acknowledged.[41]

An evaluation of the New York and Chicago relocation case histories suggests that slum clearance was seen as a physical clearance program that mandated the eradication of decrepit structures under the Housing Act of 1937 with little concern for rehousing the site occupants. This was partly as a result of the relatively high vacancy rates that existed in the depression-swept cities. Relocatees in New York and Chicago had a choice of finding other quarters for themselves, moving into public housing projects if they were eligible, or accepting apartments offered by tenant listings bureaus.

Interest in the problems of relocation was limited to the handfuls of housing cognoscente and the relocatees themselves. But the threat of another war soon overshadowed any further consideration of domestic problems including the implication of relocation programs on impacted peoples.

Relocation Housing during World War II

By 1940, the nation was again gearing its industrial production for defense purposes and anticipating related housing problems. The special relocation problem experienced in World War I had been the need to provide shelter for displaced populations—that is, for families and individuals who, in the main, temporarily relocated to areas where work was plentiful.[42] On July 21, 1940, F.D.R. created the Office of Defense Housing Coordinator within the Advisory Commission of the Council of National Defense. It was to plan a defense housing program to be built through private enterprise but with the help of appropriate federal agencies. The major legislative vehicle for creating such housing was to be the Lanham Act, which ultimately provided 945,000 publicly assisted housing accommodations of all types.[43] Both permanent and temporary public housing was built for war workers near naval yards and defense plants. After the war, the Act permitted the conveyance of permanent projects to housing authorities for use as low-rent emergency rehousing developments. Some 267,000 trailers, barracks, and quonset huts were thus supplied to educational institutions, local communities, and nonprofit groups as war surplus housing for use by discharged military persons.[44]

In commenting on the political implications of shelter built under the Lanham Act, one author surmises that due to the exigencies of World War II, much of the political criticism of the housing built during World War I was missing. Furthermore, this time better than half the dwelling units were built by private contractors.[45] As a result, the philosophic debate over private versus public construction of housing was minimized. The compelling national need for housing for defense workers supplanted the rhetoric over "socialized housing."

Significance of Housing and Relocation

The period between the two wars may be viewed as an era of slow but growing awareness of the extent of some social problems in America that were heightened by the worst economic crisis ever faced by this nation. This understanding served as a catalyst for federal intervention in the prevailing laissez-faire, marketplace attitude towards the national economic and social structure.[46] One expression of this growing federal interest was in slum clearance and public housing that was supported first by socially oriented reformers and then by organized labor. These programs were regarded as vital ingredients in an elixir concocted to restore economic health. Under such dire economic circumstances and with "one third of the nation ill-housed ..." the original privately oriented individualistic economic philsophy—practically part of the marrow of the nation—was modified. Social programs were adopted based upon a growing acknowledgement of public responsibility for fighting the depression by providing jobs, money, social security, and housing for those in greatest need. Once the economic emergency started to recede, however, so did congressional interest in swallowing this new philosophic brew. The mid-term election of a conservative Congress in 1938 indicated a slowdown of New Deal reform activities, but not before the nation's conceptual understanding of housing were expanded whereby: (1) private homeownership was defined as an ultimate national and individual goal, (2) the use of private institutions for mortgage lending was backed by federal guarantees of loans, (3) slum clearance was established as a joint federal-local responsibility, (4) low-rent public housing was identified as an employment stimulus and as an aid to slum clearance, and (5) the provision of housing was acknowledged for those who were relocating to work in war industries.[47]

Federal involvement in urban development, housing, and relocation programs from 1917 to 1945 served as launching pads for later probes in these newly charted areas of public endeavor. But public intervention in providing war housing may be viewed as a temporary tactical or strategic shift in housing policy with little long-range significance. This is so because the intensity of the housing need during both world wars was so apparent as to mute much debate and discussion about the philosophic implications of federal activities in providing shelter. Faced with the ultimate issue of national survival, war housing was seen as an essential component for national survival. At the end of both wars, this strong motivation lapsed. For the federal government moved to dispose of its housing inventory by selling it to the original occupants, or to cities, nonprofit organizations, and private individuals interested in purchasing same.

The implications of the slum clearance and public housing programs are somewhat different from the war housing programs. The PWA program of Harold Ickes was primarily designed to "prime the pump" while incidentally providing the education and experience for the significant Housing Act of 1937. Preceding the adoption of this seminal law, there occurred a heated debate in Congress on the place of the federal government in the field of housing and slum clearance. Advocates and adversaries were aware that the adoption of this Act signalled an extension of federal interest and concern in an area far beyond its relatively passive role of earlier times. It meant a transformation in the nature of the relationships between the state and the localities in support of the "ill-housed one-third of a nation." The fight was bitter and acrimonious since traditional banking and real estate interests were being threatened by a fundamental shift in the responsibility for providing decent shelter to the poor. Congress finally acknowledged this to be a public sector responsibility, thereby moving ahead toward enlarging the democratic goal of social equality and individual betterment.

Summary

Up to World War II, slum clearance and public housing legislation was the direct result of the tireless efforts of a small band of housing pioneers. Their activities led to a broadening of the social vision of the nation by focusing attention on the problems of the city slum-dweller. In opposition to this social attitude stood those corporate enterprises that were supported by a philosophy of *laissez-faire* and *caveat emptor* as acceptable economic guidelines for business activity. Not until this individualistic politico-psychological milieu was radically challenged in the 1930s was there to be a modification in the attitudes of the majority of the people. Under the duress of high rates of unemployment, now the middle-class as well as the poor suffered. As a result, the Weberian, Protestant ethic that hard work brings its own rewards was viewed critically, for it didn't seem to matter how hard or how long one worked or wanted to work. Uncontrolled economic forces apparently could rot the diminished fruits of any man's labors.

This change in popular social attitudes was filtered through Franklin D. Roosevelt who crystallized them in the form of new social legislation that up to this time had largely been ignored. The untested programs of slum clearance and public housing were a part of the Depression-propelled movement towards greater social and individual equity. Early twentieth-century reformers and writers such as John Debs, Jacob Riis, Theodore Roosevelt, Ida Tarbell, Sinclair Lewis, and others, helped create the philosophical and intellectual sparks. The Depression supplied the fuel. And F.D.R. provided the drivership necessary to guide new legislative vehicles designed to advance the cause of greater social democracy.

Relocation per se was neither a largely known concept nor an issue then, since the Depression masked any absolute shortage of urban housing. The doubling-up of families to save on rent provided sufficient housing resources in the private rental sector to accommodate the families required to be relocated from slum clearance sites. Furthermore, since the ultimate objectives and goals of low-rent public housing were desirable, there were few social critics then who questioned the necessity for effective relocation programs. The newly emergent public concern with social welfare did not extend to the area of relocation. This awaited later public actions such as urban renewal, highway, and other community development programs to spark the embers of growing public concern into flames. The magnitude of the housing shortage for the poor and the minorities, in combination with the growing awareness of discrimination against them, produced an outcry from those who were directly affected.

In the post-World War II period, the demand for more housing, public or otherwise, was voiced by different interest groups at different times for different reasons. Among the first of these were returning war veterans who needed places to live. Later there were the relocatees, especially minorities, who were thrust into a private rental market in which racial discrimination was the accepted practice. The scenario was thus being written for a troubled era in relocation—a critical fifteen-year period characterized by social conflict and a growing awareness of the gaps in the nation's social programs, including relocation.

Urban Relocation, Phase II: 1946 to 1970

The Housing Act of 1949: Relocation Institutionalized

World War II served as a temporary brake on further slum clearance legislation, but in 1945, the scenes of 1935-37 were starting to be replayed. Franklin D. Roosevelt announced that improved housing had become a postwar national objective.[1] The return of some 13,000,000 military men, most of them marriageable and in desperate need of shelter, fostered a strong, large interest group in support of the newly articulated goal of more and better housing and the elimination of the nation's slums.[2] Expanded low-rent public housing and new urban development programs, originally supported primarily by social reformers and public housers, were now strongly endorsed by ill-housed veterans as well. Pitted against this coalition were the established real estate, banking, and construction groups seeking to forestall any new legislation of this nature.[3]

Harry Truman, upon assuming the presidency after Roosevelt's death, "...demonstrated his desire to become the national leader of urban liberalism" by advocating a broad program of urban development, slum clearance, and housing. His "Fair Deal" was largely derived from the New Deal and expressed his close psychological identification with the average American as well as his populist political philosophy.[4] Truman succeeded in getting bi-partisan sponsorship for an omnibus housing bill supported by Senate Democrats Robert F. Wagner, the father of the 1937 Act, Allen Ellender from Louisiana, and the Republican Senator Robert Taft from Ohio. Taft, in an appearance before the Senate Committee on Banking and Currency on March 18, 1947, put forth his philosophy thusly: "I may say that I justify Federal interference in my general theory that the Federal Government is interested to see that there is a floor under the necessities of life for all the people in this country to give equality of opportunity, particularly to the children in all fields."[5] His co-sponsorship of this bill was vital since he was considered a spokesman for the conservative wing of Republican congressmen.

Debate over the Wagner-Ellender-Taft Bill, which was renamed the Taft-Ellender-Wagner Bill (TEW Bill) when Congress was captured by the Republicans in November 1946, took place amid the failure of the Veterans Emergency Housing Program that under Wilson Wyatt, was supposed to ease the postwar housing shortage. Wyatt, the Housing Coordinator, set a goal of 2,700,000 new homes, based on what later proved to be an unrealistic assumption that a newly born prefabricated homes industry could supply 750,000 reasonably priced dwellings of the total demand. To do so, wartime price and wage controls were required to be maintained to keep down housing production costs. By 1947, these controls were lifted, whereupon Wyatt resigned since he felt his objectives were unattainable in an uncontrolled market economy. The Veterans Emergency Housing Program was abandoned because continued wartime controls were counterproductive in an expanding economy and were unacceptable to the voting public.[6]

The issue of housing remained unresolved and refocused attention on the TEW bill, which became the subject of lengthy congressional hearings. Truman used the hiatus created by the hearings to establish the Housing and Home Finance Agency as a permanent successor to the National Housing Agency. For the first time, several housing agencies such as the Federal Housing Administration and the Public Housing Administration were brought under one umbrella.[7]

The surprise election of Truman over Thomas E. Dewey in 1948 galvanized the "do-nothing" Congress to reconsider the previously stymied TEW bill that had been strongly supported by the doughty Missourian during his campaign. Truman had spotlighted national attention on this issue by calling a special session of Congress in July 1948 just to consider housing legislation. The Republican-dominated session passed an emasculated bill, ostensibly designed to encourage housing construction, that the president damned but signed. In his campaign Truman emphasized the gap between the Republican party's platform rhetoric and promises and congressional enactment of emaciated and emasculated housing pittances. Dewey's silence on this issue was counterpointed by Truman's verbal attacks, which contributed to the generally unexpected election victory of the midwest pepperpot.[8]

The president's message to Congress on January 5, 1949, featured a request for a strong housing bill. A bitter fight ensued as the original line-up of housing protagonists and antagonists released all their verbal shots. Charges of distortion and maliciousness versus claims of "creeping socialism" were aimed at whoever would listen. At one point in the House of Representatives, sexagenarian Eugene Cox of Georgia punched octogenarian Adolph Sabath of Illinois in the mouth, causing the latter's glasses to fall to the floor. The doughty Sabath returned measure for measure before peace was restored.[9] Paradoxically, both men were Democrats but they marched to the tune of different pipers; one rural, the other urban.

On June 29, an amendment in the House to cut out the public housing component of the bill failed by a vote of 209 to 204. Finally, after much debate, the TEW bill was passed 227 to 186. Taft called it a historic occasion; Truman observed that the nation had adopted a national housing policy by assuring every American family a decent home in a good environment. The highly controversial Housing Act of 1949 became law on July 15[10] with a declaration that

The Congress hereby declares that the general welfare and security of the Nation and the health and living standards of its people require housing production and related community development sufficient to remedy the serious housing shortage, the elimination of substandard and other inadequate housing through the clearance of slums and blighted areas, and the realization as soon as feasible of the goal of a decent home and a suitable living environment for every American family thus contributing to the development and redevelopment of communities and to the advancement of the growth, wealth and security of the Nation.[11]

Congress, bombarded by the waves of protest from the underhoused veterans of World War II and their suffering relatives, passed the most comprehensive piece of legislation affecting housing and community development. Carried by the same currents was an expanded low-rent public housing program long advocated by professional public housers.[12]

Of particular interest here are two sections—Titles I and III—of the 1949 Act from which flow the relocation responsibilities towards households and businesses. Title I, the urban renewal title, provided for loans of $1,000,000,000 and grants of $500,000,000 for planning urban renewal projects. It also provided for the federal government to pay two-thirds of the aggregate net project costs, thereby making it financially attractive for a community to plan the redevelopment of a project area and to dispose of the land to private developers at a substantial "write-down" in costs.[13]

Recognizing that slum clearance by itself was inoperable without providing for decent low-rent housing, Congress, in Title III, provided for 810,000 new low-rent dwelling units as relocation housing resources. These units were to be built over a period of six years. Although Title I required that all families displaced by urban renewal slum clearance projects be relocated into standard, decent, safe, and sanitary dwellings, Title III, which dealt with public housing projects, had no such detailed constraints. As noted earlier, limited financial assistance was provided to families on public housing sites and then only as an incidental cost and not as a right. Assistance in the form of moving expenses and a month's rent were permissible expenses when needed to move a family off-site.[14]

This new Act was implemented very slowly as "the formidable task of converting its high goals into actual houses and cleared slums was beset by many difficulties."[15] At the end of Truman's term, 43 months after the passage of the Act, only 26 urban renewal projects and some 60,000 of the 810,000 low-rent public housing units were in construction, which represented "starts" of only 7.5 percent toward a goal of 60 percent by then. The elaborate administrative processes required to make Titles I and III operative, a growing public indifference resulting from an easing of the housing shortage for veterans during the 1950s, and the never-ending opposition of the real estate groups, all diminished the initial enthusiasm and support engendered by the passage of the Act.[16]

Later Legislative Amendments

The election of Dwight D. Eisenhower in 1952 ended Truman's Fair Deal. It had failed to resolve the housing dilemma but had nevertheless brought it into sharper focus. The new Republican administration subsequently called for a review of the nation's housing policies that led to these policy modifications in 1954:[17] (1) the Urban Renewal Administration was created as a constituent unit of the Housing and Home Finance Agency, (2) emphasis shifted from an individual project approach for slum clearance to the concept of an effective program for eliminating blight through rehabilitation wherever feasible, thereby presuming to limit the problems of relocation, (3) a new relocation housing resource was adopted, Section 221 housing, permitting thirty-year loans of up to 95 percent of value to nonprofit groups, (4) a new requirement called for a Workable Program for community development, which included a relocation component based on a communitywide evaluation of relocation resources balanced against needs, (5) and a directive was issued requiring a local public agency's relocation plan be approved by the Housing Administrator. The amended Act also cut down to 35,000 the number of public housing units permitted to be constructed annually.[18] This contravened the original objectives of the 1949 Act to provide public housing as a relocation resource for families residing on urban renewal sites.

In an attempt to shake the slum clearance and public housing program from its apparent lethargy, in 1956 a Democratic-controlled subcommittee of the House Banking and Currency Committee, after public hearings, charged in a report that the urban redevelopment program was hopelessly bogged down in administrative bungling as the problems of slums and urban blight remained unresolved: "It is generally conceded that new slums are still being made faster than the old can be redeemed."[19] The report stated that a large-scale public housing program was needed to relocate those 40 to 50 percent of the families displaced by urban renewal who were eligible for low-rent public housing. Concern was expressed for (1) families who move to places unknown, thereby failing to have the adequacy of their new homes certified, (2) the differing definitions of standard housing used by the cities, (3) the evident relocation of some families into substandard units, and (4) the lack of financial assistance for businesses. The lack of housing for minority groups was also considered and a pious hope was expressed that adequate solutions for this unyielding problem would be forthcoming.[20] The investigation was among the early storm warnings directed at urban renewal and was a precursor of more to come from various sources.

In 1956, Congress, for the first time, authorized relocation payments to relocatees as a right rather than as means for expediting the redevelopment program. Local public agencies could choose to pay reasonable and necessary moving expenses of up to $100 for families and individuals and $2,000 for businesses, which would be fully reimbursable by the federal government.[21] These amounts were increased the next year to $200 and $2,500, respectively, and included a proviso for optional or alternate payments according to a fixed schedule of moving expenses. In 1959, the $2,500 limit for commercial relocation payments was increased to $3,000.[22] Furthermore, grants up to two-thirds of the cost were provided to cities for preparing community renewal plans that were required to include a relocation component to serve as a guide and schedule for local redevelopment programs.[23]

Urban Renewal and Relocation under Attack

The early ripples of discontent swirling about urban redevelopment resulting from its negative effects on families and businesses, grew to a tidal wave during the beginning and middle 1960s. The combined impact of relocation programs in public housing, urban renewal, and highway developments unearthed previously submerged social pathologies in the ghettos of many cities. In 1964, the House Committee on Public Works reported that of 72,920 families and individuals relocated in a recent year, 70,553, or 97 percent, were required to do so by the aforementioned programs. It was anticipated that further agency activities would increase residential relocations to 111,080 per year.[24] Since most of the public works programming was in urban areas, it followed that involuntary displacements would have to be a prerequisite for continuing the slum clearance, urban renewal, and road building programs.

About this time a few of the pioneer advocates of public housing and slum clearance began to question the validity of some of their original assumptions regarding slum clearance as a program of social betterment, for now urban renewal was becoming synonymous with "Negro removal." Public housing was also suffering from a growing disenchantment as the projects became repositories for families with apparently unending social problems.[25]

Starting in 1964, growing urban violence caused President Lyndon B. Johnson to advocate legislation and programs to alleviate social unrest in the nation. This led to the adoption of civil rights laws, the antipoverty program, the Model Cities Program, such new public housing concepts as rent supplements and turnkey programs, and enlarged relocation benefits. The social, physical, and political milieu of the 1960s was violent, smoky, and dense, as Watts in Los Angeles burned along with Newark, Detroit, and other cities. It was a time of social activism and verbal criticism. In reaction to these onslaughts, there were some attempts at innovation and change in the now tradition-encrusted social programs, such as public housing and welfare, that were carried over from the Depression. One means proposed for effectuating change was the establishment of the Department of Housing and Urban Development (HUD) as a cabinet-level agency, thereby granting recognition to the importance of the problems of urban areas and cities.[26] In the heated social climate, the appointment of Robert Weaver as Department Secretary took on added symbolic significance since he was the first black to serve at the cabinet level.

Nonetheless, the criticism continued as urban renewal programs, highways, and other public improvements aggravated the now-open wounds of the urban population—both black and white, the poor and not so poor. By way of illustration, the titles below convey much of the critical flavor of that decade: Martin Anderson wrote the *Federal Bulldozer, A Critical Analysis of Urban Renewal, 1949-1962*; James Q. Wilson edited *Urban Renewal: The Record and the Controversy*; Charles Abrams, a public housing advocate from its first days, wrote equivocally about urban renewal activities in *The City Is the Frontier*; and the Advisory Commission on Intergovernmental Relations issued a report called, *Relocation: Unequal Treatment of People and Businesses Displaced by Governments.* Both Congress and President Johnson appointed study groups to consider the problems of the cities and to suggest ways to deal with their volatile, burning issues and ghettos.

The congressional study group, The National Commission on Urban Problems in a key observation said that ". . . over most of the country, public housing programs and other forms of housing assistance to low-income families, despite all the brave talk, are still developing at a relatively slow rate, while the rates of demolition because of urban renewal and highway construction are being speeded up. Families are therefore being displaced on a large scale, and this cannot be overlooked as among the main contributing causes of urban unrest."[27] Within this context the President's Committee on Urban Housing called for a reallocation of the nation's resources to produce 26,000,000 dwelling units · by 1978 including at least 6,000,000 units for lower-income families.[28]

In an attempt to counter the growing negative mood towards the urban renewal program, Congress in 1964 took a quantum step by authorizing relocation adjustment payments up to $500 per year for two years to low-income families and individuals to assist them in meeting relocation costs and higher rentals in their new dwellings. This amount was to represent the difference between 20 percent of their income and the actual cost of obtaining decent housing. Small businessmen were also eligible to receive $1,500[29] (raised to $2,500 a year later) if their average annual net earnings were under $10,000, in addition to a payment for moving expenses.[30] In 1965, HUD programs of low-rent public housing, urban mass transportation, public facility loans, code enforcement, and demolition were all required to offer a full array of relocation financial benefits.[31]

The Housing Act of 1965 provided enhanced fiscal help for families and businesses required to relocate. For renter families, a new program of rent supplements authorized payments up to $500 over a five-month period instead of two years. In order to qualify, a family had to be either handicapped or disabled physically or occupy substandard housing. Individuals 62 years or over were also eligible for rent supplements. Funds that were approved for an additional 60,000 units of public housing included the leasing of dwellings and rehabilitated units in the private housing market. Businesses in disaster areas as well as urban renewal areas were able to qualify for loans from the Small Business Administration. That agency was also permitted to insure business leases for a ten-year period. To strengthen relocation controls, urban renewal agencies were called upon to recertify the availability of housing for relocatees immediately prior to the start of their action programs. Relocation activities stemming from the Demonstration Cities and Metropolitan Development Act of 1966 were also covered by these tighter requirements.[32]

In 1968, Congress added Sections 235 and 236 to the Housing Act; these reduced mortgage payments (and thereby rentals to lower-income families) by providing federal subsidies for the difference in interest rates between the market rate and one percent. Priorities for such housing were granted to relocatees as provided for in the 1965 Act; namely to the elderly, the handicapped, and slum dwellers. Congress also approved another increase in financial benefits to relocatees. Renter families previously eligible for additional relocation payments up to $500 over five months were now entitled to receive as much as $1,000 over twenty-four months. Homeowners were now eligible for payments up to $5,000 to enable them to acquire other modest, decent, safe, and sanitary homes. Furthermore, recording fees, penalty costs for mortgage prepayments, transfer taxes, and pro-rata taxes incidental to conveying real property were reimbursable.[33] One commentator noted, "The Housing and Urban Development Act of 1968 provides the legislative framework for the most massive and comprehensive housing and community development program since Congress first began to tinker with the subject in the early days of the New Deal."[34]

In 1969, Congress adopted two amendments relating to relocation; the Secretary of HUD was required to review a locality's relocation plan biannually for its effectiveness, and a community demolishing low- and moderate-income housing in an urban renewal area was required to build new units at least equal to the number demolished.[35] This latter requirement expressed the broadened views of Congress that the urban renewal program must assume a major relocation responsibility by providing replacement housing for its own relocatees[36] in addition to increased financial assistance.

The election of Richard M. Nixon in 1970 resulted in a shift in federal priorities away from inner-city redevelopment. New housing programs were to be designed to produce a balanced housing strategy—that is, between programs that subsidized the production of new housing and those providing a direct subsidy to families to seek out their own decent shelter in the housing market. The objective of the "improved balance" was to make use of the existing standard housing stock, thereby eliminating the mounting interest subsidy costs of the "235" and "236" program while still providing a direct subsidy for rent payments to low-income families, including relocatees.[37] This strategy implied a decreasing emphasis on slum clearance activities and the relocation problems associated with such programs. This revised approach was tacit acknowledgement by an admittedly conservative Republican administration that the federal government had some obligation to provide suitable shelter for people with low incomes.

The Federal Highway Program

Another program in urban areas that generates relocation activities of some magnitude is the highway program. The Federal-Aid Highway Act of 1962 authorized states to make payments of relocation expenses not to exceed $200 per family or individual and $3,000 to a business concern, farm, or nonprofit organization.[38] In addition, the Act required state highway departments to give satisfactory assurances that relocation advisory assistance would be provided to the relocatees. Federal highway trust funds, previously restricted to property acquisition and road construction, were now capable of being tapped for payments for loss of personal property or the cost of moving same for tenant relocation, loss of business, diversion of traffic, and other items of damage or value. This modified an earlier legal doctrine that payments not generally compensable in eminent domain were not considered reimbursable costs by the federal government.[39]

Since the federal law merely authorized the states to provide relocation benefits by the state highway departments, adoption of its provisions was not universal. By December 1964, only twenty-two states were paying moving expenses. Of these, fifteen limited their payments exclusively to federal-aid highway programs, thereby denying payments to relocatees of state or locally financed highway programs.[40] Federal highway displacement activities at that time involved 32,395 families and individuals or 44.4 percent of the total annual urban displacements in the mid 1960s.[41] The passage of even this relatively mild form of financial aid for relocatees was not without misgivings on the part of some state highway officials and lobbyists for the highway program. There were objections that tenant relocation payments consumed funds that should be used to provide additional miles of roads. California highway officials wrote that early relocation planning by families, resulting from timely and adequate notice to vacate, was sufficient to overcome relocation problems. Furthermore, the use of funds collected from highway users through gasoline taxes, license fees, and other sources, raised a legal issue regarding their allocation for relocation payments.[42]

Congress was subject to the same public pressures against urban highway programs as against urban renewal programs; a classic illustration was the fight over highways in Boston. *The New York Times* of July 25, 1971, states, "An unusual coalition organized to resist highway construction here has moved Massachusetts to the verge of a basic change in urban transportation . . . [and] has led to a virtual stoppage in major highway construction and airport expansion in the area."[43] As a result, Congress, in the Federal-Aid Highway Act of 1968, mandated that relocation payments and advisory assistance should be provided to all persons displaced in accordance with the provisions of this Act.[44]

The following types of payments were authorized for families (1) actual reasonable moving expenses, or (2) a moving expense allowance not to exceed $200 per a fixed schedule approved by the Secretary of the Department of Transportation, and (3) a dislocation allowance of $100. For businesses or farms, moving expenses up to $25,000 or optional payments were allowed in an amount not to exceed $5,000. This was to be based upon an average of two years net earnings provided the business couldn't be relocated without suffering a loss of patronage and was not part of a chain operation. For homeowners, a payment for replacement housing no greater than $5,000 was authorized if another home was purchased within one year. Furthermore, if a homeowner was required to rent a dwelling unit, a payment up to $1,500 could be made over a two-year period to lease or to make a down payment on another residence. And, as in urban renewal programs, expenses incidental to transfer of property were compensable.[45] Relocation advisory services were required, including studies to determine the nature of the assistance needed by the relocatees, the availability of housing resources, and the availability of loans to businesses under the Small Business Act.

In 1970, Congress authorized replacement housing as part of the construction cost of the highway where a project was stymied due to relocation problems. Funds could be used for: (1) constructing new housing, (2) acquiring existing housing, (3) rehabilitating existing housing, and (4) relocating existing housing.[46]

Summary

The period from 1946 to 1970 may be interpreted as one of maturation, conflict, and change in community development and relocation programs as federally funded activities expanded throughout the nation's cities. Such programs as slum clearance, public housing, and community development, which had been initiated by Franklin D. Roosevelt and Harry Truman and subsequently continued or extended by their Democratic successors, were the chosen instruments for effectuating physical improvements to revive the cities. Although the Republicans under Eisenhower attempted to recast these rebuilding programs, they did not cast them aside. Furthermore, Eisenhower created still another community development vehicle for a changing urban and suburban

America by sponsoring the Federal-Aid Highway Acts of 1956 and 1958, which subsidized highway construction in urban areas.[47] By the end of 1962, the federal government was administering more than forty separate programs that required some form of financial aid for urban development. Of these more than half were nonexistent before 1950.[48]

The increasing involvement of the federal government in the affairs of the nations' cities and towns is one of the major characteristics of the post-World War II era. This was accelerated by the administrations of John F. Kennedy and Lyndon Johnson as new laws and executive orders were adopted to aid the depressed cities. New social programs were enacted in areas such as mental health, medical aid for the elderly, school aid, and the antipoverty program, which did not entail any relocation. But in some cases Model Cities activities along with physically oriented public housing, urban renewal, and highway programs, which came to full blossom, did require people to move. By their very nature, the building programs often necessitated the relocation of large numbers of households and businesses. The cumulative effects of these forced population movements resulted in a growing public clamor that virtually brought to a halt such activities and led to a critical rethinking of their effects on people. During this period, there developed the first strong public awareness that relocation[a] engendered a social and economic cost that required a positive federal government response in the form of fiscal and housing resources.

Thus, the Housing Act of 1949 gave birth to relocation as a formal, ongoing process subject to federal control. An analysis of subsequent amendments affecting relocation legislation reveals several critical factors in the institutionalization of the relocation process:

1. Establishment of relocation assistance as a right (which thereby gave it a new and firmer legal status than heretofore);
2. Successive enlargements of fiscal assistance to residential and commercial relocatees;
3. Attempts to make uniform the financial benefits flowing from the various community development programs;
4. Attempts to require a comprehensive relocation planning and rehousing component for each development program;
5. Requirements for providing counselling services to ease the myriad problems associated with moving elsewhere.

These program modifications resulted from the pressures raised by those most directly affected, the relocatees, as well as the social critics who decried the attempts to physically rejuvenate deteriorating urban areas. Joining with them

[a]Planned relocation is defined as those relocation programs requiring an approved written plan and program for the relocation of families and businesses as a condition for funding a community improvement program. Ideally the plan includes social, fiscal, and re-housing elements designed to meet individual needs.

were those interest groups in support of community development—public housers, urban renewal officials, highway builders, and local politicians—who feared the economic consequences of a slowdown or termination of their activities. They therefore supported changes and improvements in the relocation requirements as part of their programs. However, the changes in the laws for each program lacked uniformity in their financial payments and rehousing requirements. These inequities, borne of the different legal requirements among the various programs, resulted in severe financial hardships and strains on people and caused deep resentment.

The post-World War II era began with limited social knowledge and understanding special problems for which relatively simplistic physical solutions were preferred. Such complex issues were presumably capable of resolution merely by providing more public housing, eliminating the slums, and redeveloping the decaying cores of the cities. All these were and are, in effect, physical approaches to problems encompassing strong social undertones. The social implications, for which the slums were merely physical symptoms, were poorly understood. In the 1960s, some groping, halting steps, such as the antipoverty and Model Cities programs, were initiated to cope with social blight. This was in response to a growing awareness of the unmet needs of a large urban underclass residing in the slums. The concurrent civil rights movement, which had lost its charismatic leaders by assassinations also lost much of its momentum by the end of the decade. The social revolution of the 1960s, which had been ignited in large part by America's college youth and the underclass of society, ended—after a period of bloodshed, violence, and death in the cities and on some college campuses. By the 1970s, the fires of violent protest as a means for change were diminished when a majority of citizens ultimately registered their disapproval through the traditional political instrument of the ballot box.

During the period of turbulence in the sixties, relocation—a concomitant of public housing, urban renewal, and highway programs—showed some progress in providing economic and financial equity for relocatees; the first halting steps toward this goal culminated in the passage of the Uniform Relocation Assistance and Real Property Acquisition Policies Act in 1970 (Relocation Assistance Act). As noted above, congressional reactions towards increasing criticisms from relocatees and social critics took the form of progressively increasing financial benefits and provisions for additional housing resources. Such incremental advances notwithstanding, relocation was still viewed by some social critics as a prototype issue between the "haves" and the "have nots" of a socially stagnant society.[49]

The Relocation Assistance Act by itself is incapable of eliminating poverty, curing ill health, or solving the deep social problems faced by those trapped within their own experiences. It is a landmark because of its formal recognition of the financial and housing inequalities imposed upon those required to move as a result of federally supported physical constructions programs as well as its

7

Urban Relocation, Phase III: 1970 to Date

Public Hearings and Reports Preliminary to 1970

The Hearings of 1963

In 1963, the Select Subcommittee on Real Property Acquisition of the Committee on Public Works of the House of Representatives (hereafter, Subcommittee) held nationwide hearings to determine "the effects of piecemeal legislation on those persons forced to make way for public improvements."[1]

An early witness emphasized that the types of assistance available to families was denied to businesses, thereby creating an injustice to small businessmen.[2] Another stated there was no uniformity among the various federally aided programs. Human beings differ, their needs differ, and the resources required for resolving each specific situation must be tailored to meet the particular case.[3]

The Subcommittee also heard testimony about the results of a study dealing with the psychological effects of relocation on some 500 randomly selected families who comprised 20 percent of the relocation workload in a Boston redevelopment project. Transitional experiences such as relocation evidently produced an increase in the rate of "grief" suffered among some relocatees. Almost half the women and better than one-third the men were still unable to adjust to their change in physical environment two years after moving. The director of this study recommended: (1) an increase in extrinsic resources, such as financial benefits; (2) adequate relocation planning and increased services; and (3) providing for such intrinsic reinforcements as education, occupational skills, and relatively adequate income.[4] Another member of this research group was concerned with the increased rents that relocatees were required to pay, the inadequacy of agency referral services to other housing, and the lack of basic knowledge about the real costs and effects of relocation.[5]

The former Business Relocation Officer of the Boston Redevelopment Authority testified about the difficulties of small businessmen and stated that too many administrators accepted the inevitability of a business death rate from 25 to 50 percent. This viewpoint, he said, must be modified. He believed the liquidation rate of small businesses in renewal areas could conceivably be held to the normal business discontinuance rate of 8.1 percent.[6]

Still later, a Brown University professor discussed his analysis of the effects of relocation on small businessmen for a highway in Providence. He concluded that

83

some businesses, such as manufacturers and wholesalers, improved their volume after relocation but neighborhood-type stores suffered the most when displaced.[7]

In general, the 1963 hearings produced testimony about the dissatisfaction of relocatees with not only the variations in compensation and benefits available under the different public improvement programs but also the lack of social services and business counselling services for residential and commercial site occupants. Also emphasized was the urgency and need for adequate fiscal resources as well as inexpensive relocation housing and retail store space.

Despite the recommendations for substantive changes in current relocation programs, Congress at that time failed to codify these different relocation provisions because of pressures from special interest groups. Among the forces opposing change were the highway interests that feared a major diversion of trust funds set aside exclusively for road building. Some public interest organizations also opposed modification of the relocation provisions of the Highway Act.[8] This was the political environment in which the Subcommittee issued its *Study of Compensation and Assistance* on December 22, 1964.[9]

The mandate given the Subcommittee by Congress for its investigation was to undertake this work in the broad spirit of the just compensation requirement of the Fifth Amendment and the due process clauses of the Fifth and Fourteenth Amendments of the Constitution, "so that all persons affected by the acquisition of property by the United States or under Federal or federally assisted programs shall receive fair, just, and equal treatment."[10] The *Study* was later called the most comprehensive analysis of public relocation policies and programs ever to be published.[11] Its conclusions were concerned not only with relocation issues, but with required changes in the Internal Revenue Code and an analysis of the types of services that should be made available to relocatees from other government agencies.[12]

The Subcommittee's key conclusions and recommendations concerning relocation are as follows:

1. Federal and federally assisted programs require an "astoundingly large" number of displacements. For each year from 1964 through 1972, there is expected to be relocated approximately 183,000 separate owners, 111,080 households, 17,860 businesses, and 2,310 farm operations plus the disruption of an additional 1,350 farms.

2. Market value payments for property taken under the Fifth Amendment do not compensate for moving personal property, moving families, looking for replacement properties, closing costs on replacement properties, losses incurred as a result of forced sales, increased rent payments, increased costs to purchase new properties, and a host of other costs.

3. By federal judicial interpretation, *all tenants*—residential and commercial—are not entitled to receive compensation. About 77,860 relocatees, or 59 percent of those affected, will be tenants and the majority of the residential tenants are

poor. For example, in September 1963, the Urban Renewal Administration reported that 54 percent of its displaced families are eligible for public housing. Distressingly, in 68 urban renewal areas, 29 percent of the families had incomes below $2,400.

4. Retail businesses suffer the greatest loss from relocation especially if their customers are from the impacted project area. As stated earlier, the mortality rate for businesses in relocation programs in the recent past was 31 percent compared to 8.1 percent for all business in the United States.

5. Lack of adequate financing, advice, and counselling contribute to the high rate of business discontinuance.

6. There are vast differences in the compensation provided for by federal legislation under various programs.

7. Present administrative requirements for relocation benefits are too cumbersome. Fixed payment schedules and simplified procedures would save money and would encourage prompt payments.

8. Loan assistance should be available to businesses not directly in public improvement programs but, which, because of the nature of their locations, are adversely affected by such programs. Therefore,

It is recommended that the Congress declare the policy that owners and tenants of property acquired for public programs conducted by the Federal Government, or with the assistance of Federal funds, shall be afforded fair and equitable treatment on a basis as nearly uniform as practicable; that owners and tenants shall be fairly compensated for their property and for other losses and necessary expenses incurred because of such programs; and that every reasonable effort shall be made to prevent hardships to persons caused to move from their homes, farms, or places of business, or to lose their employment or to suffer other economic injury as a direct result of such programs.[13]

The Subcommittee in its *Study* lay down the gauntlet to Congress—which remained neglected for four years.

The Report of 1965

In January 1965, the Advisory Commission on Intergovernmental Relations issued a report on relocation that was based heavily on the Subcommittee's work. In addition, this report contained the results of a survey of relocation engendered by such local activities as street improvements, public buildings, and code enforcement programs. This survey, which was undertaken in conjunction with the Conference of Mayors in the summer of 1964,[14] showed that the inadequate supply of private and public housing was the single most important obstacle to an expeditious relocation program. It also observed that the housing market must be evaluated on a broader geographic basis—such as a metropolitan area—so long as it is convenient to places of employment, trade, and individual neighborhood choices. This study emphasized the social aspects of relocation by noting "the degree to which relocation is successful, particularly for the most vulnerable displaced groups, depends on such other governmental programs as housing, public welfare, and aids to small business," and concluded by suggesting that such desirable federal objectives as improved housing, helping to upgrade the lives of the socially and economically underprivileged, and helping small business could be enhanced through the relocation process.[15]

The Hearings of 1969

For about four years there was no further positive congressional activity toward rationalizing the relocation process. Then, on November 29, 1969, Congressman George Fallon of Maryland, Chairman of the House Committee on Public Works, introduced a bill to establish uniform policies for all federal and federally assisted land acquisition programs. There followed a series of hearings and testimony from witnesses in support of the bill. In a declaration, the Committee gave this philosophic rationale for equitable legislation:

As the thrust of Federal and federally assisted programs has shifted from rural to urban situations, it became increasingly apparent that the application of traditional concepts of valuation and eminent domain resulted in inequitable treatment for large numbers of people displaced by public action. When applied to densely populated urban areas, with already limited housing, the result can be catastrophic for those whose homes or businesses must give way to public needs. The result far too often has been that a few citizens have been called upon to bear the burden of meeting public needs. . . . In short, this legislation recognizes that the Federal Government has a primary responsibility to provide uniform treatment for those forced to relocate . . . and to ease the impact of such forced moves.[16]

The unanimously approved Committee bill on relocation, while philosophically broad and comprehensive, actually stresses economic and fiscal reforms as the major instruments for providing equity to all persons. Nonetheless, it calls for a humanitarian program of relocation compensation, advice, and assurance of the availability of decent, safe, and sanitary housing as well as a uniform policy on real property acquisition practices. Perhaps most important of all, it gets to the heart of the dislocation problem by providing some means to increase the available housing supply for displaced low- and moderate-income families and individuals. "The Congress can only provide such tools. Their effective use depends upon the attitude and skill of the officials in the executive branch of the Government responsible for their administration."[17] Congress promptly adopted the bill, changing its attitude of neglect once the highway interests began to understand the need for gaining public support for highway programs by liberalizing relocation aids and land acquisition policies.[18]

The Uniform Relocation Assistance and Real Property Acquisition Policies Act of 1970[19]

After close to ten years since the original hearings and debate, the Uniform Relocation Assistance and Real Property Acquisition Policies Act of 1970 now provides for essentially a new financial relocation policy by making available for the first time adequate funds to absorb most of the direct fiscal costs of relocation. This law can be viewed as a vehicle for correcting financial injustices. It is also a codifying instrument replacing a series of previously inchoate planned relocation policies and programs.

The Act begins with a Declaration of Purpose calling for uniform and equitable treatment of persons displaced from their homes, businesses, or farms. Title I comprises the General Provisions and the definitions under the Act.[20]

Title II is probably among the most important titles of the Act for it provides for substantial payments to any displaced persons. The following are its major relocation provisions.

Section 202—Actual Costs. A displaced person may receive: (1) actual reasonable expenses in moving himself, his family, business, farm operation, or other personal property; (2) actual direct losses of tangible personal property in moving or discontinuing a business or farm operation, but not more than the reasonable expenses that would have been required to relocate such property; and (3) actual reasonable expenses in searching for a replacement business or farm. Payments for direct losses of property are allowed where a person who is displaced from his place of business or farm operation is entitled to relocate his property, but does not do so.

The details of financial compensation to all classes of occupants are at first glance overwhelming and confusing. Undoubtedly many administrative refinements will have to be introduced into the system. But more significant is the fact that this law moves in the direction of being responsive to the particular financial needs of site occupants who are required to relocate. In this sense, the Act may be considered the initial step on the road toward individual economic equity and justice.

Section 202—Fixed Payments. In lieu of actual moving costs, fixed payments may be approved as follows: (1) for residential displacement, a moving expense allowance may be established by the administering agency of up to $300, plus a flat dislocation allowance of $200; (2) for business and farm displacement, a fixed payment for moving in an amount equal to the average annual net earnings[a] of the business or farm operation, except that such a payment may not be less than $2,500 or more than $10,000. The fixed payment for a business may be granted if the federal agency head determines that the business cannot be relocated without a substantial loss of its existing patronage and it is not a part of a chain store operation.

Section 203—Replacement Housing for Homeowners; Replacement Housing Payments. Besides payments for moving and related expenses, a displaced homeowner who owned and occupied a home at least 180 days before the start of negotiations for his property is eligible to receive a replacement housing payment not to exceed $15,000. These payments can be made only to homeowner relocatees who purchase and occupy decent, safe, and sanitary dwellings within a one-year period from the moving date.[b]

Replacement housing payments compensate for additional costs that include: (1) a replacement housing differential, which is an amount to bridge any gap between the acquisition payment for the dwelling under a "market value" standard and the actual reasonable cost for a comparable dwelling that is decent, safe, and sanitary and is located in a generally desirable area with regard to public utilities and public and commercial facilities and services, reasonably accessible to places of employment, and available in the private market to all persons; (2) compensation for less favorable financing, which includes such considerations for payment as (a) the amount of the unpaid debt at the time of acquisition of the real property, (b) the length of the remaining term of the mortgage at the time of acquisition, (c) the prevailing interest rate currently charged by mortgage lending institutions in the vicinity, and (d) the present worth of the future payments of increased interest (computed at the prevailing interest rate paid on savings deposits by commercial banks in the general area in which the replacement of dwelling is located)[c]; and (3) compensation for settlement costs, which is an amount to compensate for reasonable costs for title searches, recording fees, and other closing costs incurred in the purchase of the new unit, but not for prepaid expenses.

Section 203—Mortgage Insurance for Replacement Housing. If conventional financing is not available to a displaced owner for replacement housing, the head of any federal agency may insure such a mortgage provided it is eligible for insurance under any federal law administered by the agency. The administrator may also bypass any requirements under such a law relating to age, physical condition, or other personal characteristics of eligible mortgagors.

---

[a]The term "average annual net earnings" is defined as one-half of any net earnings of the business or farm operation before federal, state, and local income taxes, during the two taxable years immediately preceding the taxable year in which such business or farm operation moves from the real property acquired and includes any compensation paid to the owner, his spouse, or his dependents during such two-year period.

[b]Defined as beginning of the date on which he receives from the federal agency final payment of all costs of the acquired dwelling, or the date on which he moves from the acquired dwelling, whichever is the later date.

[c]To facilitate the administration of these provisions, the determination of the amount of the payment may be based upon a schedule adopted by the federal agency administrator.

Section 204–Replacement Housing for Tenants and Others. In addition to payments for moving and related expenses, tenants are also eligible for a housing replacement payment not to exceed $4,000 toward: (1) an amount necessary to lease or rent decent, safe, and sanitary housing for a period of four years (the unit must be adequate to accommodate the household and must be located in a generally desirable area in regard to public utilities and public and commercial facilities and reasonably accessible to the place of employment); or (2) an amount necessary (a) to make a downpayment for the purchase of housing and (b) to cover reasonable acquisition expenses (including title searches, recording fees, and other closing costs) of a decent, safe, and sanitary dwelling with standards established by the federal agency head. While the maximum payment may not exceed $4,000, if more than $2,000 is required, the tenant must match any amount in excess of $2,000 by an equal amount of his own funds in making the down payment.

In this section, Congress indicated a desire to offer a unique and obvious incentive to purchase housing and to encourage homeownership among renters as well as homeowners. In essence, part of the financial resources of community development programs can be utilized to broaden the nature of shelter available to renters. Through this incentive approach, the renter relocatee is encouraged to feel that he too can own a piece of society's real estate.

Section 205–Relocation Assistance Advisory Services. Relocation assistance advisory services are offered not only to any person displaced but, at the determination of the administrator, to any person occupying property adjacent to that acquired, if he is caused substantial economic injury. Each relocation assistance program must include such facilities and services necessary to: (1) determine the needs, if any, of displaced persons, for relocation assistance; (2) provide current and continuing information of the availability, prices, and rentals, of comparable decent, safe, and sanitary sales and rental housing and of comparable commercial properties and locations for displaced businesses; (3) assure that, within a reasonable period of time prior to displacment, suitable housing will be available, *equal in number to the number of households who require such dwellings* [italics added] and reasonably accessible to their places of employment; (4) assist a person displaced from his business or farm operation in obtaining and becoming established in a suitable replacement location; (5) provide information concerning federal and state housing programs, disaster loan programs, and other federal or state programs offering assistance to displaced persons; and (6) provide other advisory services to displaced persons in order to minimize hardships to such persons in adjusting to relocation.

Section 205–Coordination of Activities. The heads of relocation agencies are required to take positive action to assure the coordination of relocation activities with other project work and other planned or proposed governmental actions in the community or any of the outlying areas that may affect the carrying out of relocation assistance programs. Furthermore, by Executive Order, the heads of federal agencies are required to consult jointly to prepare a set of uniform procedures to implement this Act. This practice was originally initiated under the direction of the Office of Management and Budget to include all the agencies involved in planned relocation programs. On April 13, 1973, this coordinative function was transferred by the president from the Office of Management and Budget to the General Services Administration.[21]

Section 206—Housing Replacement by Federal Agency as Last Resort. This section states that no person shall be required to move from his dwelling for a federal project unless replacement housing is available. To guarantee that such housing will be available, if a federal or federally assisted project cannot proceed to construction because of the lack of replacement, sale, or rental housing of the required standards in the neighborhood or community in which the project is located, then the head of the federal agency can undertake such action as may be necessary *to provide such housing by using funds authorized for the project* [italics added]. Furthermore, heads of federal agencies may, whenever practicable, utilize the services of state or local housing agencies to provide the necessary housing facilities.

In what is potentially the most substantive and far-reaching section of the Act, Congress mandated that decent housing must be provided by all agencies responsible for community development programs—such as highway construction and urban renewal, to mention two. This section provides the fiscal resources for supplying sufficient low-income housing units to meet the needs of the relocatees if such accommodations are in short supply.

Section 212—Administrative Flexibility. To enhance uniform assistance programs and effective administration, a state agency can enter into relocation planning and execution contracts with any individual, firm, association, or corporation or with any government agency having an established organization for carrying out relocation programs. Wherever practicable state agencies may contract for the services of other state or local housing agencies or other agencies with experience in the administration of programs of this nature.

Congress provided here a more flexible tool for cutting through the thicket of bureaucracy by recognizing there is no "one best way" for administering a humane, effective planned relocation program. The state agency head is charged with the responsibility for evaluating competing approaches and systems and choosing that system or service that will provide the most effective assistance.

Section 215—Planning and Other Preliminary Expenses for Housing. The head of any federal agency administering a project requiring relocation is authorized to make loans as part of the project cost to nonprofit, limited dividend, or cooperative organizations or public bodies. Such loans may be up to 80 percent of necessary and reasonable expenses to be incurred in planning, prior to the availability of financing, if such housing is to be constructed or rehabilitated for those displaced. Nonprofit groups are eligible for loans with no interest, while loans to profit-oriented sponsors bear a market interest rate.

Section 216—Relocation Payments Not Subject to Federal Tax. Payments received under this Act are not to be considered as income for the purposes of the federal Internal Revenue Law, for eligibility under the Social Security Act, or any other federal law.

Section 217–Displacement by Code Enforcement, Rehabilitation and Demolition Programs Receiving Federal Assistance. Any person who moves as the result of a rehabilitation, demolition, or concentrated code enforcement program under Title I of the Housing Act of 1949, or a comprehensive city demonstration project under Title I of the Demonstration Cities and Metropolitan Development Act of 1966, is considered to be displaced as the result of the acquisition of real property for such a program or project. This makes such a person eligible for the full range of relocation benefits provided for displaced persons in Title II of this bill.

Section 301–Adequate Notice. The construction or development of a public improvement should be so scheduled that, to the greatest extent practicable, no person should be required to move from a dwelling (assuming a replacement dwelling will be available), or to move his business or farm operation, without at least 90 days' written notice of the date by which such a move is required from the head of the federal agency.

The elements of due process—written notice, public hearings, and an appeals procedure—that are traditional in American judicial processes are fairly new to some federal administrative agencies.[22] Here, for the first time in the laws governing relocation, mandatory processes and procedures are spelled out for all agencies involved in relocation programs.

Evaluations by Agencies

The effects of the Uniform Relocation Assistance Act appear to vary according to its particular sections and the agency involved in its administration. One immediate benefit, as noted, has been to codify and make uniform the previously varying rates and forms of financial aids among all those agencies whose activities require such relocation programs. Despite these improvements, concern was voiced at a Relocation Institute in 1971 and at other relocation meetings over the effect the increased costs of relocation would have on local communities.[23] Whereas previous urban renewal legislation provided for the federal government to pay in full the direct expenditures for relocation, now the Uniform Relocation Assistance Act and the Housing and Community Development Act of 1974 require that all direct relocation payments shall be part of project costs. This means that local decision making regarding the choice of projects is now subject to be influenced by the costs of relocation as an intrinsic factor. This new variable may tilt a community to select a less costly project instead of a more socially oriented alternative program since the latter may engender greater relocation costs. Thus, what may be better in the long run may be forced to yield to what is less costly immediately.

The urban renewal director of one village of 40,000 in New York stated this new federal requirement would result in an additional cost of $240,000 to cover the relocation expenses of a current project. While the cost will vary, depending upon the nature of the relocation workload, it is evident that the Uniform Relocation Assistance Act and the Community Development Act can be counterproductive if decisions on community improvements are made exclusively on a fiscal calculus rather than on broader perspectives that include social considerations as well.

Although relocation payments by all agencies during the fiscal year 1972 totalled more than $109,000,000 to over 50,000 claimants,[24] this record payment to relocatees is blemished. An audit by the General Accounting Office indicates that some communities failed to make relocation payments to eligible households and that in other cases such payments were insufficient to reimburse the displacees for moving expenses.[25] Another audit revealed cases of discrepancies in the amount of payments resulting from different interpretations of the Act, thereby negating the purposes of same. Furthermore, questions were raised about the coordinative efforts of the Office of Management and Budget.[26]

The second annual HUD report on relocation emphasizes a need for greater coordination among the various agencies. It states that current efforts are not responsive to the problems created by competing relocation activities, and cites the lack of adequate housing stock and the untimeliness of replacement housing. This report is also critical of the failure of the Office of Management and Budget to provide uniform reporting systems. The agency requests additional staff to review relocation submissions and indicates a need to provide training programs for relocation personnel at the federal and local levels.[27]

Generally HUD believes the new Act is favorably received by displaced residents and businesses, but it notes some adverse reactions stemming from the lack of proper information about the type and scope of the payments. The report states, however, these problems are being corrected. One area still causing problems is the need for some form of dislocation allowance for small businesses in addition to moving expenses since the new Act eliminates this provision of the Housing Act of 1949, thereby creating an additional financial burden on the retail merchants.[28]

The Department of Transportation (DOT) report to the President on their third year under the Act is more sanguine: "their experience indicates the relocation policies and programs are being very favorably received by those persons being displaced and communities affected by federally assisted highway projects."[29]

President Nixon's transmittal letter of 1973 summarizes the reactions of 28 agencies affected by the Act: "While the limited experience under the Act has not permitted a comprehensive survey of its effect on the general public, the principal reporting agencies agree that most of the people displaced by federally related activities were pleased with both their new relocation and their benefits.

The agencies attributed this favorable reaction to the increase in relocation benefits provided under the Act."[30]

A comparison of the fiscal impact of the HUD and DOT relocation programs immediately before and after the passage of the Uniform Relocation Assistance Act is shown in Tables 7-1 and 7-2. Differences in the nature of the benefits before and after 1970 make some of the comparisons difficult, but some general observations are possible.

Moving expense payments to families, based on submitted bills, have almost doubled under the new Act. Payments based on a fixed schedule have almost quadrupled, while financial payments to individuals are even greater.[d] Businesses, nonprofit organizations, and farmers have also received substantially greater financial benefits since moving expense payments in each of these categories have also increased significantly. The HUD second annual report states that direct relocation costs for the fiscal year 1972 are $44,000,000 while administrative costs are $12,000,000, which total $56,000,000 for their relocation program. The number of claims paid during 1972 was 25,870, for an average direct payment of $2,181 per claim at an administrative cost of $460 apiece.[31]

An evaluation of the financial payments by the Department of Transportation since 1970 also shows an increase in all categories but not nearly in an amount as significant as for the HUD program. This reflects the fact that the Federal-Aid Highway Act of 1968 already provided many of the benefits later incorporated in the 1970 Act. DOT direct relocation payment therefore increased earlier than those of other agencies. For example, their replacement housing payments went up sixfold from October 1, 1969, through September 30, 1970. An average of $2,348 was paid to almost 6,000 owner-occupants under the 1968 law. Comparable payments on rental units increased tenfold, averaging $912 apiece.[32] Table 7-2 compares DOT direct relocation payments for the fiscal period immediately prior to 1970 and thereafter.[33]

There appears to be some validity to the HUD recommendation for coordination and uniformity, especially in reporting essential data, since presently it is not possible to compare the direct relocation payments of various agencies due to the different classification of benefits. A subcommittee in the General Services Administration has been established to deal with this issue among others.

There is only one case reported among the 28 agencies where replacement housing under Section 206 (a) of the Act was required.[34] Furthermore, no loans were made to any nonprofit organizations under Section 215, which possibly reflects the relative newness of the Act. Because of its recency, it is premature to make any judgments about the usefulness of these two sections.

---

[d]The effects of inflation on moving costs must be considered as a factor. This would diminish the magnitude of the differences but not enough to negate the conclusion that increased financial benefits are being paid.

Table 7-1

Average Relocation Payments by the Department of Housing and Urban Development Immediately Prior to and Following the Adoption of the Uniform Relocation Assistance Act of 1970

Category	Cumulative Average Through Fiscal Year 1971			Category	Fiscal Year 1972[f]			
	Families	Individuals	Businesses		Families & Individuals	Businesses	Nonprofit Organizations	Farms
Moving Expenses[a]	89	60	2,376	Moving Expenses Actual Costs	186	4,467	1,605	38,123
Relocation Adjustment Payments[b]	388	411	N.A.	or Costs Per Fixed Schedule	335	N.A.	N.A.	N.A.
Replacement Housing Payments[c]	4,452	4,296	N.A.	Payments in Lieu of Moving Expenses	N.A.	2,894	2,410	—
Additional Relocation Payments[d]	631	693	N.A.	Locational Search Costs	N.A.	872	390	—
Small Business Displacement Payments[e]	N.A.	N.A.	2,331					

[a] Includes loss of property, 1956 to 1971 averages.

[b] 1965 to 1968.

[c] 1968 to 1971.

[d] 1968 to 1971.

[e] 1964 to 1971.

[f] Under Uniform Relocation Assistance Act of 1970.

Sources: Data through 1971 derived from HUD, *1971 HUD Statistical Yearbook* Washington, D.C., Table 73, p. 79. Data for 1972 derived from HUD, *Second Annual Report, Uniform Relocation Assistance and Real Property Acquisition Policies of 1970*, Washington, D.C., Exhibit I, Table I, U.S. total HUD programs, unpaged.

Table 7-2

Average Relocation Payments by the Department of Transportation Immediately Prior to and Following the Adoption of the Uniform Relocation Assistance Act of 1970

Category	October 1, 1969 through September 30, 1970				Fiscal Year 1972[a]			
	Residentials	Businesses	Non-Profit Organizations	Farms	Residentials	Businesses	Non-Profit Organizations	Farms
Moving Expenses	239	2,842	721	544	368	3,009	1,027	809
Replacement Housing:								
owner	2,348	N.A.	N.A.	N.A.	2,593	N.A.	N.A.	N.A.
renter	912	N.A.	N.A.	N.A.	1,131	N.A.	N.A.	N.A.
Incidentals	84	369	41	33	187	569	140	51

[a]Under Relocation Act of 1970.

Sources: Data for 1969-70 derived from *1971 Annual Report on Highway Relocation Assistance*, p. V. Data for 1972 derived from DOT, *Annual Report, P.L. 91-646, Uniform Relocation Assistance and Real Property Acquisition Policies Act of 1970*, July 1, 1971, through June 30, 1972, Exhibit II, unpaged.

Evaluations by Critics

Opinion about the virtues of the Uniform Relocation Assistance Act are by no means universal. Chester Hartman, critical of the basic concept of planned relocation, states: "the new Federal legislation can at most postpone the day of reckoning by offering substantial financial benefits which will be eaten up in a few years but will at least serve to mute or soften the protests of displacees. In its failure to deal directly with the underlying housing shortage, the new legislation may be described as an attempt to buy off displacees with what in effect are large bonuses."[35] This critique assumes a universe of low-income owner and tenant relocatees unable to secure decent housing, which is not necessarily valid. DOT relocation data for 1971-72 indicates that 25 percent of the homes or apartments of relocatees are valued below $6,000 or with a rent value under $60 monthly; 42 percent were between $6,000 to $15,000 or had a rent value from $61 to $110; and 33 percent were valued over $15,000 and had a rent value above $110. It seems reasonable to state that based on these criteria at least one-third of the DOT relocatees can be classified as middle-class households. Furthermore, DOT estimates only 17 percent of their relocatees were nonwhite,[36] thereby supporting the observation that in the main their relocation families are more affluent than those in urban renewal programs described below.[37]

Comparable data from HUD by race, age, and type of tenure, is based on reports from less than 70 percent of their local public agencies although the reports cover 1,200 projects. These data indicate that the majority of the households in urban renewal sites are black or Spanish surnamed elderly renters, but not overwhelmingly so as one might be led to believe. Thus, of some 13,000 relocatees in 1972,[e] about 7,100 are black or had Spanish surnames and represented approximately 55 percent of the total. Of some 3,900 households 62 or over, about 1,800 are black and 243 are Spanish surnamed. The total of elderly black and Spanish surnamed relocatees represent slightly more than 52 percent of all the elderly. Tenants total close to 9,000 while homeowners total 4,000. Tenants represent approximately 70 percent of the claimants.[38] Although the HUD study suggests that subsequent reports may yield different statistical patterns, it seems reasonable to conclude that based upon this data,[39] their households also demonstrate differential economic and social characteristics, thereby belieing global statements about the unsuitability of financial benefits for relocatees.

For middle- and upper-income families, significant cash benefits that enable them to seek out suitable replacement housing in the private sector may be an appropriate response to their needs. For low- and moderate-income families, especially minorities, subsidized housing of various types as well as other social

eCompared to 18,000 payments by DOT, presumably representing a like number of relocatees.

programs are required. However, the generally limited supply of reasonably priced, decent shelter, coupled with the limited mobility of minority families resulting from various exclusionary housing practices, creates a problem of adequate and timely replacement housing. Given such social restrictions, relocation housing resources in various rent ranges in the private and public sectors are required. Furthermore, handicaps of ethnicity or age cannot be compensated for primarily with fiscal assistance. While Section 206 of the Uniform Relocation Assistance Act is available to deal with these and other problem situations by authorizing a displacing agency to serve as "the houser of last resort," its effectiveness remains to be demonstrated.

Despite its critics, the passage of the Uniform Relocation Assistance Act has added substantive financial and useful rehousing tools toward a more equitable relocation process. It settles the earlier issue as to why relocatees should bear the financial costs and inequities resulting from programs presumably designed to benefit the community at large. It affirms that they should not be forced to sustain financial losses; that any such suffering shall be ameliorated by adequate financial compensation and supported with sufficient and appropriate rehousing resources. Although this is a somewhat limited goal in terms of the comprehensive, planned relocation process to be described later, nevertheless it represents a quantum advance over previous relocation policies.

Summary

Relocation programs in the United States developed as a consequence of an expanding federal presence in a growing society—most particularly, an urban technological society. Given the historic backdrop of the land disposition programs out of which "macro-relocation" policies grew, the intervention of the federal government in urban development appears to be an inevitable consequence of the changing nature and scale of American society. The nature of this change is illustrated by modifications in community development programs. Whereas they were once broad and amorphous (in both a geographic and programmatic sense) befitting the growth needs of an expanding individualistic agricultural economy, today these programs are far more specific and are designed to deal with the issues, problems, and felt needs of a post-industrial society. Given these conditions, new local urban community development policies and programs were mandated by Congress in response to the pressures generated by special interest groups supporting such activities.

Some of these new urban-oriented programs produced certain counterproductive social effects that fully surfaced in the 1960s. Thus, slum clearance, urban renewal, Model Cities, highway development, and other tools for urban problem solving brought in their wake some unanticipated and unintended costs: the relocation of many people with varying needs for housing, financial aid, and social services. This discovery led to a growing awareness of the lack of certain resources, such as information and knowledge, social programs, and money, to deal with the problems unearthed. This resulted in a diminution of relocation and redevelopment activities.

Unlike the Indian and Japanese relocation programs that were authoritarian by design, the relocation programs associated with community development activities tend to stem from democratic roots. This is because they were originally conceived as a means for alleviating specific crisis situations affecting people directly. Their original intent was social, as in slum clearance, war housing, and urban renewal programs, or at least neutral, as in highway development and other public works programs.

In contrast to the aforementioned acts of forced Indian and Japanese removal, there have been continuing relocation planning and program modifications and adaptations in order to minimize any ill-effects on relocatees. Although none of the community development programs produced anything like full-blown democratic models of "micro-relocation," nonetheless the incremental system of enlarged benefits for relocatees has resulted in a gradual evolution towards a more democratic relocation model. This includes the recent adoption of the Uniform Relocation Assistance and Real Property Acquisition Policies Act. This Act helped create financial equity in the relocation process. It is suggested here that this provides a nucleus for the development of enlarged housing and social components that can enhance individual growth in a dynamic post-industrial society. This, then, is the true significance of the Uniform Relocation Assistance Act: a base upon which other resources can be placed to further the goal of fairness and social equity for the individual relocatee.

We shall next consider the criticisms leveled at various relocation programs to determine their validity and relationship to the current relocation scene. By so doing, we hope to arrive at sounder and more effective social and administrative models of planned relocation that incorporate broader social perspectives, for the clarion calls to revolt against relocation are still strident today. Relocation, inveighs Hartman, "... is a prototype issue of the powerless poor facing powerful interests, public and private, economic and political, in what amounts to a battle over turf."[40] Is this a legitimate call to arms or is this a Quixotic-like campaign being waged against old and tired issues? For that matter, were the relocation issues that contributed to the traumas of the sixties fully relevant even then? If so, are they still germane or have other problems arisen to replace this conventional wisdom? Is it true that "short of a major redistribution of power and resources in the society, the most that can be done is to describe fully the costs and benefits involved in relocation, analyze the way the system operates, and prevent official deception from becoming the accepted truth"?[41] This conspiracy theory of government views many public actions as fraudulent and tends to denigrate the role of government in American society. But another hypothesis is postulated here: given the growing interest of the state in the affairs of society, and despite the erratic behavior of our government in relocation activities, a transformed, planned relocation system can serve as an instrument for enlarging social equity by promoting the growth and fulfillment of the individual.

**Part III:
Relocation: Issues and
Implications**

8 The Impact of Relocation on People

Small Businessmen

In 1958, the *New York Post* featured stories about the harmful effects of relocation on small businesses on the site of the proposed Lincoln Center for the Performing Arts. A spokesman for storekeepers forced to give up their locations, their customers, and their local reputations said, "We've been here twelve years, and what we have accomplished is to establish good will. That's our stock in trade. Without it we couldn't be in business."[1]

Fifteen years later, a headline in *The New York Times* read, "For Business, Urban Renewal Can Be Lethal," for " '. . . when urban renewal arrives small businesses are driven to the wall,' cries the small merchant. When this project is completed, space will be provided for 20 stores to replace the 325 which were on the site originally."[2] During the decade and a half between the two stories, there was a significant loss of small businesses attributable to public programs for rebuilding America's cities.

William F. Slayton, Commissioner of the Urban Renewal Administration, in 1963, stated then that the business death rate caused by urban renewal projects tended to be approximately equal to three or four years the annual normal business death rate of 10 to 11 percent found in blighted areas.[3] As damaging as the relocation process itself, was the prevailing attitude among those officials involved in community development programs that small retail businesses were marginal and, therefore, their ultimate failure was inevitable. On the basis of this fatalistic philosophy, it was simple enough to justify a business discontinuance rate of 25 percent or more as the price to be paid for redeveloping the nation's cities.[4]

This received doctrine is verified by several studies that showed a high percentage of business failures with few if any plans or programs to ameliorate this condition. In 1958, the Fordham University urban renewal site in New York City included 90 small storekeepers, many of whom were marginal and whose incomes were derived almost exclusively from the area residents. These retailers registered a dissolution rate of 45.4 percent. By way of contrast, only 24.5 percent of the 383 businesses on the adjoining Lincoln Center site went out of business. This difference in attrition is attributable in part to the fact that the Lincoln Center stores were located on a major street and near a subway station. As a result, they were exposed to more customer traffic which made them better off financially. Thus, they were able to weather the storms and stresses of

103

relocation more successfully. In this study, the more marginal, neighborhood retail businesses failed at almost twice the rate of the more broadly oriented firms.[5]

A study of the relocation of small businesses in Providence, Rhode Island, from 1954 through 1959, in many respects replicates the Fordham and Lincoln Center experience. Of 363 establishments, about one-third were from urban renewal projects and the remainder from highway programs. Approximately one-fourth were food stores, one-fifth jewelry or jewelry-related manufacturing units, while the remainder comprised other retail stores and services. The food stores were located mainly on the urban renewal sites; the jewelry firms, on the highway sites. Business losses varied by type of business; from a high of 51 percent for retail food stores to a low of 21 percent for other types of stores. Urban renewal business losses approximated nearly 40 percent of that universe whereas highway losses were 30 percent.[6] These differences reflect the greater marginality and the local neighborhood character of the food stores on the renewal sites as compared with the regional jewelry manufacturers on the highway locations.

Overall, there was a marked negative reaction to the entire relocation process, but this varied significantly in relation to one's ability to stay in business. Given their lesser economic strength, retailers from the urban renewal site expressed more negative feelings toward relocation than highway displacees. A majority of those that succeeded in relocating responded favorably to their move; one-third reported more business at their new locations, while less than one-fourth expressed dissatisfaction with their progress. Here again, economics was the crucial variable, with retailers registering the least sense of satisfaction.[7] The fundamental issue raised by the author of this study is "... whether the aggregate gains are worth not only the aggregate social and economic costs, but worth the individual costs as well."[8]

A study on *The Impact of Dislocation from Urban Renewal Areas on Small Business* elicited nationwide responses to the relocation experience.[9] This work pointed out these major problems universally faced by small businessmen:

1. The time lags between the announcement of plans and formal acquisition processes resulted in business losses as tenants started to move from the area.
2. Inadequate authoritative information resulted in rumors rather than facts.
3. Difficulties were encountered in securing new locations at reasonable rentals.
4. There was inadequate compensation for moving.
5. The failure to compensate for loss of good will and for retiring from business was noted.
6. There was a lack of readily available sources for financing new operations.
7. The economics of urban renewal resulted in the inability of businesses to return to the redeveloped neighborhood because of new high rents.
8. Relocation officials were unable to offer meaningful, substantive help.

Over the years these discordant themes were repeated with only minor changes of emphasis.[10] Robert Weaver, HUD Secretary, stated in 1966 before the House Select Committee on Small Business that "... probably the most significant single element in a business relocation program is the degree of service provided to help the business reestablish."[11]

To what extent has there been any amelioration of these problems of small businessmen? Are their earlier complaints still unanswered or are they no longer an issue? For analytic purposes, the issues may be classified as (1) financial, (2) information and educational, and (3) social.

Financial Issues

Beginning in 1956, Congress provided increasing amounts of financial assistance for moving expenses and property losses for commercial occupants of urban renewal sites.[12] With the passage of the Uniform Relocation Assistance Act in 1970, financial coverage was enlarged to include all businesses forced to move from all federal or federally assisted programs requiring relocation.[13] We noted earlier that in one respect the new Act is regressive. The former HUD small business displacement payment of $2,500 to re-establish the business has been eliminated. Instead, payments are permitted for either moving expenses and related costs, or an allowance of $2,500 to $10,000 based on annual net income. In some cases, this new formula is less rewarding than the payment for moving expenses plus the previous allowance for small business displacement.[14]

In 1964, Congress authorized the Small Business Administration to provide loans for 20 years at low interest rates (then at 3½-4 percent) to businesses displaced by federally financed programs. The Agency was also permitted to insure business leases for a ten-year period.

In 1968, Congress authorized DOT to provide increased moving expense payments of up to $25,000 or a fixed sum up to $5,000 in lieu of moving expenses for businesses on highway sites.[15]

The increases in financial assistance represent a significant advance under the Uniform Relocation Assistance Act. Nevertheless, there exist several unresolved, vexing fiscal problems. The question of "good will" or the reputation that accrues over the years to a business by virtue of its service and location is still considered a noncompensable item in condemnation cases, even though it is a consideration in the purchase and sale of retail businesses.[16] The issue of just compensation, interpreted in law primarily to mean payment for property taken,[17] should be broadened to include the loss of good will as well. Furthermore, this consideration should also be extended to businessmen in the immediately adjoining vicinity whose economic capabilities are adversely affected by public actions.

Another open issue is the lack of compensation to those businessmen who because of age, infirmity, or obsolescent skills are unable to re-open their businesses elsewhere. Ironically, the employees of a small firm are entitled to receive unemployment insurance benefits; their employers are not. For businessmen who comprise this group, the establishment of appropriate "out-of-business" insurance benefits is necessary and equitable.

Informational and Educational Issues

At the 1966 hearings of the Select Committee to evaluate the effectiveness of the Small Business Administration, the Executive Director of the Advisory Commission on Intergovernmental Relations emphasized the need for advice to small businessmen involved in the relocation process: "For many small businesses, relocation payments are not enough to assure their making an adequate adjustment to a forced move. These people need intensive counseling to prepare them for displacement and help them carry out their moves."[18] This theme was repeated by a spokesman for the Office of Economic Opportunity who felt the problems of small business were related to the issues of change and adaptability. He also stated that most minority businesses are usually small businesses greatly in need of basic management counselling.[19] The Select Committee recommended the following:

1. Increased counseling services;
2. Uniform relocation assistance to all businesses;
3. Lease guarantees for small business displacees by the Small Business Administration;
4. The feasibility of training small retail entrepreneurs in the service industries be investigated by the Department of Labor under the Vocational Act and the Manpower Development Training Act.

It concluded its hearings with this salient observation: ". . . the programs which the Congress has provided to offset or prevent these hardships are not always being administered in a manner which produces the hoped for result. Displacement loans are a most beneficial program, but only if those displaced know they are available."[20]

In response to some of these inequities, Congress, in Section 205 of the Uniform Relocation Assistance Act, mandated business relocation assistance advisory services to provide current information of comparable commercial properties and locations, to assist businesses in establishing in their new location, to supply information about related government programs that offer help to relocatees, and to minimize the hardships to businesses in adjusting to relocation.

In its 1972 report on the effects of the Relocation Assistance Act, HUD notes two problems that are unresolved and probably have a negative effect on all the site occupants. One is the failure to provide a workable mechanism at the local level to coordinate the relocation activities of the various federal agencies. HUD proposes a centralized relocation agency as a remedy and states there is a gap in providing an effective referral service for other federal and state assistance programs, an opinion expressed by the Comptroller-General as well.[21] This reflects the lack of trained relocation staff at the HUD regional and local levels, which is mirrored to a large extent among local public agencies.[22] This shortcoming is an indicator that the need for information and counselling and the concept of retraining the small businessman for successful relocation adjustment is still part of an open agenda.

Social Issues

Although some of the financial and informational issues which caused so much controversy in the earlier period, are close to resolution, the basic issue that transcends any community development program is still unresolved: What is the role for the small, individual entrepreneur in an increasingly functional and technologically organized American society? Exacerbated by public programs for rebuilding and revitalizing the cities, bypassed by innovative merchandising and marketing modes, and trapped with obsolescent talents and ideologies, the small storekeeper is likely to be an economic anachronism except in ethnic neighborhoods, Here his role is enlarged to include a social service as a communications center and local banker as well as a vendor of goods around whom people coalesce to receive services and information.[23]

In some neighborhoods, the taverns and restaurants function as local meeting places for groups of adults, the luncheonettes and candy stores cater to the teen-agers, while the grocery stores or "bodegas" may extend credit till payday. Until and unless there are substitutes, the ethnically oriented businessmen continue to serve a vital role as neighborhood catalysts or binders. Historically, some small businesses fulfill a role as incubators for larger ventures. Many of the nation's large department stores started in business as neighborhood variety stores. Furthermore, they may "spin-off" individuals with some entrepreneurial skills that may be utilized elsewhere in various economic activities.[24]

In summary, the local retailers play a social role as communicators in addition to their economic role as merchants, employers, bankers, and taxpayers. This added social dimension represents a loss to the neighborhood when they are forced out of business forever. If community development programs wish to perpetuate small businesses, it is necessary to create an atmosphere of mutual understanding and trust between relocation officials and affected businessmen.

This is an essential precondition before attention can be focused on the real estate, locational, financial, and management issues that are peculiar to the relocation of each displaced business.[25]

The Elderly[a]

The plight of the elderly couple or individual forced to move has drawn special attention during the past decade, particularly as a result of a grant by the Ford Foundation to study this significant problem of relocation.[26] Older people are affected by role changes that put them in a separate class unto themselves. Loss of full-time employment, loss of a spouse, reduced incomes, loss of friends, and declining physical and mental health, when added to an involuntary relocation process, creates more negative effects for them than for the younger family.[27] As wryly put by Charles Abrams, in addition to their imminent loss of shelter, the elderly are burdened with financial and emotional problems as well, and "what should be the cocktail hour of their life becomes their bitter evening."[28]

Since community development programs frequently effect the older areas of cities, their impact is heaviest on the occupants of such sections: minority groups, skid-row residents, and the residual elderly population who are the least capable of vacating familiar surroundings. Up to 1965, the elderly in urban renewal areas comprised from 10 to 30 percent of that population, with the average above 20 percent, except for rooming house neighborhoods where more than half may be elderly. Of the elderly households, approximately 50 percent are single persons.[29] And among this segment, the single elderly female predominates by comprising 60 to 85 percent of the group.[30]

Problems

The aging are an extremely heterogeneous group that includes the single woman living with relatives; the more "Americanized," financially secure female living by herself in her own home or in a hotel or rooming house; the single man living alone who is generally less dependent and has greater financial resources; and the married couple with the greatest degree of economic security who are more likely to own their own home. Withal, the financially independent elderly person capable of maintaining a home or apartment remains the ideal model for most Americans. Nevertheless, the elderly in the Ford Foundation study group perceived relocation as a threat in the following ways:

1. As a monetary loss. In the case of the homeowner, the purchase price for his home may not be equivalent to the price for acquiring another dwelling; for the renter, the increase in rent for a new unit is a continuing burden.

---

[a]Defined as those within the retirement range of 60 to 65 years and over.

Furthermore, one-time moving costs, loss of day's pay due to absence from work, and other financial woes were largely uncompensated in relocation.

2. As damaging to lifestyle. The dissolution of local friendships, removal from familiar places, and the need to recreate life patterns in relatively new and strange surroundings impose undue social costs on the elderly.

3. As resulting in inappropriate new arrangements. The potential dimunition of living space and suitable services in the surrounding environment plus the short supply of accommodations designed for the elderly require that many accept housing that may be unsuited to their needs.[31]

Solutions Under the Uniform
Relocation Assistance Act

Monetary loss: financial aid has increased in several ways, as demonstrated in the preceding analysis of the Act. A valid question may be raised, however, regarding the adequacy of some of the forms of financial aid, which are short-term in nature, whereas for the elderly, the decrease in earnings is long-term. The additional financial help has been able to mitigate the immediate costs of relocation for the elderly, but the long-term financial problem remains.

Damage to lifestyle: it is here that the relocation process continues to extract a toll. One case study details the existence of a symbiotic relationship almost equal to a natural condition of interdependence among some elderly neighbors. Forced by physical limitations and low incomes to rely heavily upon those living nearby, the elderly tend to spin a cocoon of social relationships revolving about local community organizations, which enmesh and protect their fragile existence, for the "... elderly have no daily contact with fellow-workers, or a younger family's involvement with children and have often been widowed."[32] Though this symbiosis is not universal, relocation processes tend to uproot and destroy whatever social and communal relationships may have developed among the elderly unless those among them can, if they so desire, move as a complete social unit. Sociologists maintain that the elderly especially should be allowed to remain *in toto* near their old area if they wish, alongside familiar sights, neighbors, and kin.[33] The importance of meeting their social-psychological needs in relocation is considered to be the most critical factor in achieving their beneficent relocation.[34] The act of relocation itself is traumatic. The failure to recognize characteristics such as the desire of independence and an interest in being with one's peers in a homey atmosphere close to shopping is a major fault in the relocation process effecting the elderly.[35]

Inappropriateness of new arrangements: the Housing Act of 1970 attempted to deal with still another segment of the elderly population by providing for congregate housing for those who are frail but not ill. Such housing provides common kitchen facilities, dining areas, and recreation rooms. At the end of 1972, all HUD programs for the elderly totalled 412,950 units ranging from traditional low-rent public housing to the innovative intermediate care facility. However, when measured against additional needs of 120,000 to 160,000 units over a ten-year period,[36] this achievement falls far short of the goal.[37] While the instruments may be available for providing more housing for the elderly, a recent study concluded: "It must be acknowledged that overall our present housing programs are costly, ineffective in reaching the poor, and in many ways inequitable."[38]

Continuing Needs

In essence, the failure to provide adequate and sufficient housing for low-income elderly relocatees is basically a failure of program execution coupled with a general lack of understanding of the diversified housing needs and social-psychological problems of the elderly. Within the last twenty years there has been a growing awareness of the elderly as a class whose housing requirements are not adequately served by the private market sector, a theme reiterated at National Conferences on Aging in 1950, 1961, and again in 1971. The last Conference ". . . urged that housing programs, specifically designed for the safety and comfort of the older population, be undertaken."[39]

While the outcries of financial injustice arising from inadeqaute relocation compensation may have been somewhat muted under the Uniform Relocation Assistance Act, there is still lacking a continuing flow of various accommodations designed for the elderly in a socially conducive milieu—that is, one which tends to preserve and sustain their tenuous and delicate friendships. The issues of changing lifestyles and diverse housing needs for the elderly remain to be dealt within a framework of independent living, continuing homeownership, and freedom of housing choice.[40] With the possible exception of medical attention, the elderly, and especially the black elderly, lag behind other age groups in terms of receiving a fair share of society's goods and services.[41] The essence of the problem is to establish a role and a place for the elderly in our "disposable society," which all too frequently equates chronology with senility.[42]

Minority Groups

Minority groups have borne a disproportionate burden of the social and economic costs of community development programs in large metropolitan areas and in smaller cities.[43] Since public housing and urban renewal programs were originally designed to clear slums, it is almost axiomatic that the older, low-rent urban core areas would tend to be occupied by those with the lowest incomes and the least mobility. They would bear most of the brunt of relocation resulting from redevelopment. During the first decade of the urban renewal program (to June 30, 1959), of 65,800 families relocated, 72 percent were nonwhite,[44] thereby substantiating the expression that "urban renewal is Negro removal." Given the nature of the present movement of minorities to metropolitan areas and the core cities, it is reasonable to assume that community development activities will continue to disproportionately affect minorities and the elderly.[45] Even the limited movement of blacks to the suburbs is likely to involve only those who already have an economic and social advantage, thereby reinforcing the trend toward concentrating the poor and the socially handicapped in the central cities.[46] The combination of limited incomes and limited housing choices due to discrimination almost guarantees the movement of migrant, poor blacks and other minorities to core slum areas.

The Backdrop

That urban renewal programs were most costly to blacks was beginning to be recognized after the first few years of such activities. In a letter written in 1959 to the Editor of *The New York Times*, Jack E. Wood, Jr., the Special Assistant for Housing of the National Association for the Advancement of Colored People (NAACP), wrote:

The forced displacement of families from their homes is a necessary process in the redevelopment of our slums and blighted areas. We can no longer afford, however, to reconcile our approach to relocation in terms of the beautiful buildings and new dwelling units which come as a result; for the displacement process itself has such broad social and psychological implications. . . . that it can jeopardize the very progress which it is intended to serve.[47]

Despite this expression by the NAACP for an orderly relocation process and for solutions for the problems engendered, there is little feeling here of the intensity and bitterness later associated with relocation activities. This latent hostility was fully articulated later during the tumultuous sixties.

Robert Weaver's analysis of the initial attitude of blacks towards urban renewal helps explain in part the early low-key nature of their opposition to the program. He states: "the idea of slum clearance germinated during the depression when there were many vacancies, so that substandard properties could be torn down and families relocated with a minimum of difficulty."[48] This notion was extant during the formative days of the urban renewal program despite the contradiction of demolishing housing units without necessarily providing for their replacement.[49] Weaver notes several other factors that later created strong general concern among whites and blacks over relocation activities: (1) the increasing proportion of nonwhite tenants moving into public housing projects, and (2) the selection of urban renewal sites in some Southern and border cities that proposed to eliminate mixed residential neighborhoods to be renewed with all-white residences. As a consequence, urban renewal appeared to be an instrument for creating ghettoized public housing—a result feared by whites—and for eliminating integrated, low-rent areas—a result feared by blacks—thereby making the program undesirable to both groups.[50] Furthermore, any of the advances that occurred in relocation programming during the early developmental period were as a result of the efforts of individual relocation agencies and dedicated relocation personnel rather than the outcome of well-articulated social or legal doctrines.[51] New Haven's family relocation program[52] and the work in Philadelphia[53] and Chicago[54] on the nature of skid-row problems exemplify the application of a broader social responsibility to relocatees than that mandated by the relocation legislation of the fifties.

If the 1950s can be broadly characterized as a period of self-satisfaction, then the Kennedy-Johnson years may be called a time of growing dissatisfaction. This mood is evident in the Inaugural Address of President John F. Kennedy in which he called upon the nation ". . . to bear the burden of a long twilight struggle year in and year out . . . —a struggle against the common enemies of man: tyranny, poverty, disease and war itself."[55] Later in his Special Message to Congress and in a letter transmitting his housing and development bills for 1961, Kennedy emphasized that an ill-housed nation is not a strong nation; that an orderly and healthy urban environment is essential for a better life for all Americans.[56] He stated that all Americans should be ". . . unwilling to witness or permit the slow undoing of those human rights to which this nation has always been committed. . . ."[57]

As the social awareness and consciousness of the minorities in the nation grew, so did social militancy. Urban development and other physical improvement programs that required the relocation of people became anathema. In addition to violence, some of the conflict took the form of legal actions to stop redevelopment activities. Other methods included administrative appeals to the agencies responsible for the community improvement programs.

Legal Actions

The landmark legal case on relocation pitted the Norwalk, Connecticut, chapter of the Congress of Racial Equality (CORE) against the Norwalk Redevelopment Agency.[58] An original complaint filed in 1967 in the United States District Court for Connecticut claimed the local Redevelopment Agency did not ". . . assure or attempt to assure relocation for Negro and Puerto Rican displacees to the same extent that they did for whites. . . ."[59] It was argued that this was a denial of equal protection of the laws. The District Court decided otherwise, whereupon CORE took the case to the Court of Appeals on the grounds that the housing accommodations available to nonwhite relocatees were not equal to those of the whites due to "rampant discrimination." CORE also claimed the intent of the urban renewal program was to drive many Negroes and Puerto Ricans out of the City of Norwalk and charged that this was a denial of the equal protection clause of the Fourteenth Amendment.

The Appeals Court agreed with the argument of CORE and said: "Where the relocation standard set by Congress is met for those who have access to any housing in the community which they can afford, but not for those who by reason of their race, are denied free access to housing they can afford and must pay more for what they can get, the state action affirms the discrimination in the housing market. This is not equal protection of the laws."[60] The court tempered its approach somewhat by also stating that efforts and success at relocation will be viewed with a realistic appraisal of the problems facing urban renewal programs since too literal an interpretation of the law could hinder programs designed to enhance the entire community.[61] Nevertheless, the door was now opened for further challenge of public relocation activities,[62] a door which previously had been kept shut by the narrow view that relocatees had no legal standing to request judicial review of administrative decisions.[63]

In another key case, the City of Hamtramck, Michigan, in 1969 was accused of engaging in "Negro removal," since there was insufficient relocation housing resources for those families already displaced or about to be displaced. In reviewing the relocation plan, the District Court found it to be ineffective and issued an injunction requiring the city to prove its adequacy.[64] These successful legal attacks against relocation programs undoubtedly have established precedents for continuing judicial evaluations of relocation programs as a means of insuring equal justice to all relocatees.[65]

"Negro Removal"

The issue of "Negro removal" has often been featured by the press throughout the nation. The following story is typical. The Human Relations Commission of Suffolk County, Long Island, according to *The New York Times*, feared that racial discrimination might mar the county's first urban renewal project in the town of Huntington. Since the 183 units to be built in the urban renewal area "will not supply the minority citizens with housing sufficient for their needs, Huntington's urban renewal is now headed along the typical route of Negro removal."[66] In July, 1968, HUD was requested to hold up funds for this project because of allegations of discrimination against minorities as part of an overall pattern aimed at those who can't afford homeownership [*sic*, blacks]. The Town Supervisor termed the complaint, "the most irresponsible thing I've ever seen," while a HUD spokesman said, "if there is sufficient evidence, the Secretary will hold up funds. The charges are quite serious."[67] In March, 1969, HUD reported that its investigation revealed no serious breach of its regulations by the town.[68] The Agency withheld specific evidence since a law suit was pending charging the urban renewal project forced the relocation of 180 Negro and Latin American residents out of town or into crowded or substandard housing in town. The Chairman of the Human Relations Commission claimed the court case was a reflection on their work [HUD's] since they approved of all the things that went on in the urban renewal project.

Disregarding the accuracy or meritriciousness of specific charges, the substantive issue is that in the main, minority groups perceive the urban renewal program and their relocation as a threat rather than as an opportunity to better their life condition.

The attack against community improvement programs was nationwide. It included communities in the Midwest and Far West as well as the East. In the following instance a complaint was lodged by the Fort Madison, Iowa, chapter of the NAACP against the Iowa Highway Commission on June 30, 1970. In a letter to the Department of Transportation, the NAACP claimed ". . . the corridor which has been chosen for the Highway relocation follows the tradition of disrupting minority group neighborhoods. Those affected will be Blacks, Mexican-Americans and low-income Whites. Chosen because it is the cheapest area of the town, it is this way because the citizens of this area have been systematically denied the privilege of living in other areas of the community."[69] The National Counsel for the NAACP charged the proposed highway route would cause a disproportionate number of blacks and persons of Mexican-American ancestry to be displaced from their homes without adequate low-rent housing resources in the community.[70] An ethnic breakdown of Fort Madison, based on 1970 Census data, reveals a total black population of 429 or 3.6 percent of the city's population of 13,996 and 1,000 Mexican-Americans, representing 7 percent of the city total. The highway displacement program affects 146 households, including 23 black families, or 16 percent of the workload and 29 Mexican-Americans, comprising 20 percent of the relocatees.[71] This comparison supports the claim that a larger percentage of the total relocatees are minority families than white families, although this is a somewhat simplistic argument for denying the need for this project.

That "urban renewal is Negro removal" is still the reality and not merely rhetoric is evidenced by the relocation statistics of urban renewal programs; even though a comparison of the 1959 and the 1971-72 urban renewal data reveals a downward trend in the number of blacks and Spanish surnamed households required to move. (The 1959 figure was 72 percent while the 1971-72 figure, noted earlier, was 55 percent.)

Despite the historic truth of that clarion call about "Negro removal" and its present pejorative implications, this crucial issue can still become a positive factor in an enhanced national goal to enlarge social justice for minority groups and individuals through a planned relocation process. Provided that relocation policies and programs are designed to incorporate social as well as economic benefits, it is conceivable that some day there may be "black approval for people renewal."

Summary

Despite the gradual improvement of financial benefits and services, relocation processes have had a negative impact on several classes of people. This is so because of our failure to understand and treat the social problems uncovered by the present rudimentary process and the lack of a transformed, social and organizational system to enhance the process. As a result, negative economic and social costs have been sustained by those least capable in our society: the small businessmen, the elderly, and minorities.

Regarding the impact of relocation generally, the overriding need in the recent past has been for decent shelter at a modest price for most of those required to move. This issue is still valid. In addition to this overriding need, relocation creates a differential demand for housing dependent upon the specific needs of the relocatees. An adequate supply of decent shelter must therefore be made available at a particular time, place, and price for atypical housing groups such as the elderly, the poor white and black family, and large households. Some assert that there is no current housing shortage and point to vacancy rates above 5 percent in many cities. This assertion may be valid with regard to the typical American family. But it has little merit for the typical American relocatee whose prototype could very well be a single, elderly lady no longer capable of providing for her own needs including shelter. Thus, more suitable dwellings and business space as well, planned with an understanding of the differential needs and desires of the residential and commercial relocatees, remains a major relocation issue in the seventies as in the sixties.

Regarding the charge that "urban renewal is Negro removal," there is no doubt that this catchy phrase may be well founded. But by accepting it on its face, this value laden statement may also have resulted in the loss of major economic and social benefits to a large part of black society. Unfortunately, their opportunity to demand well-designed housing, enlarged financial aids, and effective social services as a trade-off for their relocation from core commercial and residential areas was engulfed in the conflict and rhetoric of the times. The black community may still grasp their bargaining opportunities to exchange core space for social programs of individual enhancement. This is potentially achievable since the white business society seeks to rebuild and revitalize the prime inner-city areas, while many blacks seek to acquire so much of society's skills. To exploit this opportunity requires black and white community leaders to specify this trade-off as an acceptable *quid pro quo*. If this is done, there would be created a new rubric under which specific social programs could be designed and tested to meet the needs of the relocatees as they perceive them. Given this goal in community development, then perhaps the phrase, "urban renewal is Negro removal," can become a positive cachet for American society.

The issues of relocation have not been limited only to a concern for the financial and housing needs of the relocatees. The conflict has deepened with time as additional questions have been raised regarding the social-psychological implications, the effectiveness of program administration, and alternative organizational systems for relocation. These issues will be examined next.

9 Deepening Social Conflicts

Social-Psychological Insights

A growing concern with the social implications of relocation programs appeared within a six-month period during 1960-61 in separate articles in *Commentary* by Michael Harrington[1] and Staughton Lynd.[2] They discussed social policy issues such as the need for continuing low-rent public housing and slum clearance and the failure of the urban renewal program to provide adequate shelter for the poor.

Harrington acknowledged slum clearance was a necessary concomitant of city redevelopment but was concerned that urban renewal sites were chosen strictly for economic purposes—to bring in tax revenues to financially hard-pressed cities—rather than as a means to add to the housing supply for the relocatees. The barriers to successful slum clearance, he noted, included the poverty of the slum residents and racial discrimination, both of which limited their mobility and neither of which were treated by the renewal program.[3]

Lynd argued that slum clearance had to be coupled with public housing, master planning, and a centralized relocation agency. He recommended preserving institutional structures such as churches on urban renewal sites, clearing parts of sites in order to permit some tenants to remain in occupancy pending the construction of new public housing units, and encouraging local participation in the management aspects of new projects. But most of all he stressed the need for strong public intervention and control rather than reliance on private capital as a means for curing the symptoms of our "metropolitan madness"—the slums.[4] Despite these criticisms, both writers viewed slum clearance activities as a potentially useful tool for fighting poverty and racial discrimination.

Additional insights were later forthcoming concerning the nature of the society and social structure in an urban renewal area. The effects of the relocation process on the residents were the increasing concern of social scientists here and abroad. American researchers were becoming more and more critical in the early sixties though some of their foreign counterparts were somewhat more restrained in their observations. Books and articles on the subject were generally antagonistic toward redevelopment and relocation activities. As one observer put it a few years later, ". . . urban renewal has become to the academic community and the press of the twentieth century what the 'heartless' banker of the late nineteenth and early twentieth century was to the social protesters of that era."[5]

117

The West End Studies

Among the most influential studies were those of an interdisciplinary group of psychiatrists, sociologists, and planners working under the aegis of the Massachusetts General Hospital and the National Institute of Mental Health. They utilized the West End Urban Renewal Program in Boston in 1959-59 as their demonstration laboratory.[6] Writing with the imprimateur of these two prestigious institutions, the viewpoints and conclusions of these researchers were bound to be influential, for their pioneer efforts were adding to the limited knowledge and literature then extant about the social implications and long-term effects of relocation programs.

Marc Field and Peggy Gleicher observed that a strong sense of self-satisfaction was associated with living in Boston's West End. This was the result of the close personal associations among the local Italian residents and their sense of identity to neighborhood places that provided them with a framework for personal and social integration. This study contradicted the impression that slums comprise a highly mobile population, since 25 percent of the total population had been born there. Fried and Gleicher also noted that 71 percent of the people revealed a widespread feeling of "belonging some place," of being at home in the spatial area outside the home itself,[7] which led them to observe that a sense of localism was a basic feature of working-class life.[8] Noting the urban renewal program was responsible for destroying a network of satisfying and supporting personal and social relationships in the area, they recommended careful analysis of pre- and post-relocation effects on individuals and families. This would answer the question of the costs and benefits of urban renewal on different population groups as a basis for sound planning of urban social change.[9]

Herbert Gans, in the *Urban Villagers*, expressed essentially the same idea as Fried and Gleicher. He went further by concluding the West End was not a slum despite the evidences of physical dilapidation such as garbage strewn on the streets, which was depressing.[10] He rejected the slum connotation for this area as a limited physical construct, observing the definition should be enlarged to include ". . . an area that, because of the nature of its social environment, can be proved to create problems and pathologies either for the residents or for the larger community."[11] Gans stated that the clearance program in the West End extracted heavy social and psychological losses by destroying a functioning social system. Relocation programs utilizing middle-class standards of evaluation like the physical characteristics of dwelling units tends to ignore social concerns such as a desire to move close to similar-type neighbors. In breaking up the area, the planners failed to take into account the concept of the "extended family" (the social network described earlier by Fried) and thought only in terms of the individual nuclear family. In addition, the urban renewal program was not designed to meet the housing needs of the site tenants since it required full demolition and clearance instead of rehabilitating the low-rent structures.

According to Gans, HUD programs and policies were negative, "for even if all the effects of relocation were positive, the unequal and unjust distribution of costs and benefits built into current [1960-64] procedures still could not be justified."[12] Unless proper rehousing is provided along with a plan to keep extended families together, then urban renewal should be prohibited. For if the purpose of urban renewal is to improve the living conditions of people, then relocation must become the most important part of the urban renewal process whereby the relocation plan is accorded a higher status than the redevelopment scheme.[13] This approach requires changing the current planning and programming concepts from a concern for physical regeneration to a design for human regeneration.

Fried in another paper delivered what may have been the *coup de grace* to the urban renewal program. Entitled "Grieving For a Lost Home: Psychological Costs of Relocation," the study identified relocation with the type of bereavement one usually associates with the passing of a life, thereby providing a new dimension to the emotional stress suffered by those who had been relocated from the West End. Symptoms of grief were defined as (1) feelings of painful loss, (2) continued longing, (3) a generally depressed tone, (4) frequent symptoms of psychological or social or somatic distress, (5) active work required in adapting to the altered life situation, (6) a sense of helplessness, (7) expressions of direct and displaced anger and (8) tendencies to idealize the lost place.[14]

When asked how they felt when they heard their old building was being torn down, 46 percent of the female relocatees and 38 percent of the males reported being disturbed. Fried observed that the strength of the grief reaction is proportional to the degree of one's prior involvement in the neighborhood. Some families attempt to cope with their loss by remaining physically close to the area they know, while others try to stay close to relatives and friends or even closer to their spouses.[15]

To overcome this sense of grief, to maintain a sense of continuity for the working-class relocatees, and to maximize opportunities for substantive adaptation to a new environment, Fried recommends that renewal agencies should: (1) drastically cut programs of demolition and redevelopment requiring relocation, (2) permit relocation from one section of a renewal area to another during and after renewal, (3) where dislocation is necessary, provide new areas with some spatial elements reminiscent of the old neighborhoods, (4) provide social, psychological, and psychiatric services as needed. Fried concludes that "grieving for a lost home is evidently a widespread and serious social phenomenon following in the wake of urban dislocation. It is likely to increase social and psychological 'pathology' in a limited number of instances. It is also likely to create new opportunities for some, and to increase the rate of social mobility for others."[16] His qualifications notwithstanding, the existence of the "grief" syndrome soon became part of the common coin in the literature on relocation.

Revisionist Studies

In 1962, Peter Marris, an English sociologist who was reviewing American renewal activities, observed that the current aims of the program, which strive to improve the economic status of cities, develop a cultural renaissance, and provide for racial and social integration, may be contradictory. He commented that relocation offered only marginally better, higher rent housing in very similar neighborhoods and probably worsened rather than improved or solved the social conditions of the displaced families. He suggested as possible alternatives: (1) attempting to dissolve the subculture of a slum by eliminating low wages, racial discrimination, and high rates of unemployment since it is a self-frustrating defense against a sense of inferiority; and (2) rehousing the community as a whole without disrupting it by emphasizing rehabilitation rather than redevelopment, for ". . . the universal search is for more intimate surroundings [in which] every resident is carving out of the city a social space he can master."[17] The slums analyzed by Marris however, differed from those of the West End of Boston; the former were prototype core area slums that required the dissolution of the anti-social subculture; whereas the latter was in fact socially and ethnically viable. Its social dissolution was therefore deemed a disaster.

Other analysts criticized the administration of the relocation process in urban renewal by attacking the administration and direction of the relocation program.[18] By the mid-1960s it had been broadcast that relocation and community renewal programs did not achieve the socially desirable goal of providing more housing. Instead, they destroyed cohesive working-class and lower-class neighborhoods that were inappropriately labelled as slums. The early facile generalization that defined physically deteriorated areas as slums worthy of demolition was now being replaced by an equally facile generalization regarding the social homogeneity of the slum dwellers and the negative psychological effects associated with relocation programs. Additional studies were soon to be forthcoming which modified or indeed contradicted such broad assertions.

England in many ways serves as a social laboratory and incubator for the United States on issues of poverty, housing, and employment. As a precursor of a later revisionist period, two sociologists wrote in 1961 about the effects of urban redevelopment and community change in a central city area of Liverpool.[19] They took into account the desires of some to leave the district for better accommodations while others wished to remain undisturbed where they had been born. They described the variety of social life in the district as a continuum that ranged from those who are unstable and unruly to the orderly and rooted. There was no consistent pattern regarding attitudes towards relocation and the co-existence in the district of distinct subgroups with different long-term goals for their families and themselves. Some young marrieds showed a tendency to establish their first homes in the same neighborhoods they grew up in or to live with the wife's parents. Although the presence of relatives in a locality was a real and limiting influence on mobility, it was not total in terms of the desires of some of the younger generation to move elsewhere.[20] About 61 percent preferred to remain in the neighborhood; at the same time, 39 percent indicated a relatively high desire to leave. They concluded "doubt must now be cast on all historical estimates which assess an area in terms of the firmness of its roots in the past without at the same time bringing into account the possibly quite different aspirations which the inhabitants may have for the future."[21]

The authors also noted, "It is neither self-evident that a development plan should be closely adjusted to the present social pattern and preferences, nor on the other hand, that the social life of central areas should be completely disrupted in order to fit in with what planners may believe to be the inevitable future trends . . . the problem is how to adjust the degree of disturbance to what a democratic community can reasonably be expected to approve and accept."[22] In addition to these conclusions, their study is noteworthy for its typology of voluntary relocatees according to their length of marriage (e.g., newlyweds and older households). Other recent social-psychological studies also reflect notions of differentiation: as between "ethnics" and "natives," children and parents, and nonrelocatees with like characteristics as relocatees. These more sophisticatedly-designed studies yield conclusions at variance from those of the West End because of the greater depth of their analyses.

In 1967, William Key of the Menninger Clinic in Topeka, Kansas, published a study about the effects of relocation on persons required to move in that city for an urban renewal and highway program. He hypothesized that social change results in an "unfreezing" of significant elements of the social system that may lead to stress. Coping with a stressful situation such as relocation calls for learning new roles that require the abandonment or modification of accustomed behavior. Key postulated that people could not deal satisfactorily with the changes necessitated by their required relocation and posited a theory of crisis intervention—that is, the direct opportunity to provide professional, social, and psychological help during and after relocation as a means for helping people reorganize their lives toward a more satisfactory pattern.[23] Accordingly, in Topeka counseling services were made available with the following effects:

1. On the physical quality of housing: Counselors exerted a favorable influence in reducing crowding and increasing homeownership, especially for middle- and lower-income groups, but they did not affect housing costs. Among lower-income households, money constraints limited their housing choices, therefore, more low-income housing for the poor was recommended.

2. On the emotional satisfaction with new housing: Urban renewal relocatees given counseling help most closely matched a group of voluntary movers in their degree of housing satisfaction. Counseling services were useful in advising people regarding the suitability of their new housing. Future rehousing studies should plan to evaluate the degree of housing satisfaction.

3. On family structure: The need to relocate had little positive or negative impact on family structure. Such changes as occurred were explained in terms of the life cycle of the families, although moving tended to bring families closer and increased satisfaction with family life and marriage. Counseling services did not modify in any direction nuclear family relationships or relationships with relatives. On this point, counseling may even be negative, since it may inhibit a pulling together of the family by its own efforts to meet the challenge of moving.

4. On neighborhood relationships: Here the results were mixed; urban renewal relocatees were more attached to the former neighborhood because of ties of friendship than were the highway relocatees. This may be because the former were more "people-oriented" or it may be a function of the compactness of the urban renewal area as compared to the ribbon-like highway site that cross-cut through different neighborhoods. The conclusion is that mobility—planned or voluntary—results in greater feelings of social isolation, for "the greater the investment in some facet of the neighborhood, the greater the distress and difficulty when one must move."[24]

Key then states that when the same questions posed by Fried earlier were used, in many instances his conclusions differ. Urban renewal white households were less pleased about their move than others; Mexicans were next. On the whole, almost everyone was fairly well satisfied with his present life circumstances. "The Topeka Grief Index" recorded the following results: (1) "Apparently the forced moves were very much resented, but they had no shattering or permanent effect on [people's] outlook toward life."[25] Blacks were most favorably disposed towards moving, and the younger people managed fairly well, whereas in general Mexicans and the elderly were consistently negative after they moved and were the most depressed. The majority of the people seemed capable of absorbing the effects of relocation as one more event in what was for many of them a lifetime characterized by uncertainty and deprivation.[26] The Topeka study concludes by suggesting that the relocation process does not substantially harm people, with the researcher noting that "Frankly, these findings astonished us."[27]

This study raises some question about the validity of Fried and Gleicher's theory of the interrelatedness of neighborhood social and spatial relationships with "satisfaction" in life. According to Key, in considering the social effects of relocation their methodology was suspect since they did not provide for a control group of nonmovers nor did they distinguish between different age or ethnic groups. The West End studies should therefore be considered suggestive rather than definitive.[28]

A second test of Fried's hypothesis was forthcoming in 1968 in Toronto where the social and psychological consequences of urban renewal on a group of Portuguese, "others" (including many Jews), and Canadians was studied. That investigator notes that adaptive capabilities toward change were related to class differentials and class mobility.[29] The Portuguese, who were upwardly mobile, reacted positively towards relocation; "others" were also highly mobile and tended to react favorably; whereas the Canadians, who were primarily downwardly mobile, white, lower-class welfare recipients, were less able to adapt to relocation. Thus, the propensity to cope with change may be related to one's status in society. The higher one's status, the less the dependence upon local, social, and spatial networks and vice versa. Another finding was that the weaker the social network before relocation, the greater the capability toward adjustment and adaptation; however the degree of involvement with pre-relocation neighbors and relatives does not appear to inhibit post-relocation and adaptation.[30]

Most of the Portuguese who originally said they wanted to stay in the area were basically more satisfied and happier after relocation and felt positive about the change. This was due to their ability to relocate on the fringes of the urban renewal area as compared to the scattered relocation pattern of the Italians of the West End. Interestingly, these relocatees seemed to have a stronger association and feeling towards their new neighbors than toward their pre-relocation neighbors; for their successful adaptation and adjustment was related to their ability to develop an extended network of friends in the receiving neighborhood.[31] Relocation was a positive experience for the Portuguese here; Fried's hypothesis that urban renewal destroys the close-knit network of social relationships is not supported in this case.

Regarding the adaptability of children and the effects of moving on them, relationships within the family rather than within the community tend to determine their rate of adjustment. Children who did poorly in school before relocation did so afterwards, while those who were successful earlier continued this pattern later. The Portuguese had a highly successful pattern of adaptation. Furthermore, "others" showed a high adaptive pattern based on their readiness to absorb middle-class modes elsewhere, while the native-born Canadians had a low pattern resulting from the breakup of the community and their dependence on their culture of welfare dependency.[32]

A Detroit study of a black slum in 1969 draws negative conclusions about the "belongingness" of slum life and its satisfying social and spatial networks. Despite numerous and very important social ties and other factors such as neighborhood convenience, most black residents held the slum area in low esteem and many considered it dangerous.[33]

Two recent reports tend to support the above conclusions about black reactions to the community and their desire to move. A 1969 study in Austin, Texas, states: ". . . it appears that loss of community was highly salient for some 26.3 percent but was not uppermost in the minds of the majority."[34] And in 1970, two researchers note a lack of emotional involvement among blacks within the urban renewal area. To them, it is "less a matter of preference than of limited alternatives" since they are less opposed to urban renewal and more concerned about finding other housing.[35]

Fried's hypothesis that relocation is a major crisis of transition, which few in the working-class community can meet alone successfully, seems to lack universality. More recent studies show that not all ethnic or social groups follow the same behavioral patterns. The effects of relocation on people must be differentiated according to ethnicity, social class, and family life cycle.

Relocation Results Challenged

The West End social research laboratory produced other studies highly critical of the relocation process. In 1964, Chester Hartman was concerned with the nature of the housing changes and the financial costs borne by those who moved.[36] He interviewed approximately 500 households prior to relocation and two years afterward. He then compared his results with the different patterns in location, housing type, and tenure of 33 relocation case studies spanning thirty years.

The West Enders relocated in a "shotgun" pattern throughout Boston and the nearby suburbs. Hartman considers this atypical as compared to patterns of relocation in New York and Chicago in 1933. Most of the West End relocatees moved from tenements into similar structures elsewhere, although homeowner-ship increased from 10 to 21 percent. Overall, pre-relocation densities decreased as the average number of rooms per household increased from 4.35 to 4.94; thus, 46 percent of the residents increased their space, while 54 percent remained constant. But Hartman says that increased privacy was achieved at the loss of those public communal facilities that were previously within walking distance. He suggests this issue be investigated more fully for it raises questions of planning policy. Although acknowledging a gain in the physical quality of housing after relocation, he cautions this may not be representative during the years ahead due to expected cutbacks in the public housing program.[37]

On the question of rents, over half the households were paying thirty dollars more per month after relocation, while two-fifths were paying forty dollars more. The rent/income ratio rose from 13.6 percent to 18.6 percent for the new accommodations. While many of the families bought better housing for their additional dollars, 27 percent moved into unsound housing and an equal number showed no improvement at all. Rent increases were noted in all the other reports reviewed by Hartman. He concludes that the relocation aid received by the area resident was "strikingly small," for in the West End only 15 percent got such help. Furthermore, a disturbing number of site families were reported "lost." This suggests to him that agency follow-up procedures and the lack of counselling services leading to hostility by residents may be crucial factors in the relocation process. In concluding, he notes that relocation generally has a low priority; had it been otherwise the results so far would be totally unacceptable. Relocation has made a "disappointingly small contribution" to raising the living standards of site residents elsewhere.[38]

This study raises serious questions regarding the validity of the relocation data supplied by local redevelopment agencies as shown by their failure to consider environmental factors in evaluating relocation dwellings, their built-in bias in reporting the results of their activities, and their lack of social consideration in the relocation process.[39]

Hartman's analysis contains several shortcomings including some value judgments that are not supported by his detailed but dated statistical base. Because of the time span of over thirty years, this data is subject to unreliability.[40] His study does note the following procedural and resource gaps that existed in urban renewal relocation programs in 1963:

1. The failure to be concerned with environmental surroundings in rehousing families;
2. Limited financial assistance;
3. The dilemma facing public agencies in their dual role as proponents of slum clearance and as auditors of their own activities;
4. Differences in local criteria for evaluating the effectiveness of the relocation process;
5. The failure to provide a post-relocation analytic capability;
6. The overall lack of local capability in providing meaningful relocation assistance;
7. The inability of the program to deliver the results intended of it in the way of "decent shelter in a suitable living environment."[41]

In reaction to these criticisms, the HHFA asked the Census Bureau to undertake a survey to determine the adequacy of the housing units to which families were being relocated. Some 2,300 households representing 132 local public agencies were interviewed in 1964. Their conclusions follow:

1. "The vast majority"—94 percent—were relocated into standard dwelling units. (*West End findings supported.*)
2. Although median gross rents rose from $66 to $74 and the median proportion of income spent on rent increased from 25 percent to nearly 28 percent, the median room size increased slightly from 4.3 to 4.4 rooms per dwelling unit. (*West End findings supported.*)
3. Homeownership rose slightly from 33 to 37 percent, (*West End findings supported.*)
4. Community facilities were at least as convenient to the new apartments as earlier for a majority of the households (e.g., shopping, 66 percent same or better; transportation, 77 percent same or better; church location, 55 percent same). (*West End findings supported.*)
5. Changes in employment effected only 10 percent of the households. (*Not included in West End data.*)

6. Time required for journey to work remained the same for 63 percent. (*Not included in West End data.*)
7. Self-relocation totalled 70 percent, although 90 percent of the households received counselling, financial, or other assistance from the local public agency. (*West End findings unsupported.*)[42]

The Census Bureau study confirmed that the majority of those relocated by urban renewal programs moved into better accommodations with no lessening of community facilities, but paid more rent than before. This result supports one of the major goals of the Housing Act of 1949: to upgrade the standard of housing for those who must vacate areas designated for slum clearance.

Not content to let the matter rest here, Hartman then proceeded to challenge the conclusions of the Census study by noting:

1. The study did not consider those who moved prior to actual land-taking.
2. It omits single-person householders.
3. It does not analyze its results as between metropolitan centers and small cities and towns.
4. The percentage of income paid toward rent after relocation is "disturbingly high."
5. The report fails to compare pre- to post-relocation overcrowdedness.
6. The study lacks a useful, working definition for standard housing.
7. There is no data on how many families relocated into areas slated for later public improvement.
8. The study was undertaken by one government agency at the behest of another and there is doubt that it is bias free.[43]

Hartman's disregard of the positive results of physical renewal programs and his emphasis of the negative aspects of relocation found widespread support among the critics of urban renewal as he concludes: "Those who are active in the relocation field, have a great obligation for searching for answers and correcting program deficiencies."[44] Very true, but "those who are critics of relocation also have a serious responsibility—to seek out all the relevant facts to support criticism, to abjure the use of half-truths and innuendo's and to discuss more fully the areas of concern for possible future study."[45]

While most of the issues raised by Hartman deal with the procedures and processes of relocation, he indeed notes two substantive and significant deficiencies: (1) deficiencies in the supply of decent suitable shelter, and (2) the lack of social services. For in the present decade as in the past, these critical issues still remain unresolved.

"Centralized" versus "Decentralized" Relocation

Another issue is the debate over "centralized" versus "decentralized" relocation services. This problem is a microcosm of the larger struggle for the decentralization of public services and the demand for community participation in public programs.[46] Several different administrative models for relocation programming have evolved in the past, each related to a particular ideology about the nature of the relocation services to be provided. Philadelphia originally viewed relocation activities as another form of social services and contracted with the Department of Public Welfare to administer its program. New York City considered this function a form of real estate activity and provided for sponsors of urban renewal sites to contract for relocation services with private real estate agencies. Chicago viewed relocation as an administrative issue and in 1962 established a consolidated Tenant Relocation Bureau under a new Department of Urban Renewal.[47]

When one considers the impact of relocation on small businessmen, the elderly, and minority groups, the recurrent demand for changes in relocation structure programming and processes as a means for minimizing human discomfort is understandable, notwithstanding the inadequacy of a change in form alone. New York City presents a dramatic case study of this "shadow" conflict in which organizational form looms larger than program substance.

The Conflict

New York City's urban renewal program was initially placed under Robert Moses, it's "master-builder." Following the passage of the Housing Act of 1949, Moses, philosophically at odds with the local and national urban renewal bureaucracy, preferred to operate through an organizational instrument designed, perfected, and responsive to himself. Despite its broad appellation and, "public" association, the Mayor's Committee on Slum Clearance operated like a private corporation. There was little if any open disclosure, no attempt at representativeness, and little responsiveness to the local needs or the pressures of various interest groups. In keeping with this classical closed administrative system, those private consultants who served Moses faithfully and well in his other building ventures such as the Triboro Bridge and the Queens-Midtown Tunnel, could be expected to be called upon for their services in urban redevelopment.[48]

Private relocation firms that earlier helped relocate families for local public improvements were thus assigned a similar role in urban redevelopment. In this unique approach to relocation, the sponsors were required to pay all administrative and organizational costs and direct relocation expenses for the tenants on their sites.[49] The New York pattern was atypical in two respects: (1) some financial assistance, albeit rudimentary, was provided to relocatees even though this was not then mandated by the Housing Act of 1949; and (2) the New York City Housing Authority, the Department of Real Estate, and the Title I Slum Clearance Program each maintained independent, separate relocation organizations with different relocation payment schedules.

Given the bewildering diversity in administration and financial aids, Moses added to the frustrations of the relocatees and community groups by ignoring them in his decision-making processes, thereby arousing their wrath. Eventually this disdain led to a loud public demand to eliminate the Mayor's Committee on Slum Clearance and to establish a centralized relocation agency, presumably as a means to guarantee the more effective delivery of services.[50] In response to growing public pressures, Mayor Robert F. Wagner in 1954 asked the Planning Commission to review the city's relocation policies. Four members of that seven-man Commission approved continuing the decentralized concept of relocation, but not without strong dissent from the remaining three.[51] To resolve the deepening political crisis, the report of the Commission was reviewed by Dr. Luther Gulick, the City Administrator, who supported the majority view on the grounds that diversified relocation services would produce more action and less hardship and that the real need was not organizational—such as the form of the relocation agency—but substantive—the necessity to safeguard tenants' rights.[52]

But this analysis did not settle the issue, and in 1955, Wagner appointed a blue-ribbon "Mayor's Committee for Better Housing" to further study the problem. It recommended not a central agency, but rather a central nerve center or focal point of responsibility in city government to collect housing and relocation data; the requirement of a demonstration by each public agency of the feasibility of relocation; and the development of uniform standards for rehousing, financial assistance, and similar administrative devices.[53] Robert Groberg, then of the National Association of Housing and Redevelopment Officials, reports that in 1956 the Community Service Society surveyed nine private and civic organizations and their consensus, in opposition to the Mayor's Committee, was that relocation procedures were highly unsatisfactory and should be changed. They felt there should be a central relocation office under city auspices to relocate all families from all the public improvement sites, with the possible exception of those sites under the New York City Housing Authority.[54] The controversy continued unabated and indeed grew as the pace of urban renewal activities increased in the city.

In this heated climate of crisis, the Mayor in 1959 appointed a special research group headed by J. Anthony Panuch to evaluate what by then had become "New York's Number One Problem"—relocation. The Panuch Report was the first thorough work dealing with relocation in New York City. The report describes "The Many Faces of Relocation," such as:

1. Relocation as a problem of shelter—the relationship of housing need and supply;
2. Relocation as a political problem—the fact that clearance programs tend to organize communities with strong, strident, and vocal opposition;
3. Relocation as a sociological problem—the unresolved questions about "the lost families," "problem families," integration, skid row, and other problems.[55]

Panuch felt that establishing a huge bureaucracy to handle relocation could not possibly answer the problems raised above. "At best, it would complicate a complex problem and jeopardize any rational attempt at its solution. At worst, and in determined hands, such an agency could readily lend itself to the socialization of all housing in the City."[56]

Panuch suggested three controlling principles in setting up an equitable relocation program:

1. The city must be responsible for insuring fair and equitable treatment for all;
2. Regardless of the source requiring relocation, all programs must provide equality before the law for all;
3. The city "... must accept responsibility for supervising compliance by all agencies responsible for relocation...."[57]

The report concludes by noting that a central relocation bureau was the wrong issue. More critical is the establishment of fair and equitable relocation policies and an agency to enforce such policies. "Given the right policies and the right people, the organization of relocation, in my judgment [Panuch's] should be *decentralized* to the maximum extent possible...." The role of the city agency should be to supervise, coordinate, and enforce an equitable relocation policy to be established by law.[58]

On the basis of the recommendations in this study, Mayor Wagner appointed a Deputy Commissioner for Relocation within the Department of Real Estate to carry through its program objectives. Presumably this issue was settled. But not for long. A series of new scandals erupted, involving the method of selecting sponsors for Title I sites, which finally led to the dissolution of the Committee on Slum Clearance. The mayor replaced it with the Urban Renewal Board, which he established earlier to develop the city's West Side Urban Renewal Plan. This dramatic power shift also resulted in changing the nature and selection of urban renewal sponsors—from speculative entrepreneurial developers or institutions, to poorly funded local community groups.[a] The new sponsors, in need of adequate financial resources to pay for the costs of a relocation program and the demolition of property, presented these arguments: (1) relocation should be the responsibility of the city, not the sponsors, and (2) a central relocation agency should be responsible for providing relocation services as a public service and at public expense.

Wagner agreed, and proceeded to establish a central relocation agency with authority to relocate the site tenants and to pay the costs of such a program, thus providing the requisite public financial resources to support the community organizations in their new roles as urban renewal project sponsors.[59] A new centralized Department of Relocation was set up in 1967, thereby pacifying the

[a]This fulfilled the primary objectives of nine key citizens groups that led the fight for a centralized relocation agency.

public interest and local community groups that had been demanding this approach for over ten years. The first Commissioner of the Department of Relocation was Herman Badillo, the previous Deputy Commissioner of Relocation in the Department of Real Estate.[60]

Implications

While the New York City case study is unique and interesting, it has broader implications. "Centralized" versus "decentralized" relocation was not the basic issue. Political power was the "gut" issue. Relocation merely served as the "lightening rod" or symbol for many of the political controversies in which urban renewal had become embroiled, for the form or structure of a relocation organization is of little consequence in building low-rent dwelling units, in providing social services, in making more dollars available to the poor, in creating a sense of dedication and purpose in a relocation staff, or in motivating site occupants to take an active role in planning and programming their relocation activities so as to be able in some way to determine their own destinies.

In this instance, the argument over the form of the relocation agency served as the stalking horse for a larger, more fundamental issue: power under a classic oligarchy versus community control and the power that flows from it, "for . . . ," says Panuch, ". . . what the consumer of a public service needs is a voice in the way the service is performed. How to provide a way for that voice to be heard is the issue and neither centralization nor decentralization is really relevant."[61] In planned relocation, the real issue is the extent to which these processes make a meaningful, positive impact on the lives of those affected.

Summary

The earliest social critics wrote of modifying urban development to fulfill its original goals of providing new housing resources for the poor through instruments of public intervention. But the pioneer social-psychological findings that coincided with the beginnings of physical and social upheaval helped create an unfavorable climate for programs that required the relocation of people. This changing, negative attitude was bolstered by the attacks launched on the effectiveness and credibility of those agencies responsible for administering the urban renewal program. Concern was expressed about the following:

1. Whether planned relocation processes actually provided better housing for relocatees;
2. The reliability of the relocation data base;
3. The overall lack of social awareness among planners and administrators;
4. The relative merits of centralized versus decentralized relocation agencies.

By 1968, several significant steps taken by Congress affected relocation. These included enhanced financial benefits under the highway and urban renewal programs, and the addition of sections "235" and "236" to the housing program. Furthermore, HUD urban renewal policies were modified to require one new unit of low-income housing to be built for each such unit demolished. At the same time, newer and more sophisticated social-psychological studies concerned with the impact of relocation on people were demonstrating the weaknesses of the earlier research. A revisionist point of view was evolving—one reflecting an awareness of the differential effects of planned relocation on the various population subgroups who live in renewal areas.

This was the paradox: increasing federal aid, offered to communities on a scale unsurpassed since the Depression, was accompanied with a growing disillusionment and rejection regarding the efficacy of such help. The application of new and untested social programs was not succeeding. The social problems were more complex as the needs of the poor and minorities were far greater, while the knowledge required to cope with increasingly complex social issues was limited. Well-motivated attempts to redistribute some of society's goods and thereby enhance social democracy were perceived as "too little and too late."

The potential of human betterment resulting from transformed programs of planned relocation were never realized as this process came under heavy attack. Accordingly, the mere existence of conflict over issues of relocation revealed a "program conceived in callousness," designed to remove people from their "fury," with little regard for the financial and social-psychological damages they suffered. Furthermore, an ineffective system for delivering even the available pittance of services created additional hardships on relocatees. The conclusion: halt all community development programs till their emphasis shifts to concern for human growth. This interpretation of the relocation happenings in the sixties failed to consider the changing nature of the program during that decade that ended with the passage of the Uniform Relocation Assistance Act. This Act can now serve as the pedestal in enlarging city rebuilding from a narrow concern for physical problems to include social problems as well, thereby broadening its base.

We next consider the implications of economic theories in community development and how such rebuilding activities can provide programs designed to enhance individual growth and human betterment.

10 The Implication of Economics

In the main, economists have been interested primarily in the quantitative, property re-use and fiscal characteristics of urban renewal or highway programs. This is so because these concerns lend themselves more readily to "hard" fiscal analysis sooner than do the "soft" social programs, such as relocation. One can more readily determine the costs of land assemblage, property disposition, and demolition, than fix a cost for the traumas caused by involuntary relocation.

Nonetheless, several economists have considered the social or relocation implications of urban renewal in terms of social policy, by making use of applied welfare economics such as benefit-cost analysis. But few have attempted to link social policies of enhancing the individual's capabilities through better education, health, or on-the-job training with concomitant economic benefits to our society. For increases in our national wealth have been the result of advances in knowledge, labor productivity, capital accumulation, and education and from improved use of our manpower resources.[1] Indeed, increasing our productive capacities *ceteris paribus*, increases the gross national product (GNP).

Because of the symbiotic relationship between urban renewal and relocation, the application of economic theory to the former has had an influence on the latter. Our concern here, however, is not with the entire spectrum of economics and urban renewal or community development. It is limited to the interface of economics with social policy and relocation for which urban renewal programs serve as our models. We shall also consider the implications and effects of welfare economics on relocation so as to be able to forge improved social instruments for benefiting both the individual relocatee and the larger society.

Economics and Social Analysis

In 1964, Martin Anderson in *The Federal Bulldozer* analyzed urban renewal from the standpoint of social policy as well as economics when he wrote: "The consequences of a typical federal urban renewal project are often harsh. People are forcibly evicted from their homes, businessmen are forced to close their doors, buildings, good and bad, are destroyed—all in the name of an appeal to some higher 'good," the public interest."[2] Then he goes on to place his full faith in the free enterprise system as the vehicle for achieving a better-housed America. According to Anderson, urban renewal did not deliver any significant

133

social benefits because: (1) relocatees did not increase their incomes, (2) discrimination is still practiced, and (3) social problems remain unresolved.[3]

One can agree that these desirable objectives may not have been fulfilled by the urban renewal program. But these were not the original goals of that program, which, according to Anderson, were to (1) eliminate substandard and other inadequate housing through the clearance of slums and blighted areas, (2) stimulate housing production to relieve the housing shortage, and (3) realize the goal of a decent home in a suitable living environment for all.[4]

The original purposes of the 1949 Act were largely physical—that is, the emphasis was on planning and housing so as to transform the city environment. The goals perceived by Anderson include several that are essentially social. This difference in interpretation helps explain in part the low marks he gives urban renewal. Furthermore, it is difficult to understand how in the short run private enterprise can be expected to go it alone to increase incomes, eliminate the practice of discrimination, and solve social problems. Over time, it is the public sector that has become more pervasive in these areas. This public concern for the social growth of the disadvantaged can reasonably be expected to continue whereas this has not been of primary interest to the private sector.

The American Enterprise Institute for Public Policy Research recently sponsored a study of urban renewal by John C. Weicher that is based upon a review of renewal literature. He observes the typical relocatee is "worse off," for the urban renewal project harms the poor and helps the rich by raising the price of housing for the former while it lowers it for the latter. This is the result of increasing the pressure for inexpensive rental units on the existing housing market because of the lack of new construction to replace the slums at acceptable rent/income ratios for the various components of the population that comprise the demand. Although he concedes an increase in the quality of housing occupied by relocatees, he qualifies this result by quoting a Chicago study that notes the fact that given the poor housing in the urban renewal area, it would have been difficult for the relocatees to find worse housing elsewhere. While the quality of housing may have improved, the quantity may have decreased since single persons or even families may have had to double up. Dedensification and redesigned land use patterns are among the important qualitative changes overlooked by Weicher as he concludes: to claim the relocatee has improved his housing is to substitute the judgment of the government for that of the individual as to what is best for him. According to Weicher, his findings are in large measure supported by the West End study, which he recognizes are controversial.[5]

This 1972 report disregards two significant changes affecting relocatees: the HUD requirement for replacement housing adopted in 1968 and the passage of the Uniform Relocation Assistance Act in 1970. To arrive at the above conclusions on the basis of one case study, without considering the effectiveness of substantive policy changes, must of necessity yield misleading conclusions about the efficacy of relocation and renewal activities. To eliminate time dimensions and ignore the physical upgrading of our cities reveals a faulty understanding of urban renewal as a continuing process.

Both authors display a conservative bias in their work. Anderson posits a set of social goals for urban renewal that it was never structured to achieve. He then recommends resolving social issues through the aegis of private enterprise, which has shown little interest or capability in resolving the dilemmas he poses. The study by Weicher is a "heads I win, tails you lose" proposition, for, he says, the benefit of an increase in housing quality is achieved at a cost of higher rents coupled with the lack of inexpensive or poorer housing elsewhere. Indeed, asks Weicher, who is to say that a family must move into better accommodations? This study is limited since it fails to take into account the real and potential fiscal and housing benefits flowing from the recent modifications of housing and relocation policies.

In sum, it may be granted the effects of many early relocation programs essentially were economically and socially counterproductive for the relocatees. In the initial stages, the urban renewal program was just evolving and hence failed to provide adequate financial compensation and inflicted varying social costs, especially if cohesive social neighborhoods were destroyed. Nonetheless, it does not follow that early program failures, due in large part to a lack of social sensitivity, the inability to forecast outcomes, and the inflationary condition in which they occur, should cause desirable, social, and physical goals achievable only through slum clearance and housing betterment to be abandoned. Rather, the critical issue should be to demonstrate how an enhanced social purpose through planned relocation can serve to achieve these goals so that the few no longer are required to bear the costs for the many.[6] This can be achieved through social programs that encourage the economic growth of the individual and society.

John Rawls, in his theory of "compensating benefits," states that *inequalities of wealth and authority are permissible only when they result in improving the condition for all and especially for the poor.* Unlike utilitarian economics, this construct rules out justifying institutions in which the hardships of the few are offset by the greater good for society. This approach may be expedient, but the democratic ethic of equality of opportunity and rewards commensurate with effort must suffer if some must have less in order for the rest to prosper. "But," says Rawls, "... there is no injustice in the greater benefits earned by a few provided that the situation of persons not so fortunate is thereby improved."[7] From this and other postulates, Rawls derives his theory of justice as fairness, whereby that which is *right* takes precedence over that which is *good*. To state it differently, just and fair ends are primary, with just means to be used for achieving specific social objectives, for today in planning, distributive effects are paramount.

Another concept is worth noting here since it underlies benefit-cost analysis.

This is the notion of "economic efficiency," also referred to as Pareto optimality. In this construct, *the results an individual achieves in maximizing his well-being as he perceives it is accomplished without diminishing the well-being of any other person.*[8] At the very least, one person's gain does not impose a cost on another.

We now have two benchmarks for evaluating various program outcomes; one is derived from ethics, the other from economics. They are similar in the sense both agree that none should suffer for anyone to benefit. They differ in degree since the ethical concept conceives of benefits to *all*, even though these may be disproportionate, whereas the economic notion conceives of a benefit to *some* although at no cost to others. While both may be deemed acceptable, of the two, the ethical appears to be the more desirable since all stand to gain, albeit not equally.

Benefit-Cost Analysis

Benefit-cost analysis incorporates the second concept, "economic efficiency" (Pareto optimality), as the criterion for evaluating public policy programs.[9] According to Nathaniel Lichfield, such analyses should include:

1. A statement of program goals against which the proposals designed to meet them can be judged;
2. Direct and indirect beneficiaries, and measurable and nonmeasurable benefits;
3. Direct and indirect costs, and measurable and nonmeasurable costs;
4. The use of an acceptable discount rate in the calculations to account for the time factor required to achieve a given goal;
5. Measurement of all factors in money terms wherever possible;
6. Descriptions of those qualitative elements that do not lend themselves to measurements in money terms;
7. Development of a set of social accounts that identifies who benefits and who loses;
8. Distinguishing real costs from transfer costs, which in the latter case the dollars move from one side of the ledger to the other;
9. Identifying constraints that limit the achievement of goals;
10. Considering alternative uses for the proposed expenditure of resources.[10]

The approach is in essence an elaboration and application of capital budgeting and cost accounting. In addition, it also identifies constraints and alternatives as well as beneficiaries and losers. In this common-sense method, the measurable benefits are added and the costs are subtracted. If the balance is positive, the program is deemed to be economically feasible. If not, presumably it is dropped unless the community places a greater value on the less calculable social benefits than on the calculable costs. In this respect benefit-cost analysis can be assumed to have influenced urban renewal and its concomitant activity, relocation.

An Early Attempt

James Mao in 1966 posed this question: given that the present urban renewal program is supposed to provide a superior pattern of resource allocation, improve housing conditions, and bolster the fiscal health of the city, will a particular project result in a reduction of monies spent on fighting fires, disease, crimes, and juvenile delinquency?[11] To the extent that renewal and relocation activities save the city money that would ordinarily have to be spent for such services, this savings represents a tangible economic benefit deriving from a social improvement. Furthermore, the elimination of the slums reduces the total resources required to be devoted to such areas.[a]

In considering the costs of relocation for a particular project, Mao suggests that in addition to direct money payments, there also are incalculable costs flowing from the disruption of people's lives. He then draws up a balance sheet as shown in Table 10-1. On the benefit side, there are considerable dollar savings

Table 10-1
The Social Costs and Benefits of Urban Renewal

Benefits	Costs
1. Better allocation of resources	1. Survey and planning costs
a. Increase in property values	2. Administrative expenses
b. Value of public improvements	3. Demolition cost
c. Aesthetic and cultural value of planned communities	4. Value of improvements demolished
2. Social implications of slum clearance	5. Cost of public improvements
a. Reduction in crime, disease, fires and juvenile delinquency	6. Relocation costs
	a. Economic
b. Improvement in housing welfare	b. Noneconomic
c. Savings in the costs of municipal services	7. Land value write-down
3. Improvements in local finances	

Source: James C.T. Mao, "Efficiency in Public Urban Renewal Expenditures Through Benefit-Cost Analysis," *American Institute of Planners Journal* XXXII, no. 2 (March 1966): 96. Reprinted with permission.

[a]Arguments of this nature were originally used to support the public housing program.

for the city in protection and health services that result from slum clearance activities. His research also verifies that relocated families had to pay an extra cost for their new accommodations. This was true for homeowners and renters alike. But of 437 original site households, 275 were interviewed to find out their reactions to relocation. Of these, 85 percent stated they benefited from moving.

According to Mao, the dollar value of the acquired improvements, plus the other cost factors in Table 10-1, exceed the benefits by somewhat more than one million dollars. Does this mean the project is inefficient? Not necessarily, for if the *intangible* benefits to the city exceed the costs, then the project is efficient.

It is beyond our purpose to consider all the economic ramifications of this work, but the social analysis suffers since: (1) it assumes the dispersal of the relocatees eliminates the costs for protection and health services, which is not necessarily so, for it may merely redistribute these costs among different areas; (2) it does not take into account the differential effects of the relocation process on the elderly, large families, minority groups, and small businessmen; (3) it does not consider the consequences of the spillover effects of relocation onto the surrounding communities; and (4) it does not come to grips with the problem of placing a dollar value on the intangible social elements in the analysis. Despite these flaws, the Mao study is a positive start toward quantifying some of the benefits and costs for a specific urban renewal project.

A Landmark Study

What could be considered the major work in this area is Jerome Rothenberg's *Economic Evaluation of Urban Renewal* published in 1967.[12] In measuring the effects of urban renewal, the author uses for his criteria the maximization of welfare among the impacted population, rather than the maximization of property values. His salience is social; his tools, financial and economic.

This analysis takes into account explicit and implicit goals in slum clearance and alternate means for achieving them. It identifies those who benefit and those who lose from demolition programs, their direct and indirect costs, the discount rate to account for time, and it makes use of descriptive material where quantitative data is unavailable. The author considers the major goal of urban renewal to be the elimination of blight and slums.

Slums generally represent a suboptimal use of property because (1) one slum building may have a deleterious impact on an entire neighborhood due to its "ripple effect";[13] (2) slums represent an immoral or socially disapproved use or may be the inadvertent result of government policies (private owners are rewarded for their "innovativeness" in maximizing income by conversion to illegal uses along with the failure of the city to enforce codes and other legal standards); (3) the slums create excessive social costs (slum residents are forced to live in firetraps, under overcrowded, unhealthful conditions in crime-ridden areas that may generate personality problems for them). For these reasons, the elimination of slums may produce an overall social benefit, but whether this benefit is better achieved through less surgical approaches such as spot clearance, code enforcement, and fiscal policies is subject to examination, according to the author.[14]

However, slum clearance creates certain direct physical and social costs borne by the relocatees. Those attributable to physical characteristics result from the actual demolition of slum buildings, which requires the relocation of residents elsewhere at higher rentals. Social costs arise from the destruction of friendship networks in the slum community and the requirement that relocatees must vacate from their first choice of housing location for what may be a less preferred alternative.[15] Rothenberg notes, however, that the elimination of inexpensive rental units can be compensated for by providing additional low- and moderate-income housing. Financial losses can also be dealt with by additional compensation. More and better social services and the correction of inequities arising from the delivery of agency services is also possible. The insoluble problems stem from the disruption of communal ties and the need to move to a secondary location. For this latter problem, the relocation process today offers few alternatives. This socially disruptive influence reflects upon the desirability of total clearance as the major tool in urban renewal.[16]

In summary, the social benefits to all presumed to flow from slum clearance includes the removal of fire hazards and health-impairing conditions and a decrease in crime and in personal instability. The costs to the relocatees include higher rents elsewhere, and the destruction of social capital such as neighborhood friendships and established communal ties to organizations and neighborhood facilities.

At this point, the author acknowledges the difficulty in quantifying the social aspects of slum clearance with several statements such as ". . . costs and benefits are extraordinarily difficult to measure, and their existence is subject to intense controversy . . . [or] in most cases the problem is either that it is not clear exactly what should be measured, or that even if it is known, measurement is inaccessible."[17] This is so because (1) the relationships between slums and social costs is interrelated with other causal factors; (2) outcomes are hard to interpret; (3) it is hard to isolate specific influences of other interrelationships; (4) the important effects are truly long-run ones (the more minor relationships that are more easily perceived are short term); and (5) even when the effects are isolated, it may be impossible to place a dollar or market value on them.[18]

After these disclaimers, Rothenberg then proposes several methods for measuring the relationships between social problems and slum life. This would include regression analysis to factor out family from neighborhood influences and to provide a comparison of slum with nonslum data. He recommends comparative studies in the following areas:

1. *Fire hazards.* costs here can be established by comparing the total value of fire damages plus fire prevention services in slums versus nonslums on the basis of the costs per $1,000 of assessed valuation.

2. *Health hazards.* Two factors must be considered for comparisons: the differences in protective and therapeutic services and the differences in morbidity and fatalities. Household samplings may also be required to elicit the health data required. Another difficulty here is placing a dollar value on the cost of illness and death. Diseases most closely associated with slum characteristics—such as overcrowded living conditions, lack of heat and hot water, poor ventilation, rodent and insect infestation from poor garbage disposal, and the like—include acute respiratory infections, infectious children's diseases, infectious and noninfectious skin diseases, minor digestive diseases, injuries caused by accidents in the home, and lead poisoning. Costs here may be calculated by totalling the incidence and dollar value of such diseases on the basis of days lost per capita from work or school and morbidity and mortality rates.

3. *Crime.* Family characteristics such as poverty, poor education, and housing conditions must be factored out. Crimes per capita is the dependent variable; income, median education level, overcrowding and dilapidation are the independent variables. The problem here is to determine the essential characteristics for setting up the equation.

4. *Personality problems.* Broad, qualitative judgments will be required here for there are few if any satisfactory measures of the quantity or cost of the neuroses or psychoses suffered by slum residents. Nonetheless the failure to take this factor into account can impart a downward bias when estimating the benefits from slum clearance.[19]

Although Rothenberg does not compute dollar amounts for these social costs in his case study, he observes that the social component is probably the most important in determining the future of urban renewal. Where dollar values can't be calculated, surrogates may be applied such as the number of fires, illness days, deaths, murders, and the extent of neuroses. Unable to compute these values, he simply represents the benefits with plus marks in his algebraic equation.[20]

In considering the overall effects of redevelopment, the author concludes that other approaches to urban renewal may be cheaper. Rehabilitation, for example, extracts much smaller resource and human costs than does redevelopment, although it eliminates far fewer units of slum occupancy and minimizes the physical scope of community planning. Accordingly, he recommends the program be modified to include a mix of the two approaches since this will reduce the disruptive effects of relocation.

We note here an important distinction between different levels of rehabilitation. The consequences of "gut" or total rehabilitation in occupied buildings has the same immediate effect on people as total clearance; their relocation. Partial or "cosmetic" rehabilitation does not require people to move but causes temporary inconvenience and hardships. Nevertheless what is foreseen here is a shift in focus from the physical to the social—from an emphasis on land use and spatial planning to the problems of slum residents. Their welfare would be the primary goal of the program, supplemented by physical planning related to meet their needs.[21]

This analysis suffers in the area of social costs much as the Mao study does, for the dispersion of certain of the health and criminal pathologies is improperly equated with their elimination. The inability to place a cost on what is concededly the most significant component of a benefit-cost analysis is a vital methodological flaw. Anthony Downs also adds that the locus of decision making in urban renewal is essentially political and not economic. The desire to maximize social welfare ignores the need to identify specific groups of the polity who stand to benefit or lose from urban renewal or community development activities.[22] Consequently, the heavy reliance on fiscal evaluation in benefit-cost analysis limits its usefulness in urban renewal and like programs; for this program is as much a political and social one as it is economic or physical, and it contains moral overtones as well. This inability to cost out social components limits its application as a viable tool for measurement and evaluation, and must perforce limit its use in policy setting where fiscal constructs are the major inputs.

The implications of benefit-cost analyses on relocation cannot be determined. In conjunction with more traditional types of economic analyses, it is reasonable to assume however, that they have been critical factors in hastening the demise of urban rebuilding as a program originally designed to provide the physical elements of the good life.

Investment in Human Capital

The revived interest of economists in considering capital investments in people is in part explained by their puzzlement over the variances in rates of economic growth among some Western and non-Western societies. This concern about human capital was expressed in an earlier time by several economists including Adam Smith. He considered the acquired and useful skills of people as part of the capital resources of the country. In response to later critics, H. von Thünen averred that the concept of capital as applied to man did not degrade or impair him. Despite these disclaimers, subsequent economists have held that it is neither appropriate nor practical to apply the concept of capital investment in people because of its dehumanizing connotations. By so doing, the application of this idea has been inhibited until recently.[23]

Within the last decade there has been a growing awareness that peoples of the world differ enormously in their productive capabilities. This is largely related to environmental factors such as the individual's accumulation of knowledge and his maintenance of good health.[24] The understanding of this relationship has opened at least one door, for the inability to account for the differences in economic growth rates among various groups and countries may be resolved once increases in human capital are taken into account when other resources are deemed to be equal.

Increasing the resources and productivity of the individual affects his future real and psychic income and well-being. Investments for such purposes may take the form of additional schooling, better health, on-the-job training, migration to more economically productive locations, and an enhancement of one's knowledge and information about employment markets.[25] Theodore W. Schultz believes that most of the differences in earnings among people reflects differences in the amounts invested in them. Furthermore, changes in the investment ratio among classes are basic factors in reducing inequalities in income distribution.[26] The concept of an investment in human capital is relevant to planned relocation, for it contains the seeds of redistributive economics that is incorporated in the theory of justice. In this sense, it offers broader and hopefully more acceptable goals for transforming the relocation process as it is known today.

The growth of quality in human resources includes an economic and social dimension, for the economic betterment of the individual is one of the major sources in accounting for our national economic growth. It also indirectly serves to equalize the social differences in our society, thereby enhancing the basic social goals of our democracy as well. Accordingly, the possibility of augmenting "human capital" will be discussed here for its application in planned relocation programs.

Education

Investments in education expands knowledge, raises incomes, and increases productivity. Additional schooling also has desirable external effects. It influences the children of the educated to emulate their parents, it benefits employers seeking an intelligent labor force, and it strengthens democracy by creating a better informed electorate.[27]

In considering the benefits derived from education, Burton Weisbrod distinguishes those that are specific to the individual from those that are general to society. Among the specific benefits are the following:

1. *Direct financial returns.* People with more education earn more than those with less. This is true even after one subtracts the income lost or foregone by persons while attending school. After accounting for one's rank in high school intelligence test scores and father's occupation, at least some part of the additional earnings of the more educated is directly attributable to that education.

2. *Financial option return.* This concept includes two components: the additional income resulting from completing a given level of schooling (as above) and the value of the "option" to obtain still more schooling with accompanying

financial rewards. The decision to pursue a high school education involves not only the earnings derived from that achievement, but involves the value of the opportunity to go on to college, assuming the option to continue with further schooling is exercised and that it is indeed profitable.

3. *Nonmonetary "opportunity" options.* Added education permits widened job choices, possibly greater security, and chances for a different lifestyle than would otherwise be possible to attain.

4. *"Hedging" option.* This represents the increased ability to adjust to changing employment opportunities. Education may be viewed as one's private hedge against his obsolescence in the labor market. Those with greater knowledge and skills should be able to adjust more readily to changes in technology and jobs. Furthermore, the more the education, the more the benefit one can derive from on-the-job training programs.

General benefits to society include nonmarket returns such as the uses to which literacy may be put. For example, the skills required to fill out income tax forms saves the costs of hiring others for such tasks. Also, a child's involvement in school may permit the mother to seek employment. As the child grows into adulthood and becomes a parent, his children may benefit from informal "in house" educational resources.

There are other benefits to neighbors and society as children are removed from potentially destructive activities resulting from excessive idle time. The educated child may not require the community to spend as much for police protection, assuming the lesser proclivity of educated children to indulge in antisocial behavior. The lack of effective education programs in some regions requires other areas to provide supportive educational programs as when an illiterate rural family elects to migrate to an urban community.[28]

Employers also benefit from a better-educated worker as it reflects upon the quality of the output. Fellow employees gain too, for their interdependent work relationships may be enhanced by their co-worker's greater flexibility and adaptability. Communications, banking, and finance, all computer-oriented technologies, require an educated work force to sustain information flows and to deal with work problems of increasing complexity. Finally, education helps towards the social goal of equality of opportunity as individuals are better prepared to take advantage of changing work patterns and increasing leisure time.[29]

The pursuit of schooling is not achieved without incurring costs to the individual and to society. Chief among the individual's costs are the loss of earnings as a result of withdrawing from the labor market. In addition to earnings foregone, one must calculate the direct investment including the cost of borrowing money for tuition, books, supplies, lodging (as required), extra travel, and laundry expenses as well as the indirect, unquantifiable costs such as the withdrawal from family activities and leisure pursuits.

Society as a whole pays a cost as well. This is reflected in the need for additional physical facilities, the cost of borrowing money to build such facilities, the loss of income to the community from alternate forms of investment, the cost for additional faculty and supportive administrative, clerical, and maintenance staff, and the loss of tax revenues from the land on which the school is sited. Society also loses the benefits of the individual's productivity by his absence from the labor market.[30]

In calculating the returns[b] from an investment in college, two different rates must be considered—the social or societal return and the private or individual one—"for," says Gary Becker, "the most important single determinant of the amount invested in human capital may well be its profitability or rate of return. . . ."[31] An analysis of the social or societal rate of return for the class of 1949 white male college graduates shows it to be around 12.5 percent. The private or individual rate of return, after adjusting for differences in ability, seems to be at about 12 percent for this same group. This is a favorable return to both society and the individual as compared with an estimated return of 7 percent from corporate manufacturing investments. Becker also observes, ". . . that the private money gain from college to the typical white male graduate is greater than what could have been obtained by investing elsewhere."[32] The rate of returns to white, male high school graduates relative to their time investments and income foregone is even greater as shown in Table 10-2. The rate of return for college graduates did not change significantly during a twenty-year span but for high school graduates the change was substantial.

Technological advance and other changes apparently increased the demand for high school graduates even more so than for college graduates.[33] The rates of return to the 1939 group of nonwhite male college students is lower and ranges

Table 10-2
Private Rates of Return from College and High School Education for Selected Years Since 1939

Year	College Graduates (percent)	High School Graduates (percent)
1939	14.5	16
1949	13+	20
1956	12.4	25
1958	14.8	28
1959	slightly higher than in 1958	
1961		

Source: Gary S. Becker, *Human Capital: A Theoretical and Empirical Analysis With Special Reference to Education*, National Bureau of Economic Research (New York: Columbia University Press, 1964), p. 128.

[b]The rate of return is a ratio of return on investments (expenditures) to costs; $r = k/c$.

from 10.6 to 14 percent in the South and from 6.6 to 10 percent in the North.[34] This may suggest that nonwhite male high school graduates have less incentive than their white counterparts for going to college, but not much less.[c]

In the short term, these returns exceed that from other kinds of investments since people with more education earn greater salaries. In addition, the long-term psychic return increases as one's opportunities for growth is enlarged through continuing education. The transfer of a familial heritage of education also has positive implications for the family and society as well. An extensive educational investment in human beings shows a good positive pay-off with an immediate and long-term benefit to the individual and society. The growth in human capital through investment in education demonstrates the application of Rawls' theory of mutual benefits as well, even though the benefits may indeed be disproportionate.

Good Health

Good health as an investment rests on the assumption that people are improved as productive agents by maintaining their state of physical well-being and that such outlays show a positive return in the future.[35] Health and education are interwoven since the ability to go to school and to work is dependent upon one's good health. Loss of days due to ill health reduces the effectiveness of the investment in education. By increasing life expectancy, there is a reduction in the rate of depreciation in investment in education. On the other hand, an increase in production through improved education increases the return on a major investment in health.

Outlays for health accrue in part to the individual and to society. The prevention of a communicable disease benefits both. This improvement in health status in turn contributes to the growth in productivity. The reduction in disease creates a yield in the form of an additional and healthier labor force with consequent savings on health expenses in the future. Furthermore, there is a gain in the additional output derived from a healthier and longer-living worker.[36]

Sickness extracts a cost in three ways: (1) through death and the permanent loss of productivity of the person, (2) through disability and a loss of working time and finally, (3) by debility, or the loss of productive capacity while at work.[37] The benefits from good health comprise the increase in output attributable to the eradication of a disease or the extension of life.

One investigator estimates that work loss due to illness ranges from 2.24 to 4.5 percent of total work time. In 1960, the average work days lost due to illness

---

[c]The higher rate for nonwhites in Southern colleges may be explained by the greater opportunity provided black college graduates to offer their services to a relatively large but more restricted market there. Similar monopolistic opportunities may not be available in the North.

totalled 5.6 per person. The labor force in that year was 13,000,000 more than it would have been had the death rate not declined since 1900. With 1920 instead of 1900 as the base year, the labor force was 6,000,000 more than it would have been otherwise. Reduction in mortalities created these additions to the labor force and added to the labor product. At 1960 average incomes, the value created by the 13,000,000 who survived added $60,000,000,000 to national income. (The value for the 6,000,000 survivors totals $28,000,000,000.) The sixty-year decline in death rates accounts for over 10 percent of the overall 3 percent growth rate in the economy.[38]

In 1963, the U.S. Public Health Service calculated the direct and indirect costs of mortality and morbidity.[39] Direct costs included the prevention, detection, treatment, rehabilitation, research, training, and capital investment in physical facilities. Indirect costs such as earnings lost due to illness and premature death, as well as the presumed earnings of housewives were also figured. Excluding the intangibles of pain and suffering, the total economic costs for illness for that year were estimated at $58,000,000,000. Of that sum, approximately $34,000,000,000 went for medical care and services and $24,000,000,000 represented wages lost due to premature deaths, disability, and illness. (This includes $3,000,000,000 for the lost services of housewives.)[40]

On the basis of such costs, an investment in raising the health levels of people can be expected to produce a positive economic return to the individual and to society. Any reduction in the costs of medical care permits the redistribution of funds for other purposes that may also be needed. Any extension in longevity of life or the creation of a state of well-being in the individual results in a more productive and more useful worker. Indeed, the economic and social benefits flowing from good health may be viewed as significant and worthwhile objectives.

On-the-Job Training

Enhancement of individual capital through on-the-job training allows a worker to maintain his skills in an advancing technological society. Such training includes formal and informal programs taught under real work conditions.[41] As with education, on-the-job training includes direct and indirect costs. Direct outlays for training are incurred by employers who must provide instructors and facilities, and by employees who work for less while learning. Indirect costs such as foregone incomes and profits must also be counted. The investment in training one person at work is somewhat higher than the cost for providing him with an equivalent amount of schooling. As implied previously, there seems to be some correlation between the level of on-the-job training and the level of schooling completed by the individual: executive training programs are available to college graduates; apprentice programs are designed for grammar or high school graduates. As crucial as formal schooling appears to be in our society, even more dollars are invested by private firms and public agencies in on-the-job training programs. However, the rate of return to the individual for taking part in on-the-job training is somewhat less than that from a college education.[42]

Although the above characteristics generally apply, there are significant differences in how the money is spent for training. The sums provided for training female employees total about one tenth the amount invested in males, thereby reflecting the fact that employers expect that most females may not work for a very long time. This limits the return to the employer from an investment of this nature. Since his return is lessened, so is his investment in female-oriented training programs.[43]

On-the-job training programs are similarly limited for blacks because firms and employers prefer to invest in those who require the least resources to enhance their individual capital. Because formal school training lowers the costs of on-the-job training, the better prepared an individual is prior to his employment, the cheaper it is to train him at his job. Unfortunately, this results in negative consequences for the poorly educated, poorly trained black worker, for given the economic rationality of investment theory, white males are better and cheaper training investments for a firm than black males. Unfortunately, economic rationality only serves to widen the disparity that already exists between the "haves" and "have nots" of our society.

A growing disparity in the distribution of investment in human capital may make economic sense, but it also perpetuates the cycle of inequality. This gap can be overcome by public policies and programs designed to distribute more equitably the investment in people. By supporting the training of the disadvantaged, their human resources can be increased, thereby more nearly equalizing black and white incomes and promoting social stability.[44] Furthermore, the increase in human capital is really an increase in national capital as well, as reflected in a rise in the gross national product.

Migration and Information

Some exploratory work has been done in treating migration and job information as investments that increase human capital. The assumption here is that migration resulting from knowledge about alternative employment possibilities elsewhere will lead to higher-paying jobs, thereby increasing human capital.[45]

As with education, health, and on-the-job training, these activities incur direct and indirect costs. The direct costs include the additional expenses for food and lodging away from home, as well as the costs for travel in search activities and the expense of transporting one's goods to a new location. Indirect costs include the income foregone that must be calculated for the search itself, for moving, and while learning a new job. Incalculable expenses, which also play a part, include the cost of ending friendships and whatever social networks existed in the old environment as well as those involved in creating new ones elsewhere. These are psychic costs. Psychic benefits may also be incurred, like the positive differences in moving to a warmer or healthier climate. The benefits may also include those derived from moving into a more prestigious community, if this should result from a change in locale.[46]

The age of the worker is crucial in establishing the private rate of return for search and migration activities. Longer life expectancies for a young worker increases the present value of his future returns. Also, the probability that one's work skill will be obsolete elsewhere is less critical when one is young. A younger worker can more easily absorb the costs associated with his search, relocation, and retraining activities than his older counterpart since he can amortize his financial costs over a longer life span.[47]

The ability to migrate is therefore a form of human capital, as is the information a person possesses regarding the jobs available in different labor markets. If information of this nature induces an individual to move to a better job elsewhere and permits him to make greater use of his talents or to develop new ones, then he has successfully capitalized on his information. Society gains as well as the individual, for this information and knowledge permits a more efficient distribution and allocation of the labor force.[48] Thus mobility and information as utilized to take advantage of job opportunities may result in the enhancement of the human being by adding to his capital resources.

In an analysis of major proportions, Edward F. Denison identifies five variables as crucial to our economic growth during the past forty years. These include: (1) advances in technical knowledge; (2) increases in the amount of work done; (3) the input of capital (inventories and nonresidential structures and equipment); (4) education of the work force; and (5) improved use of human resources in shifting from farming and nonfarm self-employment.

From 1929 to 1969, national income grew at an average annual rate of 3.33 percent.[49] The findings in Table 10-3 show the relative percentage contributed by the aforementioned variables to this annual increase in our national income. Approximately one-third of the increase in our growth rate is the result of advances in technology, management, and organizational knowledge. It is reasonable to assume that on-the-job training programs have played an important role in the prominence of this factor. The increase in work done due to a larger labor force contributed almost 30 percent. This is the result of additions to the work force by women, part-time students, and the increase in the total population available for work. Capital goods increases accounted for nearly 16 percent of the growth rate while the fourth largest contributor was the increase in the average amount of education by workers, totalling 14 percent. The improved use of labor by migration from less productive farm employment to more highly productive industrial jobs added 10 percent to the national growth rate.[50] Of these five major components, four represent an enhancement in

Table 10-3
Variables Affecting National Income, 1929-1969

	1929-1969
Potential National Income	100.0
(1) Advances in knowledge and not elsewhere classified	31.1
(2) More work done except education	28.7
(3) More capital goods	15.8
(4) Increased education per worker	14.1
(5) Improved resource allocation	10.0
(6) Dwellings occupancy ratio and irregular factors	0.3

Source: Edward F. Denison, *Accounting for United States Economic Growth, 1929-1969* (Washington, D.C.: The Brookings Institution, 1974), p. 130.

human capital while one (capital goods and inventories) represents an increase in physical capital.

The dominant role played by individuals in increasing the total wealth of the nation is indeed impressive and significant. This factor is usually ignored or unrecognized in many discussions dealing with social programs, their costs, and their consequences. Significantly, the investment in human capital appears to have been of greater worth than investments in physical capital in raising national wealth during the last two generations. This could also be an indicator of a change from a technological to a service-oriented American society.

Positive Implications

Investment in human capital is an attractive, compelling concept for it appears to bring benefits to all of society as well as to the individual. According to Lester Thurow, investments of this nature are desirable for the following reasons:

1. *Human capital may be likened to a pure public good.* Since the private sector cannot provide for certain essential services basic to all, then the public sector must compensate here. National defense, environmental protection, universal education, and good health are some illustrations of a public good. Universal education, for example, promotes social stability and communal and individual well-being. As one benefits, so all benefit. An investment in human capital therefore incorporates the elements of a pure public good.

2. *Society may prefer to redistribute incomes in a specific manner.* Private sector investment decisions appear to widen the economic and social disparities among groups. Society may wish to close this gap. This can be done by direct

transfer payments or by investing in human development. The former is more expensive since it requires a continuing subsidy and provides for little if any personal enhancement. The latter may require a higher initial investment but chances are the economic and social rewards from developing an individual who gains self-respect through work far outweighs the initial investment.

3. *Human capital may be viewed as a merit want.* Society may feel that a minimum level of education or subsistence is necessary. Accordingly, it may require that one achieve a basic level of education or earnings, even where the individual may feel otherwise. These values may not necessarily be as important to the individual, but are deemed critical by society.

4. *Society's information about the future stream of costs or benefits from an investment in human capital may differ from that of firms or individuals.* The government may decide to make social investments for the future well-being of society to offset what appears to be imperfect current knowledge by the private sector and by individuals. Enlarged training programs in health services or other service jobs based upon forecasts of future societal needs, demonstrate the application of this notion. Furthermore, the government may be able to far better afford the cost of risk and the uncertainty of training than can firms, institutions, or the individual.[51]

Negative Implications

There appear to be sound economic justifications for programs that invest in the enhancement of the individual.[52] But before assuming that investments of this nature are *the* panacea for society, some negative implications should be noted. Several economists are concerned with the concept of "returns on investment" in human beings, for this implies a consideration of alternative possibilities. Some may weigh an investment in education against an investment in shopping malls or athletic stadiums. "Mixed" or primarily social investments may be equated as "business propositions" where the "rate of return" is a fundamental consideration.[53]

Some values deemed vital to all include an ethical or moral content that preclude financial "trade-offs." In addition, such "trade-offs" are premised on the continuing stability of tastes and resources. The concept of stability, however, runs counter to the purpose of change-creating social programs that contain large elements of uncertainty. Also, there is no firm basis for calculating *a priori* the nature or amount of the "pay-off" from such programs, for much of the future value of an educated citizenry depends to a large extent upon the availability of employment.[54] This in turn is related to an unknown future demand.

All these factors cast doubt on the appropriateness of this benefit-cost calculus over a long term. Furthermore, the investment itself may modify the environment that is dependent upon it, thereby yielding a result altogether different from the one initially expected. For example, how does one measure and evaluate the benefits from an education that enhances the economic life of society and then may be put to use for militaristic rather than humanistic global adventures? To avoid the possibility of distortions to programs resulting from an indeterminate future, changes must be moderate or incremental so as not to negate goals or objectives based on an assumption of continuity.[55]

Fiscally determined "rates of return" are useful for the present where a more or less societal steady state exists, but for long-range decision-making purposes, quantitative analyses must yield to decisions "...that are judgmental and strategic but are no less real despite their inability to be measured."[56]

This cautionary note applies not only to investments in human capital for which justification is sought via economic "rates of return," but to all benefit-cost analyses that also attempts to quantify the variables of social and physical programming.

Summary

Various economists have had incalculable but influential effects on urban development and relocation programs. One major economic interpretor of the social aspects of urban renewal argued against objectives that were at best implicit; another omitted the consideration of time, which is critical to the renewal agenda (this oversight resulted in faulty conclusions); and others applied benefit-cost techniques that are presently more useful for physical than social analysis. Failing to develop rigorous fiscal measures for social gains or losses, they have substituted descriptive data or have proposed instead several other avenues for future research.

A most recent economic approach, investment in human capital, appears to be the most promising. This theory seems to meet several criteria: enhancing the individual's potential for economic growth, enlarging social justice, and adding to the country's capital wealth. But even here caution must be exercised. Concern for the technical hardware (e.g., "rates of return," "discount rates," "future income streams," and the like), while important, should not be allowed to outweigh the moral imperative implicit in the growth of the human being and the enlargement of social justice in our society.

This reservation notwithstanding, the successful application of the concept of investment in human capital through the medium of planned relocation provides the latter with a new set of socially and economically desirable objectives and programs. In promoting this kind of growth in the individual, society stands to gain as well from the spillover effects of such human development.

Although it is not yet widely recognized, there is a real economic benefit to society coincident with the social betterment of the individual. Recent detailed economic analyses have measured the relative contributions of the social, fiscal, and physical subsectors to the growth of our economy. Especially in the case of advances in knowledge (through education, on-the-job training, and job mobility) and increases in the size of the work force (resulting from among others, better health and longer life), these social inputs to the national economy help explain our ability to sustain and even increase our national level of economic growth. By enhancing our human capital, we are really investing in and increasing our national capital.

The early economic concepts of community development made their own contribution to furthering the understanding of public policy, but none utilized a holistic approach in integrating social and economic theory. Current economic analyses tend to achieve this meld by including in national wealth the sum of the contributions by the various social sectors of society as well as the more traditional economic sectors. In this context, the national good is the sum total of individual and communal goods, and national wealth is truly an index or expression of all these goods. Also, in ignoring the consequences of social programs, we tend to overlook additional economic benefits. The multiplier effects of increased individual consumption and production also contributes to an enhanced GNP, for the investment in human capital plays a larger role than investment in physical capital in raising both per capita income and our total national wealth.

It seems wise therefore that public policies in relocation be adopted that enhance the social and economic capabilities of the individual relocatee by means of his or her social growth effectuated through the planned relocation process. Programs of this nature would therefore reinforce community rebuilding activities via a cohesive, coordinated assault on the problems of the underutilized, unfulfilled individual forced to live in a decaying physical environment. It would also avoid the economic and social waste that characterized unplanned relocation efforts in the formative years.

Part IV:
Transforming Relocation

11 A Social System for Enhancing the Individual and Society

An Historic Perspective

The dynamics of natural population movements and relocation programs demonstrate the growing role of the state in support of such activities. In the light of past events it is reasonable to expect federal involvement to continue and even expand. This is true despite the Nixon-Ford approach to community development, which seeks to remove the federal government from direct intervention in the details of local decision making.[1] In one respect, this shift is only in form rather than substance, for the amount of dollars and the basic activities they support are still largely determined by one major source, the federal government.

Although the amplitudes of federal control and direction may vary from time to time, in our increasingly complex society, federal intervention is required to redistribute our economic and social goods. This is necessary in order to counteract those inequalities that are deemed to be undesirable in contemporary America, in terms of both the ethical values inherent in the American constitutional system and the operational dictates of a resource-scarce society.

The Enlarging Role of the State

Students of city growth may differ about the reasons, but the record is clear that people have had a tendency to cluster on an ever-increasing scale to satisfy their essential needs and desires.

Starting with the earliest civilizations, mobility and relocation processes have been influenced in varying but increasing degrees by the state. In this country the role of the federal government in its earliest days was simultaneously indirect and direct. This is to say that families and individuals were encouraged to migrate from Europe and elsewhere, and from the east coast to west of the Alleghenies by cheap land policies. This culminated in the Homestead Act of 1862, which provided up to 160 acres of land at nominal cost after five years of residency. A policy of rewarding the most mobile members of American society was deemed to be in the public interest as a means for settling the western lands.

In order to fulfill this public policy it was necessary for the federal government to intervene directly to force the Indians to vacate their lands. This

155

epitomizes an extreme in federal intervention in the relocation process, for in this case it was backed by the use of arms. The land and Indian policies and programs of the nineteenth century demonstrate that relocation processes can be measured on a continuum ranging from democratic to authoritarian.

More recently, in the battles against the Depression and in two world wars, direct federal involvement in natural relocation processes was deemed to be essential. In the former case, there was a need to resettle and rehouse America's destitute farmers and urban slum dwellers while in the latter the need was to provide living quarters for war production workers. In both these instances, to be sure, the purpose for relocation contrasted with that in the previous century; neither the desire to raise money from land sales or encourage resettlement, nor the extermination of another culture, but the overriding necessity to deal with compelling social problems. The relocation of the luckless farmers and slum dwellers was based upon a newly perceived concern for the lowest third of the nation, a concern which justified federal activity in areas heretofore never considered appropriate. Nevertheless, the two centuries, with two contrasting objectives, were both characterized by governmental intervention.

Still other cases of federal involvement in relocation programs display this increasing interest, also springing out of the dissimilar motives. The emotionally and economically inspired forced removal of the Japanese-Americans during World War II displays extremely negative aspects of public policies in relocation. Paradoxically, this was followed by the socially motivated urban redevelopment program that derived its roots from the social welfare philosophy of the New Deal. In both these cases, the federal role was paramount, on the one hand to protect the state from presumed acts of sabotage, on the other to revitalize the physical environment of the nation's deteriorating cities. This difference in program motivation is vital to an understanding and interpretation of relocation activities and its consequences.

The passage of the Housing and Community Development Act on August 22, 1974,[2] attempts to restructure the form of federal-local relationships by assigning to local communities some power to decide what types of community programs shall be supported with federal funds. This should not be considered a diminution of federal interest in relocation, since all community development activities are still obligated to comply with the Uniform Relocation Assistance Act. What is different is the provision for local options in determining the content of the community development package. In the area of relocation, the federal government has chosen to limit its responsibility as the community's "watchdog." The pragmatic effects on relocation are likely to be more procedural than substantive. This is so because the terms and conditions of specific relocation programs are based upon the requirements mandated by the community development programs selected by local governments.

It follows, therefore, as our society becomes more complex, more interrelated, and more dependent, "the inexorable expansion of the Federal government as the dominant device for social guidance will be a major factor in the increasing rationalization of society."[3] One can conclude that the federal role in future relocation activities will continue to be significant, but its purpose and function can be expected to vary from one time to another.

Duality in Relocation Process

It should not be assumed that this continuing federal involvement in relocation will, *a priori*, fulfill the social and economic growth needs of the individual and promote social justice in our society; nor that the opposite is true. The preceding pages on the relocation history of the United States illustrates the dichotomous nature of this process as it shifts back and forth from democratic to authoritarian modes. At times it has displayed these characteristics simultaneously through different programs, a circumstance neither ideologically nor pragmatically acceptable to a democratic society. As we comprehend more fully the effects of such programs, we can increasingly plan them along democratic lines.

Relocation must be transformed into a process designed to capitalize on the opportunity thus afforded to improve the quality of life for both the individual and society. As a consequence, its methods and purposes must encompass dual needs—those of the impacted people and the entire community as well—since the current welfare economics model, which is based upon the notion that public intervention is justified when the overall communal benefit outweighs the individual cost, can no longer be deemed acceptable. In order to be fair and just to all, the new social welfare model must be of direct benefit to the individual as well as the larger society, although the extent to which each benefits need not be equal.

The removal of the Indians for the benefit of the white settlers dramatically demonstrates how the same relocation process can be perceived oppositely by different peoples at the same time. To the Indians, their removal meant the annihilation of their culture at the hands of an authoritarian government. To the white settlers, it represented an opportunity for their individual enhancement, the development of a populist-oriented government, and the enlargement of democracy. This contradiction has a milder and more contemporary analogue. In describing the early relocation process in urban renewal, a renowned city builder opined, "you can't make an omelette without breaking the eggs." While the use of this metaphor offends our notions of fairness and justice, it reveals a viewpoint that unfortunately has some degree of acceptance in our culture.

The internment of the Japanese during World War II was earlier described as "one of the most spectacular breakdowns of government responsibility in our history." It exemplifies the extremes that even a democratic government will go to in the name of "national survival." Had the real issue been national survival instead of ethnic prejudice, there might have been some grounds for this precipitous act. But the fact that no such step was taken in Hawaii, with its much larger percentage of Japanese, makes this doctrine suspect. In this relocation process, both the means and the latent ends—the removal of a highly competitive and successful ethnic group from its land and wealth—were clearly authoritarian.

Perhaps the most idealistic application of democratic means and ends in relocation were the rural resettlement programs promoted by the New Deal. Unfortunately, these attempts in expanding democracy were largely unsuccessful, for the programs were perceived by Congress as promoting a communal, cooperative concept. These goals were premature since they challenged the American stereotype of the free, independent, and self-reliant yeoman farmer of the nineteenth century. In addition, the visionary dreams of the program administrators, when joined with their failure to produce the requisite housing units, spelled the end of this experiment in enlarging social justice.

Unfortunately, many post World War II relocation experiences also failed to satisfy the prerequisite of fairness to all through democratic means and ends. As these activities in city rebuilding burgeoned in the 1960s, they were successfully challenged by the impacted populations. This resulted in many relocation program modifications requiring increasingly adequate fiscal and rehousing resources. The protests finally resulted in the passage of the Uniform Relocation Assistance Act in 1970.

This Act is only a prologue. Planned relocation programs must play a far more important role in enhancing life; they can no longer serve merely as handmaidens to the physical reconstruction of urban areas. The transformed purpose of planned relocation must be to enhance the capability of each individual to become a more productive member of society. When redesigned to serve this new end, a planned relocation process should no longer be perceived as a threat to the community and individual; rather, as it moves towards these new social goals, it should be viewed as a vital component of an acceptable process to combat both human and physical stagnation.

Relocation as an Evolving Process

The inability of present-day critics to view relocation as an evolving social process has placed it temporarily in eclipse alongside other social endeavors such as the antipoverty and Model Cities programs, for in Washington today the urban condition is no longer considered critical. Domestic economic problems have displaced the incomplete social agenda. According to one observer, ". . . the 'urban crisis' of the nineteen-sixties is over."[4] This attitude is reflected in the latest legislation from Washington dealing with urban problems.

The Housing and Community Development Act of 1974 displays a bias toward the *physical* renewal of urban neighborhoods. Under the new Act, Model

Cities grants are scheduled to be phased out. To the extent these activities deal with the "software" of social problems, the future funding of such activities is uncertain. Although 20 percent of the funds allotted to a community may be used for nonphysical, service activities, this sum is allowable only if federal funds from other sources are not available.[5]

Under these circumstances, planned relocation as a process capable of enhancing the individual could be cast aside as the "Cinderella of Community Development" activities. Those who suffer most from socially and physically debilitating slum environments may be able to hope for the physical regeneration of their areas, but little more beyond this. The new approach is piecemeal and fragmented, while the need is comprehensive. As federal officials proclaim the end of the urban crisis and translate this expression into law, one can only hope this judgment is indeed accurate for the consequences of misjudgment and self-delusion can result in much the same type of damage to our cities tomorrow as the lack of understanding in the past contributed to their demise today.

The potential of the planned relocation process as a vehicle for individual growth has never been truly put to the test in its entirety. Transforming this process to include social components must become the basis for wide experimentation in community development programs. This process must be viewed as an open social system whose output—a more capable, productive individual—makes a direct contribution to our national wealth. The planned growth and relative stability of our society must include social as well as economic and physical dimensions; it must include the enhancement of people as well as neighborhoods.

An Open Social System

Planned relocation as a functioning open system envisions a full bundle of intermediate and long-range social services to increase the productive capabilities of the individual. It also encourages the re-establishment of a social community where this objective is deemed desirable by the relocatees. The participation of the residents is a critical part of this open system that translates peoples' desires and needs into programs designed to attain specific ends.[6]

This innovative relocation process is achievement-oriented. Its major thrust is toward fulfilling social objectives designed to increase human performance as well as the more traditional physical and fiscal forms of relocation assistance. It is a dynamic, evolving process that is sensitive to the needs of the household and business community it serves. Under its new mandate, it responds to human beings ahead of grand physical designs.

Planned relocation, structurally conceived here as an open social system, is a new way of viewing the organization of the relocation process. Figure 11-1 is a schematic presentation of an ideal model of such an open, planned relocation

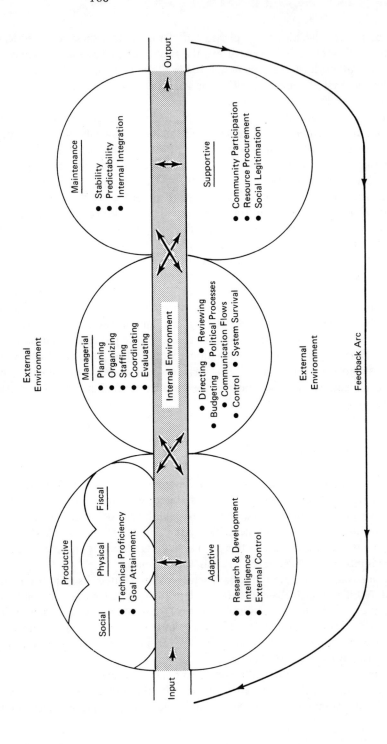

Figure 11-1. Model of Ideal Open System Organization.

system. This social-psychological approach incorporates several subsystems, task units, and broad concepts. The subsystems perform the following general functions (specific functions will be described later):

1. *Productive Functions*, which are concerned with technical or work proficiency and the accomplishment of tasks. Production is achieved by transforming human energy within the system through a division of labor determined according to task specifications and standards.
2. *Supportive Functions*, which are concerned with system means and ends such as procuring resources, dispensing services, and obtaining social support and legitimation. These are achieved by controlling resources and by creating a positive image in the community, thereby influencing the social structure. Legitimation is attained by molding organizational and societal attitudes in the outside environment.
3. *Managerial Functions*, which are concerned with compromise, control, survival, and the coordination and direction of all the subsystems. It also seeks to enhance its environment and to enlarge its functions by the use of sanctions and authority. This is accomplished through making more effective use of its resources.
4. *Adaptive Functions*, which are concerned with issues of external control and internal change via research and development, and planning and intelligence services. This subsystem makes recommendations for changes to management.
5. *Maintenance Functions*, which are concerned with organizational stability and predictability by mediating between the demands of the task and human needs, thereby keeping the structure in operation. This is done by formalizing behavior through standardized procedures, setting up a rewards system, and socializing and integrating new members into the organization.[7]

The open system organization is also characterized by its structural capacity to absorb feedback from its environment, to correct its errors and omissions, and to adapt to changes in its surroundings, thereby enabling the entire system to survive.[8] This theoretical framework permits us to understand planned relocation from an enlarged perspective, as an open and responsive social process. We shall attempt to incorporate the essential functions and concerns of planned relocation within the theoretical framework just described. A word of caution is appropriate here. Some of the functions and concepts might conceivably be placed in two of the subsystems or may not seem appropriate for any of them. This is an ideal model of an open relocation system, which is still largely an abstraction. Only after it has been tested and applied can one say with some certainty which of the functions and tasks are better performed elsewhere. We next consider various operational problems within the framework of our theoretical construct.

The Productive Subsystem: Social,
Physical, Fiscal, Technical Proficiency,
Goal Attainment

This subsystem incorporates three basic functions of planned relocation: the social, physical, and fiscal. Of these, the social unit is the most important. It is responsible for establishing and maintaining the necessary linkages between the site residents and those outside agencies offering required skill-training programs. This includes the entire educational establishment from technical institutions to grammar and even graduate schools. Private and quasi-public organizations that offer on-the-job training programs also come within its orbit. In addition to skill-imparting organizations, this unit maintains links with job-finding organizations. This is a critical connection that must be nourished by the relocation agency.[a] Educating and training for a limited or nonexistent job market not only wastes human talent but creates a hoax that could lead to the demise of the entire planned relocation system.

Essentially the same linkages must be developed by the relocation staff in the health field as in education, on-the-job training, and job information. Once the health needs of the relocatees have been determined, the supervisor responsible for the delivery of these services must bring together the people and the health institutions. This may require the assignment of several health practitioners to relocation field offices as well as referrals to the home base of the health institution.

The methods for delivering the above services can be as varied as the kinds of organizations themselves. These services can be provided for by contract, by staff, or a combination of these forms. Methodology is a mechanical problem. This should not be confused with the substance, or the content of programs. The prime objective here is to insure the effective delivery of required social services to the impacted residents.

It is also expected that services of this nature, will be incorporated in all development programs in which relocation is a prerequisite. Furthermore, they should be made available beyond the period of physical relocation until such remedial help is unnecessary. Unlike its predecessor programs, the planned relocation process does not envision an abrupt termination of essential social services upon the relocation of the household. Indeed it should be designed so as to be able to provide its social program output within the new physical milieus of the relocatees. In this process, the spatial change is but one phase of a total process of human development.

The second unit in our productive subsystem provides rehousing services, including residential as well as commercial resources. The nature of the

[a]The concept of the "linch-pin" or the "man in the middle" is an important element of organization theory. See Rensis Likert, *New Patterns of Management* (New York: McGraw-Hill, 1961).

rehousing "mix" is jointly determined by the policy-making managerial and supportive subsystems. Once the data base is known, a rehousing program should be designed to meet the needs of all the relocatees. Their demand for housing should be fulfilled in several ways: under Section 8 of the new Housing and Community Development Act, under Section 206 of the Relocation Assistance Act—the "houser of last resort" clause or under any other housing legislation which is effective in meeting the housing demand.

It is crucial that community organizations, and especially relocatee groups, participate in policy-making relocation processes. It is their vital interests that are at stake. Furthermore, their participation is the keystone of a democratic relocation process that is envisioned here. In fact, the Housing Act requires adequate citizen participation as a prerequisite for federal assistance.

The fiscal unit of the subsystem is concerned with establishing and validating the financial needs of the relocatees and processing their relocation claims. Although the Relocation Assistance Act spells out in detail the amounts to be paid by the types of occupancy, it does not consider the effects of inflation on the purchasing power of the relocation dollar. To compensate for this, the present allowances should serve as the baseline for financial assistance. These allowances should be reviewed annually by HUD and modified to reflect any fiscal erosion, thereby sustaining the value of the financial compensation.

The Supportive Subsystem: Community
Participation, Resource Procurement,
Social Legitimation

The supportive subsystem is perhaps the most crucial in terms of creating and maintaining community support for social programs. Through the medium of a locally created Board of Directors or a Citizens Advisory Council (organizational units may represent a spectrum from control to advice), a strong political force must be established to exert pressure to support appropriate levels of social services. This policy-setting or policy-recommending group also has the function, among others, of legitimating the agency's activities to the outside world. By so doing, it should help to smooth the path for the fiscal flows needed to support the various social programs required by the relocatees.

Under the block grant method of allocating federal funds, there is the possibility that, as in revenue sharing, fiscal displacement will occur. This means that some communities may fail to give proper emphasis to social services in their use of revenue-sharing funds.[9] Although it is expected that the neediest communities will benefit the most under the block grant approach (as determined by their "needs score," which is based upon population, a double-count for poverty, and housing crowding), there may be local struggles to control the use of the dollars. One recent analysis of cities in the Middle Atlantic region reports that "... few of the cities with such functions (human resources) have demonstrated any genuine effort to integrate social with physical and economic development. This fact is disappointing to the intent of the legislation; even though social services are lowest on the list of funding priorities (limited to 20 percent for social service administration after other federal resources have been used), there was the legislative hope that there would occur, at least, the coordination of traditional urban renewal with traditional Model Cities social programs."[10]

Experience with Model Cities programs in New York and elsewhere is an indicator of the potential power struggles that could develop among community groups.[11] Care must be exercised to insure that the least organized, the elderly poor, are equitably represented in the distribution of block grant funds, for even among the poor, the competition for limited resources could result in a distribution based upon power instead of need.

In its supportive role, the neighborhood board or committee plays a seminal part in understanding and countering the power plays of the more politically sophisticated. As middlemen and local power brokers, they serve as links between those who may be less and those who may be more actively involved in local political processes.

The Managerial Subsystem: Direction, Coordination, Control, System Survival

Perhaps the most important characteristic of the managerial subsystem is its ability to develop and apply policies and programs that serve to enhance the individual relocatee. To some extent this is dependent upon the nature of the leadership provided by this component of the organization. In order for planned relocation to function effectively, a new breed of manager is required. He or she must be a person who is achievement oriented, knowledgeable, innovative in ideas, and with charismatic qualities that induce others to willingly subject themselves to the manager's direction.

Several students of leadership have each identified the "leader" in different terms such as the "entrepreneurial type," or as a "change agent." Others define the most effective form of leadership as a shared function within a group.[12] While the nature of the leadership role is moot, the ability to perform well in an environment loaded with uncertainty should be a prerequisite for the systems director. It is essential that the "new breed" have the ability to manage political bombardment and social change. In addition, this key executive must serve as a "linch-pin," connecting his organization with other service groups in the community.

Broader social and organizational perspectives are required as planned relocation evolves towards a new form and system. The "new breed" will therefore not only have to be able to master the traditional functions of administration (planning, organizing, staffing, directing, coordinating, and budgeting)[b] but must also be able to function and manage under conditions of continual risk and uncertainty.[13]

The Adaptive Subsystem: Research and Development, Intelligence, External Control

Embarking on a social program of the depth and magnitude described requires careful field application and continual testing to verify program outcomes. This is a function of this subsystem. Continual monitoring and evaluation of the effectiveness of the various activities is a prerequisite. Quantitative and qualitative indicators of effectiveness must be developed to evaluate the output. While such indicators should include the traditional measures of cost and time, of equal or even greater significance are new indices of human enhancement through useful work, strengthened physical and emotional health and well-being, and an advancement in learning and education.

The planned relocation model must develop the capacity for rigorous testing so as to determine the extent to which each of the above elements contribute to its success or failure. This requires the use of external control groups in order to significantly compare results of the new programs.

Finally, the adaptive function is concerned with perpetuating the integrity of the system. It does so by filtering and processing reactions of the outside environment to the agency's programs. It either recommends changes in organization function to meet the demands of the outside universe, or it seeks to modify or control the external forces that surround the organization.[14]

The Maintenance Subsystem: Stability, Predictability, Internal Integration

This subsystem is concerned with maintaining the stability of the organization. As the adaptive subsystem scans the outer world for relevant intelligence about organization effectiveness, this subsystem scans its internal operations. It deals with such problems as institutionalizing agency operations, socializing personnel in the mores of the organization, and establishing a rewards system. Internal auditing of organizational operations are among the means by which it attempts to maintain stability and predictability.[15]

---

[b]Luther Gulick's famous acronym POSDCORB describes the responsibilities of the traditionalist-administrator; see Luther Gulick, "Notes on the Theory of Organization," in Luther Gulick and L. Urwick, eds., Papers on the Science of Administration (New York: Institute of Public Administration, 1937), p. 13.

The Feedback Subsystem:
Information Input, Negative
Feedback

Inputs into an open system comprise not only raw materials as in factories, but information and signals about the outside environment. Information input enables the organization to adjust to changes in the external environment. Negative feedback permits it to correct deviations from its goals by adjusting its programs. It is this capacity for self-correction that distinguishes an open from a closed social system. If it fails to react to its negative feedback, it will eventually fail as an organization. To prevent this from occurring, continual research such as attitude polling and other reaction indicators are required, for it is this sensitivity to its environment that will help perpetuate its existence.[16]

The open relocation system just described is now in the testing stage in one community in a modified form.[17] Our ideal model incorporates a series of transactions between individuals, groups, the organization itself, and the outside environment. It is a fluid, dynamic conceptual scheme which incorporates a broad range of social services within an open system organizational design.

The oversize bulges in the schematic for the social unit and the supportive subsystem indicates their importance relative to the other subsystems. The managerial subsystem serves as the integrative, coordinating element for all the subsystems. The productive subsystem is the "line" component. It is responsible for the delivery of the essential social, physical, and fiscal services. The adaptive subsystem has a "radar-like" function of continually scanning and testing the external environment and reporting its findings to the managerial component. Lastly, the maintenance subsystem is responsible for promoting internal harmony by integrating the various roles and creating a universal set of behavioral norms for the individuals comprising the organization.

The value of this type of organizational mode over the more traditional, Weberian Bureaucratic Model is that it is cast in a democratic pattern. It seeks to serve rather than dominate. Its ethic is based upon program effectiveness, defined as the ratio of output to input. It does not forego efficiency and economy, but these classical standards are now enhanced and subsumed under new yardsticks; adaptability, effectiveness, responsiveness, and responsibility. This open approach to the relocation process is designed to promote the capabilities and well-being of its constituents, the relocatees, along with the reconstruction of the cities.

A Social Policy

If we are to achieve the social goals put forth above, then a firm legislative declaration—a Social Bill of Rights—is essential now. It would be naive to expect any congressional or presidential statement on this subject to change the nature of events in our restless and largely individualistic society. In fact, earlier declarations have been mainly consigned to history's slag heaps. Nevertheless, a firm moral commitment from our elected leaders can serve as "earnest money" by underwriting their good faith. It can also serve as a yardstick for evaluating and measuring our progress in enlarging social democracy. Finally, it could unify our drifting society by providing the nation with a sense of direction and purpose.

Defining the National Purpose

Franklin D. Roosevelt in 1944 was concerned with the discontents engendered by fighting a massive war on two fronts. Faced with the need to inspire the people to make even greater sacrifices, he used his annual message to Congress as a clarion call. In introducing what he labelled a "second Bill of Rights," he said, "...Some individual freedom cannot exist without economic security and independence."[18] This address contained several social and economic goals that are still germane and must be considered today. These include such rights as:

1. The right to useful work;
2. The right to earn enough to provide adequate food and shelter;
3. The right to a decent home;
4. The right to adequate medical care and the opportunity to enjoy good health;
5. The right to a good education;
6. The right to adequate security from unemployment, sickness, accidents, and the ravages of old age.[19]

In 1948, the newly created United Nations adopted a Universal Declaration of Human Rights, which also has served largely as a statement of moral principles. This Declaration surpassed the goals earlier enunciated by F.D.R. in its statement of political, economic, and social rights for all.[20]

The lofty aims stated in these declarations may have only slight substance, but they have great moral significance for they help create a state of mind that makes lesser national goals unacceptable. As a result, to a society that has established full employment as a major economic objective, a 10 percent unemployment rate is intolerable, and even a 6 percent rate is not acceptable.

Rhetorical shortcomings notwithstanding, Congress should adopt a "Social Bill of Rights" to serve as a standard against which to measure legislative acts and social programs.

Legislative Actions

As part of an overall package of social legislation, Congress should follow in part the model provided by the Employment Practices Act of 1946 and its proposed successor, the Equal Opportunity and Full Employment Act of 1976.[21]

The 1946 Act established a Council of Economic Advisors and requires an annual economic report by the president. As Bertram Gross and many others have suggested, Congress should create a Council of Social Advisors and require the president to submit an Annual Social Report.[22] There may not be available as yet the same degree of preciseness in quantifying and evaluating social progress as there is in recording economic trends. It is important, however, to institutionalize at the highest level of government an interest and responsibility for the advancement of social knowledge and trends in the United States. Furthermore, an Annual Social Report by the president would go far toward sensitizing the nation as to the value of enhancing our human capital. It could also help restructure our national priorities as expressed in federal budgetary allocations.

The Employment Practices Act of 1946 failed to provide for a linkage between the individual and the job. Its effect was mostly symbolic, marking a permanent, historic change by government away from a "laissez-faire" attitude toward unemployment. The proposed Equal Opportunity and Full Employment Act is far more integrative. It is primarily a *job guarantee* measure.[23] It achieves this by creating a link between the individual and the job, which is significant. The Bill calls for specific jobs to be provided by the Job Guarantee Office within the renamed United States Full Employment Service. The latter agency would fund private and public job programs that would be approved by local Planning Councils in Cooperation with Community Job Boards.[24] A program of this nature could provide a very deft "fit" with planned relocation activities. Relocatees in need of employment could be linked to jobs funded by this program such as construction work engendered by the Housing and Community Development Act.

The Bill also creates a Standby Job Corps to absorb workers temporarily when more suitable jobs are not readily available. It also includes mandatory bi-annual funding, creation of a National Commission for Full Employment Policy Studies, and the right of the individual to seek redress through the U.S. District Courts.[25]

As the Medicare program attempts to create a minimum acceptable level of health care for the elderly, the Full Employment Act strives for a similar goal in employment. It deals with one of the most fundamental human rights, the guarantee of a job. In this way it seeks to affirm the worth of the individual to society as a productive being rather than consign him to a role as a nonproductive outcast.

Hubert H. Humphrey, a supporter of full employment, raises this question: "How can genuine full employment best be sustained without inflation?"[26] He calls for a full production and employment economy based upon a model of the United States that would consider economic variables such as production, employment, investment, foreign trade, distribution of wealth, and income. He also includes in his model domestic goods and services in short supply such as housing, mass transit, daycare, health, education, scientific research, and development of the arts. This approach could be useful in establishing, at least on a theoretical level, the appropriate "mix" needed to sustain truly full employment, growth in the GNP, an increase in social services and the employment of the arts. At the same time, it would be designed to maintain a damper on inflation.

Much of the legislative framework is already in place to support the social programs to be linked to planned relocation. The Elementary Secondary Education Act of 1965 represents the most comprehensive single commitment since the Morrill Act of 1864 to further the development of educational programs. Title I, for example, was designed to provide funds to those school districts whose children are educationally deprived. It is this title that has supported the Headstart program. Title II provides funds for school library resources and other educational materials. Title III supplies monies for Adult Education courses in reading, writing, and arithmetic for those over eighteen years old. The Act also authorizes grants for initiating, expanding, and improving services for physically handicapped children. A Bilingual Education program deals with those children with limited English-speaking ability who are in greatest need of educational assistance. It also pays for the Dropout Prevention Program.

As in the area of academic education, federal legislation is available to support vocational and manpower training programs. The Manpower Development and Training Act provides vocational training to unemployed and underemployed adults and youths. It attempts to upgrade their work skills to meet market needs. The Vocational Educational Act supports vocational training in high schools and community colleges. Many of these activities include work-study arrangements thereby providing on-the-job training to its recruits. There are many more specialized and experimental manpower and vocational programs, some under the Comprehensive Employment and Training Act of 1973, which can be dovetailed into planned relocation programs.

In the field of health care, the Comprehensive Health Planning Act, the Community Mental Health Center Act, and Medicare legislation comprise a basic bundle of health services. The early extension of Medicare to include all age groups appears likely. What is needed now is a better method for penetrating the old urban core areas to deliver essential medical and mental health services. In this field, as in other service areas, better coordination appears to be the major order of business. In 1970, a Senate study noted that increased costs resulted from the ineffective delivery of health services and the duplication of efforts as expenses for these services continue to rise twice as fast as the cost-of-living.[27]

The next legislative requirement is to amend the Relocation Assistance Act so as to link social services to planned relocation. This Act now provides two of the three critical components delineated; physical (rehousing) and fiscal (relocation benefits). To this should be added the legislative mandate that social services are an integral component of the Act. There should be an emphasis on requiring social services as a means for encouraging individual growth and social democracy. This would provide the missing function needed to complete the circle of services to the relocatees. The Act should also call for the development of planned relocation programs on an experimental basis, subject to rigorous field tests and evaluations to establish their effectiveness. Program modifications based upon local and individual needs should be encouraged. The planned relocation process should be conceived as an evolving one, with experimentation and testing a continuing part of the entire process.

Accountability and Effectiveness

To those who raise a question of program costs, this new approach should not require the immediate expenditure of additional funds. What is probably more politic is the application of monies already authorized, but unappropriated or unspent. Communities and programs demonstrating lesser capabilities for delivering needed services,[28] should be called upon to yield their allocation of funds toward the creation of a new financial pool. This pool could then be used to fund the various social programs deemed to be required in the test communities. Since the transformed relocation process is viewed as continually evolving towards a new form or process, vast programs requiring huge expenditures are not now in order; rather, demonstration relocation programs are called for that would include the basic triad of services: social programs, rehousing, and fiscal compensation.

Our immediate purpose is to establish the relative effectiveness of various combinations of concentrated social service delivery programs to impacted households and businessmen. Once their efficacy has been demonstrated, then a more universal application of this approach would be established. In other words, instead of relocation functioning as a shifting, purposeless change, the planned relocation process would function as an incubator for testing various methods for delivering social services, as well as a means for enlarging the capabilities of people.

As expressed here, the open social system would function within a framework of national social policy that calls for:

1. A congressional or presidential "Social Bill of Rights";
2. Passage of an act establishing (a) a Council of Social Advisors, (b) an Annual Social Report by the president, (c) an organization for sponsoring basic social research and monitoring social progress in the United States;
3. Passage of the Equal Opportunity and Full Employment Act;
4. Linkages between social legislation in such fields as education, health, on-the-job training and the like, with the planned relocation process;

5. Amending the Uniform Relocation Assistance Act so as to mandate the delivery of social services as an essential component of the Act;

6. Appropriating funds from other underutilized programs to provide for continuing field tests adapted to meet local needs until effective models are developed.

Such models should serve to enhance the growth of the individual and foster social democracy. This then is the concept—the development of a positive social policy within a democratic philosophical and administrative framework designed to overcome the historic blunders and insults of past generations. This is the goal—to enhance the deprived person so as to benefit society and the individual. And this is the rationale—only in the renewal of people and the reaffirmation of their worth can our society hope to achieve its major purpose: the creation of a social and physical environment in which each person is able to strive successfully toward achieving his own destiny within the mainstream of a democratic society.

Notes

Notes

Introduction: The Transformation
of Relocation

1. This theme is dominant in Gideon Sjoberg, *The Preindustrial City* (Glencoe, Ill.: The Free Press, 1960).

2. Frederic L. Paxon, *History of the American Frontier, 1763-1893* (Boston: Houghton-Mifflin, 1924), pp. 100-25.

3. Thomas Jefferson, "First Inaugural Address," March 4, 1801, in Henry Steele Commager, ed., *Documents of American History* (New York: Appleton-Century-Crofts, 1963), pp. 186-8.

4. Paxon, *History of the American Frontier*, pp. 130-3.

5. Don E. Ferenbacher, *The Era of Expansion, 1800-1848* (New York: John Wiley & Sons, 1969), p. 38.

6. Audrie Girdner and Anne B. Loftis, *The Great Betrayal, The Evacuation of the Japanese Americans During World War II* (New York: The Macmillan Co., 1969).

7. See *Of Utmost Good Faith*, ed. cited by Vine Deloria, Jr., (San Francisco: Bantam Books, 1972) for the case of the American Indian against the federal government. For the Japanese case, see Bill Hosokawa, *Nisei: The Quiet Americans* (New York: William Morrow, 1969), and Eugene V. Rostow, "The Japanese-American Cases: A Disaster," *Yale Law Journal* (June 1945):489-502.

8. On land disposition, see Paxon, *History of the American Frontier*, and Roy Robbins, *Our Landed Heritage, The Public Domain, 1776-1936* (Lincoln: University of Nebraska Press, 1962).

9. On relocation, see Philip Schorr, "A Search for Social Equity, The Uniform Relocation Assistance and Real Property Acquisition Policies Act of 1970," *Right-of-Way* (February 1972):32-39, and Philip E. Sieber, "Uniform Relocation Act Can Be a Force for Citizen Support of Community Development," *Journal of Housing* (September 1972):455-6.

10. This notion is developed more fully in a later chapter (e.g., Tönnies, Weber, Wirth, and Greer).

11. See Paul Conkin, *Tomorrow a New World: The New Deal Community Program* (Ithaca, N.Y.: Cornell University Press, 1959).

12. See Richard S. Kirkendall, *Social Scientists and Farm Politics in the Age of Roosevelt* (Columbia: University of Missouri Press, 1966), and Sidney Baldwin, *Poverty and Politics: The Rise and Decline of the Farm Security Administration* (Chapel Hill: University of North Carolina Press, 1968).

13. See various relocation reports issued by the Tennessee Valley Authority, especially *A Study of Population Relocation for Land Between the Lakes*, 1970.

14. See Langdon W. Post, *The Challenge of Housing* (New York: Farrar & Rinehart, 1938), which is a prototypical work.

15. See statements of Maxwell Tretter and Robert Weaver, "professional housers" closely identified with the first days of slum clearance programs and also the earliest relocation assistance activities of the Chicago and New York City Housing Authorities that follow in later pages.

16. See Paul F. Wendt, *Housing Policy—The Search for Solutions* (Berkeley and Los Angeles: University of California Press, 1963).

17. U.S. Congress, House of Representatives, Select Subcommittee on Real Property Acquisition of the Committee on Public Works, *Study of Compensation and Assistance For Persons Affected by Real Property Acquisition in Federal and Federally Assisted Programs*, 88th Congress, 2nd Sess., 1964 (hereafter cited as Study of Compensation).

18. See Michael Harrington, *The Other America, Poverty in the United States* (Baltimore: Penguin Books, 1962).

19. For example, on small businessmen, see Basil G. Zimmer, *Rebuilding Cities, The Effects of Displacement and Relocation on Small Business* (Chicago: Quadrangle Books, 1964). On the elderly, see Paul L. Niebanck and John Pope, *The Elderly in Older Urban Areas* (Philadelphia: Institute for Environmental Studies, University of Pennsylvania, 1965). On the poor blacks, see *Norwalk CORE v. Norwalk Redevelopment Agency*, 395 Federal 26920 (1968).

20. See Marc Fried, "Grieving for a Lost Home," in Leonard J. Duhl, M.D., ed., *The Urban Condition, People and Policy in the Metropolis* (New York: Simon and Schuster, 1969), and Herbert Gans, *The Urban Villagers* (New York: The Free Press, 1962). For another viewpoint, see William Key, *When People Are Forced to Move; Final Report of a Study of Forced Relocation* (Topeka, Kansas: Menninger Clinic, 1967).

21. See Chester Hartman, "The Housing of Relocated Families," *Journal of the American Institute of Planners* XXX, no. 4 (November 1964); Robert P. Groberg, *Centralized Relocation: A New Municipal Service* (Washington, D.C.: National Association of Housing and Redevelopment Officials, April 1969); and Richard T. Le Gates, *Can The Federal Welfare Bureaucracies Control Their Programs: The Case of HUD and Urban Renewal* (Berkeley: Institute of Urban and Regional Development, University of California, May 1972); The Housing Authority of the City of Raleigh, North Carolina, *Model Relocation System: A Systems Approach to Relocation Planning and Service Delivery* (Raleigh: North Carolina State University, 1974); and Martin Anderson, *The Federal Bulldozer, A Critical Analysis of Urban Renewal, 1949-1962* (Cambridge, Mass.: M.I.T. Press, 1964).

22. See Charles Vereker and John Barron Mays, *Urban Redevelopment and Social Change* (Liverpool, England: Liverpool University Press, 1961).

Chapter 1
Relocation in the Urban Context

1. V. Gordon Childe, *Man Makes Himself* (New York: Mentor Books, 1951), pp. 48-49.

2. Ibid., pp. 74-86. Studies of relocation activities in some urban renewal programs also reveal this characteristic of the proximity of children to parents. See for example, *Final Report on Family Relocation–Government Center Project Area* (Boston: Boston Redevelopment Authority, December 1963), p. 25.

3. Ibid., p. 87.

4. Ibid., pp. 87-114.

5. V. Gordon Childe, *What Happened in History* (England: Penguin Books, 1954), pp. 104-88.

6. Stuart Piggott, "The Role of the City in Ancient Civilizations," in Robert Fisher, ed., *The Metropolis in Modern Life* (New York: Russell & Russell, 1955), p. 10.

7. Gideon Sjoberg, *The Preindustrial City* (Glencoe, Ill.: The Free Press, 1960), pp. 1-15.

8. Henry Frankfort, *The Birth of Civilization in the Near East* (New York: Doubleday, 1956), pp. 90-120.

9. Childe, *What Happened in History*, p. 198.

10. Lewis Mumford, *The City in History* (New York: Harcourt, Brace & World, 1961), pp. 1-30.

11. Ibid., pp. 34-57.

12. Childe, *Man Makes Himself*, p. 104.

13. Mumford, *The City in History*, p. 260.

14. Ibid., p. 264.

15. Fritz Rörig, *The Medieval Town* (Berkeley: University of California Press, 1967), pp. 113-5.

16. H.L. Beales, *The Industrial Revolution 1750-1850* (New York: Augustus M. Kelley, 1967), p. 30.

17. Adna F. Weber, *The Growth of Cities in the Nineteenth Century: A Study in Statistics* (Ithaca, N.Y.: Cornell University Press, 1965), pp. 31-32. All numbers are rounded for convenience. This work was originally published in 1899 for Columbia University by Macmillan Company.

18. J.R.T. Hughes, "Industrialization–Economic Aspects," *International Encyclopedia of Social Sciences*, Vol. 7 (New York: Crowell, Collier and Macmillan, 1968), p. 252.

19. Ibid., pp. 258-59.

20. Daniel Bell, "The Post-Industrial Society," in Eli Ginzberg, ed., *Technology and Social Change* (New York: Columbia University Press, 1964), p. 44.

21. Ibid., p. 44.

22. Peter F. Drucker, *The Age of Discontinuity: Guidelines to Our Changing Society* (New York: Harper & Row, 1968), Preface.

23. Victor C. Ferkiss, *Technological Man: The Myth and the Reality* (New York: George Braziller, 1969), p. 3.

24. Zbigniew Brezezinski, *Between Two Ages: America's Role in the Technotronic Era* (New York: Viking Press, 1970), pp. 9-11.

25. Charles A. Reich, *The Greening of America* (New York: Random House, 1970), pp. 4-6.

26. U.S. Riot Commission, *Report of the National Advisory Commission on Civil Disorders* (New York: Bantam Books, 1968), pp. 203-4.

27. For a concise discussion and analysis of "Megalopolis," besides Gottman's monumental 810-page work, see Jean Gottman, "Megalopolis: The Main Street of the Nation," in Raymond A. Mohl and Neil Betten, eds., *Urban America in Historical Perspective* (New York: Weybright & Talley, Inc., 1970), pp. 275-84; also Wolf Von Eckardt, *The Challenge of Megalopolis: A Graphic Presentation of the Urbanized Northeastern Seaboard of the United States* (New York: The Macmillan Co., 1964).

28. Patricia Leavey Hodge and Philip M. Hauser, *The Challenge of America's Metropolitan Outlook, 1960 to 1985* (New York: Frederick A. Praeger, 1968), pp. 51-3.

29. Raymond Vernon, *The Changing Economic Function of the Central City* (New York: Committee for Economic Development, 1959).

30. *The New York Times*, October 16, 1972, p. 58.

31. See illustrative essays relative to the problems of New York City but applicable to every large American city as well, Robert H. Connery and Demetrios Caraley, *Governing the City: Challenges and Options for New York* (New York: Praeger Publishers, 1969).

32. An eloquent statement of this credo is to be found in an address given by President Lyndon Johnson, *To Fulfill These Rights*, Howard University, Washington, D.C., June 4, 1965.

Chapter 2
Theories of Urban Growth Processes

1. Eric E. Lampard, "Urbanization and Social Change," in Oscar Handlin and John Burchard, eds., *The Historian and the City* (Cambridge, Mass.: M.I.T. Press, 1966), p. 233.

2. Ibid., p. 246-7.

3. Amos H. Hawley, *Human Ecology: A Theory of Community Structure* (New York: The Ronald Press, 1950), p. 73.

4. Ibid., p. 74.

5. Robert E. Park, "The City: Suggestions for the Investigation of Human Behavior in the Urban Environment," in Robert Park, Ernest W. Burgess, Roderick D. McKenzie, eds., *The City* (Chicago: University of Chicago Press, Sixth Edition, 1970), pp. 6-7.

6. Ibid., p. 10.

7. Ibid., p. 17.

8. Ibid., p. 18.

9. Ernest W. Burgess, "The Growth of the City: An Introduction of a Research Project," in Robert Park et al., eds., *The City* (Chicago: University of Chicago Press, Sixth Edition, 1970), p. 49.

10. Ibid., p. 50.

11. Ibid., p. 58.

12. Ibid., p. 59.

13. See James A. Quinn, *Human Ecology* (Englewood Cliffs, N.J.: Prentice-Hall, 1950), pp. 128-38 for critical evaluations of this theory.

14. Homer Hoyt, *The Structure and Growth of Residential Neighborhoods in American Cities* (Washington, D.C.: Federal Housing Administration, 1939), pp. 4-6. See also Herman G. Berkman, "Delineation and Structure of Rental Areas, A Milwaukee Case Study," *Wisconsin Commerce Report* IV, no. 5 (August 1956).

15. Ibid., p. 112-6.

16. Lloyd Rodwin, "The Theory of Residential Growth and Structure," in William Wheaton, Grace Milgram, and Margy Meyerson, eds., *Urban Housing* (New York: The Free Press, 1966), pp. 85-91.

17. This discussion of the ghetto is based largely on Louis Wirth, *The Ghetto* (Chicago, Ill.: University of Chicago Press, Tenth Impression, 1969), and Herbert Gans, *The Urban Villagers, Groups and Class in the Life of Italian-Americans* (New York: The Free Press of Glencoe, 1962). This definition does not have universality; in terms of blacks especially, "voluntarism" is modified by racial prejudice that limits their mobility.

18. Wirth, *The Ghetto*, pp. 4-5.

19. Ibid., pp. 160-4.

20. Ibid., pp. 171-94.

21. Ibid., pp. 284-85.

22. Gans, *The Urban Villagers*, p. 19.

23. Ibid., pp. 197-228.

24. For an analysis of differential rates of ethnic assimilation, see Otis Dudley Duncan and Stanley Liberson, "Ethnic Segregation and Assimilation," *American Journal of Sociology* 64 (January 1969):364-74.

25. R.D. McKenzie, "The Ecological Approach to the Study of the Human Community," in Robert Park et al., eds., *The City* (Chicago: University of Chicago Press, Sixth Edition, 1970), p. 74.

26. Ibid., pp. 75-77.

27. Alvin Boskoff, *The Sociology of Urban Regions* (New York: Appleton-Century-Crofts, 1962), p. 119.

28. Dudley Kirk, "Population, the Field of Demography," *International Encyclopedia of Social Sciences*, Vol. 12 (New York: Crowell, Collier, and Macmillan, 1968), p. 343.

29. Dudley Kirk, *The Urban Scene* (New York: The Free Press, 1965), pp. 40-59.

30. Leo F. Schnore, "Social Mobility in Demographic Perspective," *American Sociological Review* 26 (June 1961):407.

31. Ibid., pp. 407-23.

32. Amos H. Hawley, *The Changing Shape of Metropolitan America: Deconcentration Since 1920* (Glencoe, Ill.: Free Press, 1956), p. 1 *et passim*.

33. Ibid., p. 145.

34. See Robert Presthus, *The Organizational Society* (New York: Vintage Books, 1962) for an interesting analysis of the "upward mobile" and his role in a bureaucratic organization.

35. Eshref Shevky and Wendell Bell, "Social Area Analysis," in George Theodorson, ed., *Studies in Human Ecology* (New York: Harper & Row, 1961), pp. 227-37.

36. See John Dyckman, "The Changing Uses of the City," *Daedalus* no. XC (Winter 1961):111-31, especially the section entitled "The Declining Social Importance of Space."

37. Melvin M. Webber, "The Roles of Intelligence Systems in Urban Systems Planning," *Journal of the American Institute of Planners*, no. 4 (November 1965):289-90.

38. Melvin M. Webber, "The Post-City Age," in Martin Meyerson, ed., *The Conscience of the City* (New York: George Braziller, 1970), pp. 2-3.

39. Ibid., p. 10.

40. Melvin Webber, "The Urban Place and the Nonplace Urban Realm," in Melvin Webber, ed., *Explorations into Urban Structure* (Philadelphia: University of Pennsylvania Press, 1964), p. 113.

41. Ibid., pp. 134-44.

42. Richard L. Meier, *A Communications Theory of Urban Growth* (Cambridge, Mass.: The Joint Center for Urban Studies of the Massachusetts Institute of Technology and Harvard University, 1962), pp. 50-54.

43. Urbanity is defined as a familiarity and tolerance for different life patterns along with a successful synthesis of institutions and physical forms, ibid., p. 50.

44. Ibid., p. 12.

45. Richard Meier, "The Metropolis as a Transaction-Maximizing System," in Martin Meyerson, ed., *The Conscience of the City* (New York: George Braziller, 1970), pp. 222-3.

46. John Friedmann and John Miller, "The Urban Field," *Journal of the American Institute of Planners*, no. 4 (November 1965), pp. 312-20.

47. John C. Bollens and Henry J. Schmandt, *The Metropolis: Its People, Politics and Economic Life* (New York: Harper & Row, 1965), pp. 312-72.

48. "Indianapolis Links Public/Private Development Resources," *Journal of Housing*, no. 8 (August/September 1973):389-94.

49. York Willbern, *The Withering Away of the City* (Bloomington: Indiana University Press, 1964), p. 122.

50. Ibid., p. 136.

51. Robert L. Heilbroner, *Understanding Macroeconomics* (Englewood Cliffs, N.J.: Prentice-Hall, Fourth Edition, 1972), p. 13.

52. Ferdinand Tönnies, *"Gemeinschaft and Gesellschaft,"* in William R. Taber, ed., *Man in Contemporary Society* (New York: Columbia University Press, Third Edition, 1969), pp. 247-50.

53. H.H. Gerth and C. Wright Mills, *From Max Weber: Essays in Sociology* (New York: Oxford University Press, 1946), pp. 51-55.

54. Ibid., pp. 56-70.

55. Robert Park et al., eds., *The City* (Chicago: University of Chicago Press, Sixth Edition, 1970), pp. 12-24.

56. Ibid., p. 28.

57. Louis Wirth, "Urbanism as a Way of Life," in Elizabeth Wirth Marvick and Albert J. Reiss, Jr., eds., *Community Life and Social Policy* (Chicago: The University of Chicago Press, 1956), pp. 122-5.

58. Ibid., p. 130.

59. Louis Wirth, "The Scope and Problems of the Community," in Elizabeth Wirth Marvick and Albert J. Reiss, Jr., eds., *Social Policy* (Chicago: University of Chicago Press, 1956), p. 19.

60. Scott Greer, *The Emerging City, Myth and Reality* (New York: The Free Press, 1962), pp. 41-43.

61. Wirth, "The Scope and Problems of the Community," p. 43.

**Chapter 3
Democratic and Authoritarian Models
of Relocation Processes**

1. Alexis de Tocqueville, *Democracy in America*, edited by Richard D. Heffner (New York: Mentor Books, 1956): "The chief circumstance, which has favored the establishment and the maintenance of a democratic republic in the United States, is the nature of the territory which the Americans inhabit. Their ancestors gave them the means of remaining equal and free, by placing them upon a boundless continent" [pp. 128-32].

2. Henry Steele Commager, *Documents of American History* (New York: Appleton-Century-Crofts, 1963), pp. 123-4.

3. Roy Robbins, *Our Landed Heritage: The Public Domain, 1776-1936* (Lincoln: University of Nebraska Press, 1962), p. 8.

4. Ibid., p. 10.

5. Ibid., pp. 12-13.

6. Bayard Still, ed., *The West, Contemporary records of America's Expansion Across the Continent: 1607-1890* (New York: Capricorn Books, 1961), p. 53.

7. Thomas Le Duc, "History and Appraisal of U.S. Land Policy to 1862," in Howard W. Ottoson, ed., *Land Use Problems in the United States* (Lincoln: University of Nebraska Press, 1963), pp. 10-11.

8. Leonard D. White, *The Jeffersonians: A Study in Administrative History, 1801-1829* (New York: Free Press Paperback, 1965), p. 514.

9. Still, *The West*, pp. 69-70.

10. Robbins, *Our Landed Heritage*, pp. 48-50.

11. Ibid., p. 91.

12. Ibid., pp. 172-99.

13. Ibid., pp. 200-5.

14. Ibid., p. 217.

15. Commager, "The Northwest Ordinance," *Documents of American History*, p. 131.

16. Frederic L. Paxon, *History of the American Frontier, 1763-1893* (Boston: Houghton-Mifflin, 1924), p. 160.

17. George Dewey Harmon, *Sixty Years of Indian Affairs, Political, Economic, and Diplomatic, 1789-1850* (Chapel Hill: The University of North Carolina Press, 1941), pp. 16-18.

18. Ibid., pp. 375-6; derived from Table IV, Aggregates of Lands, Compensation, Exchange, and Names of Tribes from the Origin of the Government to 1840.

19. Ibid., p. 367.

20. Arthur H. DeRosier, Jr., *The Removal of the Choctaw Indians* (Knoxville: University of Tennessee Press, 1970), p. 37.

21. Ibid., p. 49.

22. Ibid., p. 82.

23. Ibid., pp. 83-112.

24. Ibid., pp. 124-5.

25. Grant Foreman, *Indian Removal* (Norman: University of Oklahoma Press, 1932), pp. 10-121.

26. DeRosier, *The Removal of the Choctaw Indians*, pp. 118-53.

27. Ibid., pp. 132-63.

28. Foreman, *Indian Removal*, p. 252; the remainder of this paragraph in the text is derived from his pp. 120-50.

29. Ibid., p. 163.

30. Angie Debo, *And Still the Waters Run: The Betrayal of the Five Civilized Tribes* (Princeton, N.J.: Princeton University Press, 1970), pp. x, xi.

31. Audrie Girdner and Anne B. Loftis, *The Great Betrayal: The Evacuation of the Japanese Americans During World War II* (New York: The Macmillan Co., 1969), p. ix.

32. Ibid., pp. 145-72.

33. Ibid., p. 20.

34. Ibid., p. 63.

35. Alexander H. Leighton, *The Governing of Men* (Princeton, N.J.: Princeton University Press, paperback edition, 1968), pp. 68-72.

36. Ibid., p. 74.

37. Ibid., pp. 96-7.

38. Ibid., p. 47, and Girdner and Loftis, *The Great Betrayal*, p. 97.

39. Girdner and Loftis, *The Great Betrayal*, pp. 14-16.

40. Morton Grodzins, *Americans Betrayed, Politics and the Japanese Evacuation* (Chicago: University of Chicago Press, 1949), pp. 19-20.

41. Ibid., pp. 19-21.

42. Ibid., pp. 24-25.

43. Ibid., pp. 28-29.

44. Grodzins, *Americans Betrayed*, pp. 88-89.

45. Bill Hosokawa, *Nisei; The Quiet Americans* (New York: William Morrow, 1969), pp. 308-9.

46. Ibid., pp. 316-20.

47. Ibid., p. 329.

48. Ibid., p. 334.

49. Ibid,. pp. 342-3.

50. Ibid., p. 351.

51. Edward S. Corwin, *The President, Office and Powers 1787-1957* (New York: New York University Press, paperback edition, 1964), p. 227.

52. Ibid., p. 229.

53. Ibid., p. 232.

54. Ibid., p. 236.

55. Eugene V. Rostow, "The Japanese-American Cases: A Disaster," *Yale Law Journal* (June 1945):489-502.

56. Girdner and Loftis, *The Great Betrayal*, p. 482.

57. Ibid., pp. 446-7.

Chapter 4
The New Deal in Rural Relocation

1. Paul K. Conkin, *Tomorrow a New World: The New Deal Community Program* (Ithaca, N.Y.: Cornell University Press, 1959), p. 27.

2. Louis Koenig, *The Chief Executive* (New York: Harcourt, Brace & World, Revised Edition, 1968), p. 368.

3. Conkin, *Tomorrow a New World*, p. 28.

4. Koenig, *The Chief Exeuctive*, pp. 365-7.

5. Henry Steele Commager, "F.D. Roosevelt's First Inaugural Address, March 4, 1933," *Documents of American History* (New York: Appleton-Century-Crofts, 1963), pp. 239-40.

6. Richard S. Kirkendall, *Social Scientists and Farm Politics in the Age of Roosevelt* (Columbia: University of Missouri Press, 1966), p. 50.

7. Ibid., pp. 50-55.

8. Conkin, *Tomorrow a New World*, pp. 79-82.

9. Ibid., p. 97.

10. Franklin D. Roosevelt, *Looking Forward* (New York: The John Day Company, 1933), p. 55.

11. Conkin, *Tomorrow a New World*, pp. 88-95; subsistence homesteads defined, pp. 110-1.

12. Ibid., pp. 100-1.

13. Ibid., pp. 98-110.

14. Ibid., p. 116.

15. Ibid., pp. 111-30.

16. Sidney Baldwin, *Poverty and Politics: The Rise and Decline of the Farm Security Administration* (Chapel Hill: The University of North Carolina Press, 1968), pp. 74-76.

17. Conkin, *Tomorrow a New World*, p. 131.

18. Baldwin, *Poverty and Politics*, pp. 75-6.

19. Kirkendall, *Social Scientists and Farm Politics*, pp. 134-5.

20. Ibid., pp. 144-5.

21. Carl Degler, *Out of Our Past, The Forces That Shaped Modern America* (New York: Harper & Row, revised edition 1970), p. 379.

22. Conkin, *Tomorrow a New World*, pp. 143-4.

23. Ibid., p. 145.

24. Ibid., p. 146.

25. Bernard Sternsher, *Rexford Tugwell and the New Deal* (New Brunswick, N.J.: Rutgers University Press, 1964), p. 266.

26. Ibid., pp. 160-1.

27. Ibid., pp. 170-2.

28. Ibid., pp. 276-7.

29. Conkin, *Tomorrow a New World*, pp. 151-61.

30. Ibid., pp. 112-3.

31. Joseph L. Arnold, *The New Deal in the Suburbs, A History of the Greenbelt Town Program 1935-1954* (Columbus: Ohio State University Press, 1971), pp. 83-101.

32. Ibid., pp. 139-43.

33. Ibid., p. 145.

34. Ibid., pp. 162-71.

35. Conkin, *Tomorrow a New World*, pp. 324-5.

36. Arnold, *The New Deal in the Suburbs*, pp. 243-4.

37. Conkin, *Tomorrow a New World*, p. 305.

38. Baldwin, *The New Deal in the Suburbs*, p. 123.

39. Conkin, *Tomorrow a New World*, p. 185.

40. Ibid., pp. 226-7.

41. Ibid., pp. 222-8.

42. Ibid., p. 232.

43. Ibid., pp. 326-7.

44. Clarence Lewis Hodge, *The Tennessee Valley Authority: A National Experiment in Regionalism* (New York: Russell and Russell, 1938, reissued 1968), pp. 30-31.

45. Ibid., pp. 32-33.

46. Commager, "Hoover's Veto of the Muscle Shoals Bills, Message to the Senate, March 3, 1931," *Documents in American History*, Vol. II, pp. 226-8.

47. Hodge, *The Tennessee Valley Authority*, p. 33.

48. Ibid., pp. 38-40.

49. Philip Selznick, *TVA and the Grass Roots, A Study in the Sociology of Formal Organization* (New York: Harper Torchbooks, 1966), p. 5. Originally published in 1949 by University of California Press.

50. Ibid., pp. 6-7.

51. David Lillienthal, *TVA, Democracy on the March* (New York: Harper & Brothers, Twentieth Anniversary Edition, 1953), p. 6.

52. Ibid., p. 93.

53. Commager, "The Tennessee Valley Act, May 18, 1933," *Documents in American History*, Vol. II, pp. 255-7.

54. U.S. Congress, House of Representatives, Committee on Public Works, *Study of Compensation and Assistance for Persons Affected by Real Property Acquisition in Federal and Federally Assisted Programs*, 88th Congress, 2nd Sess., 1964, pp. 98-9.

55. Selznick, *TVA and the Grass Roots*, p. 104.

56. Tennessee Valley Authority, Reservoir Property Management Department, *Population Readjustment, Wheeler Area*, February 1, 1937, p. 3.

57. Tennessee Valley Authority, *The Wheeler Project*, Technical Report No. 2 (Washington, D.C.: U.S. Government Printing Office, 1940), p. 256.

58. Tennessee Valley Authority, *The Norris Project*, Technical Report No. 1 (Washington, D.C.: U.S. Government Printing Office, 1940), pp. 506-7.

59. Ibid., p. 505.

60. Tennessee Valley Authority, Reservoir Family Removal Section, *Norris Area*, September 1, 1937, p. 2.

61. Ibid., p. 3.

62. Ibid., pp. 12-15.

63. Tennessee Valley Authority, *A Study of Population Relocation for Land Between the Lakes*, September 1970, p. 1.

64. Ibid., Appendix 5, p. 1.

65. Selznick, *TVA and the Grass Roots*, p. 265.

Chapter 5
Urban Relocation, Phase I:
1918 to 1945

1. Timothy L. McDonnell, S.J., *The Wagner Housing Act, A Case Study of the Legislative Process* (Chicago: Loyola University Press, 1957), p. 7.

2. Edith Elmer Wood, *Recent Trends in American Housing* (New York: The Macmillan Company, 1931), p. 67.

3. McDonnell, *The Wagner Housing Act*, footnote 12, p. 7, especially for an interesting commentary by Senator Warren G. Harding in favor of barracks,

foreshadowing his attitude towards early federal disposition of all housing when he became president.

4. Ibid., p. 71.

5. Ibid., pp. 72-73.

6. Wood, *Recent Trends in American Housing*, p. 82.

7. Curtis J. Berger, *Land Ownership and Use: Cases, Statutes and Other Materials* (Boston: Little, Brown & Co., 1968), p. 859.

8. Henry Steele Commager, "The National Recovery Act," *Documents in American History* Vol. II (New York: Appleton-Century-Crofts, 1963), pp. 271-3. The Subsistence Homestead Program discussed earlier was based on this section of the Act.

9. McDonnell, *The Wagner Housing Act*, pp. 35-37. See *United States v. Certain Lands in the City of Louisville, Jefferson County, Ky. et al.*, 78F. (2d) 684 (1935).

10. *New York City Housing Authority v. Muller*, 279 N.Y.S. 299 (1935).

11. Mcdonnell, *The Wagner Housing Act*, p. 49.

12. Thomas F. Johnson, James R. Morris, Joseph G. Butts, *Renewing America's Cities* (Washington, D.C.: The Institute for Social Science Research, 1962), pp. 22-25.

13. Langdon W. Post, *The Challenge of Housing* (New York: Farrar & Rinehart, 1938), p. 192.

14. Wood, *Recent Trends in American Housing*, p. 280.

15. Edith Elmer Wood, "Slum Clearance—What? Why? How?", *Proceedings*, National Conference on Slum Clearance, Cleveland, July, 1933, pp. 18-24.

16. Ibid., p. 19.

17. Ibid., p. 115.

18. McDonnell, *The Wagner Housing Act*, pp. 51-119.

19. Ibid., pp. 88-89.

20. Ibid., pp. 51-87.

21. Ibid., pp. 130-2, p. 186. See also, Leonard Freedman, *Public Housing, The Politics of Poverty* (New York: Holt, Rinehart, Winston, 1969), p. 100.

22. As quoted in McDonnell, *The Wagner Housing Act*, p. 250.

23. Commager, "The Wagner Housing Act," *Documents of American History*, Vol. II, pp. 393-6.

24. U.S. Congress, House of Representatives, Committee on Banking and Currency, *Basic Laws and Authorities on Housing and Urban Development*, Revised through January 31, 1969, 91st Congress, 1st Sess., January 31, 1969. (Hereafter cited as *Basic Laws and Authorities, 1969*.)

25. Glenn H. Beyer, *Housing and Society* (New York: The Macmillan Co., 1965), p. 486.

26. *Basic Laws and Authorities*, 1969, footnote 1, p. 229.

27. P.L. 88-560, Stat. 769, 794, September 2, 1964.

28. Housing Act of 1964, sec. 405 (a), P.L. 88-560, 78 Stat., 769, 795, approved September 2, 1964.

29. Ibid., sec. 406.

30. New York City Housing Authority, *Tenth Annual Report*, Table 16, p. 120.

31. New York Housing Authority, *Fifth Annual Report*, p. 30.

32. Citizens Housing Council of New York, Committee on Rehousing of Tenants, *Report and Recommendations*, June, 1939, p. 1.

33. New York City Planning Commission, *Tenant Relocation Report*, January 20, 1954, p. 5.

34. Interview with Maxwell H. Tretter, former Counsel and Executive Director, New York City Housing Authority, 1938-1947. Langdon Post in his book, *The Challenge of Housing*, fails to mention tenant relocation as a problem facing the New York City Housing Authority.

35. Rosamond G. Roberts, *3000 Families Move To Make Way for Stuyvesant Town* (New York: James Felt & Company, 1946), p. 19.

36. New York City Housing Authority, *Eleventh Annual Report*, p. 20.

37. Statement by Herman D. Hillman, Director, New York Regional Office, Public Housing Administration, U.S. Congress, House of Representatives, *Hearings, Real Property Acquisition Practices and Adequacy of Compensation in Federal and Federally Assisted Programs*, 88th Congress, 2nd Sess., February 27-28, 1964, pp. 33-42.

38. Jack Meltzer, "Relocation of Families Displaced in Urban Redevelopment: Experience in Chicago," in Coleman Woodbury, ed., *Urban Redevelopment: Problems and Practices* (Chicago: The University of Chicago Press, 1953), pp. 409-11.

39. Ibid., as cited in footnote 2, page 411.

40. Ibid., p. 411-12.

41. Ibid., p. 413.

42. Miles L. Colean, *Housing for Defense, A Review of the Role of Housing in Relation to America's Defense and a Program for Action* (New York: The Twentieth Century Fund, 1940), pp. 32-38.

43. Jack Levin, *Your Congress and American Housing, The Actions of Congress on Housing from 1892 to 1951* (Washington, D.C.: U.S. Government Printing Office, 1952), P.L. 849, October 14, 1940, pp. 16-18.

44. Ibid., p. 21.

45. Beyer, *Housing and Society*, pp. 474-5.

46. Michael D. Reagan, *The Managed Economy* (New York: Oxford University Press, 1963), pp. 1-5.

47. Paul F. Wendt, *Housing Policy: The Search for Solutions* (Berkeley and Los Angeles: The University of California Press, 1963), pp. 151-5.

Chapter 6
Urban Relocation, Phase II:
1946 to 1970

1. Richard O. Davies, *Housing Reform During the Truman Administration* (Columbia: University of Missouri Press, 1966), p. xii.

2. Ibid., p. xiii. In 1945-46 this writer was part of a coalition of returning war veterans seeking the adoption of new housing legislation by Congress. The group included such later political stars as John F. Kennedy, Robert Wagner, Jr., and Jacob Javits.

3. Ibid., p. 12.

4. Ibid., pp. 31-32.

5. U.S. Congress, Senate, Committee on Banking and Currency, *Hearings, Housing*, 80th Congress, 1st Sess., 1947, p. 13.

6. Davies, *Housing Reform*, pp. 40-58.

7. U.S. Congress, Senate, Subcommittee on Housing and Urban Affairs, Committee on Banking and Currency, *Congress and American Housing, 1892-1967*, 90th Congress, 2nd Sess., 1968, p. 55.

8. Davies, *Housing Reform*, pp. 87-100.

9. Ibid., p. 111.

10. Ibid., p. 113.

11. P.L. 171, 81st Congress, 1949.

12. Davies, *Housing Reform*, p. 117.

13. Berger, *Land Ownership and Use: Cases, Statutes and Other Materials*, p. 953.

14. Statement by Herman D. Hillman, U.S. Congress, House of Representatives, *Hearings*, 88th Congress, 2nd Sess., February 27-28, 1964, pp. 33-42, and Martin Millspaugh, "Problems and Opportunities of Relocation," *Law and Contemporary Problems* 26, no. 1 (Winter 1961):9.

15. Davies, *Housing Reform*, p. 125.

16. Ibid., pp. 116-31. See also Leonard Freedman, *Public Housing, the Politics of Poverty* (New York: Holt, Rinehart and Winston, 1969) who concludes that ". . . available evidence suggests strongly that while most people did not care deeply one way or another, the general inclination was toward a scaling down of the proposals of 1949" [p. 11].

17. President's Advisory Committee on Government Housing Policies and Programs, *Report*, (Washington, D.C.: U.S. Government Printing Office, 1953).

18. P.L. 560, 83rd Congress, August 2, 1954.

19. U.S. Congress, House of Representatives, Subcommittee on Housing of the Committee on Banking and Currency, Report 16.1, *Slum Clearance and Urban Renewal*, 84th Congress, 2nd Sess., 1956, p. 2.

20. Ibid., pp. 26-29.

21. P.L. 1020, 84th Congress, August 7, 1956.

22. P.L. 372, 86th Congress, September 23, 1959. The $3,000 limit was later raised to $25,000 by federal agency administrative determination and then incorporated into the law under the Housing Act of 1961.

23. For a typical community renewal relocation study, see Relocation and Management Associates, Inc., City of Milwaukee, *A Relocation Analysis*, 1964.

24. U.S. Congress, House of Representatives, Committee on Public Works, *Study of Compensation*, pp. 18-19.

25. Alvin Schorr, *Slums and Social Insecurity* (Washington, D.C.: U.S. Department of Health, Education and Welfare, 1963), lists 271 books and articles on problems of housing, poverty, relocation, and family relationships. See also Catherine Bauer, "The Dreary Deadlock of Public Housing—How to Break It," *Architectural Forum* 106, no. 6 (June 1957):139-41.

26. P.L. 89-174, 79 Stat., 667.42 U.S.C. 3531.

27. U.S. Congress, Report of the National Commission on Urban Problems, *Building The American City*, 91st Congress, 1st Sess., 1968, pp. 86-87.

28. The President's Commission on Urban Housing, *A Decent Home*, 1968, in U.S. Congress, Senate, Special Committee on Aging, *Developments in Aging, 1970*, 92nd Congress, 1st Sess., 1970, pp. 1-5.

29. P.L. 88-560, September 20, 1964.

30. P.L. 89-117, August 10, 1965.

31. P.L. 174, 89th Congress, September 9, 1965.

32. P.L. 754, 89th Congress, November 4, 1966; more popularly known as the Model Cities Act.

33. P.L. 90-448, 82 Stat. 476, and 477 added sec. 235; 498 added sec. 236, 90th Congress, August 1, 1968.

34. Mendes Hershman, "The Housing and Urban Development Act of 1968," *Real Property, Probate and Trust Journal*, 1968, pp. 537-44.

35. P.L. 91-152, 83 Stat. 379, 388, December 12, 1969.

36. Mary K. Nenno, "Housing and Urban Development Act of 1969," *Journal of Housing*, no. 1 (January 1970):14.

37. U.S. Congress, *Fourth Annual Report on National Housing Goals, Message from The President of the United States*, 92nd Congress, 2nd Sess., June 29, 1972, pp. 29-32.

38. P.L. 87-866, 87th Congress, October 23, 1962.

39. Letter from George Jefferson, Chief of Relocation Payments, Federal Highway Administration, Washington, D.C., October 30, 1972.

40. *Study of Compensation*, pp. 87-98.

41. Ibid., p. 18.

42. National Highway Users Conference, Inc., *Tenant Relocation and the Highway Program*, Washington, D.C., May, 1963.

43. *The New York Times*, "Drive in Boston May Bring a New Urban Mix," July 25, 1971.

44. P.L. 90-495, 82 Stat. 815, 830, August 23, 1968.

45. Title 23, Chapter 5, Highway Relocation Assistance, sec. 505.

46. P.L. 91-605, 84 Stat. 1713, 1735, December 31, 1970.

47. W. Brooke Graves, *American Intergovernmental Relations: Their Origins, Historical Development, and Current Status* (New York: Charles Scribner's Sons, 1964), p. 676.

48. Advisory Commission on Intergovernmental Relations, *Impact of Federal Urban Development Programs on Local Government Organization and Planning*, 88th Congress, 2nd Sess., January, 1964, p. 2.

49. Chester Hartman, "Relocation: Illusory Promises and No Relief," *Virginia Law Review*, 57, no. 5 (May 1971):817.

Chapter 7
Urban Relocation, Phase III:
1970 to Date

1. U.S. Congress, House of Representatives, Select Subcommittee on Real Property Acquisitions of the Committee on Public Works, *Hearings, Real Property Acquisition Practices and Adequacy of Compensation in Federal and Federally Assisted Programs*, 88th Congress, 2nd Sess., February 27-28, 1964, p. 3.

2. Ibid.; Lester Eisner, former Regional Administrator, Region 1, Housing and Home Finance Agency, pp. 3-9.

3. Ibid.; Ellis Ash, Acting Administrator, Boston Housing Authority, pp. 50-57.

4. Ibid.; Marc Fried, Director of Research, Center for Community Studies, Boston, Mass., pp. 113-5.

5. Ibid.; Chester Hartman, Staff Associate, Center for Community Studies, Boston, Mass., pp. 115-21.

6. Ibid.; John P. Alevisos, Boston Redevelopment Authority, pp. 121-31.

7. Ibid.; Basil Zimmer, Brown University, pp. 261-81.

8. See statement of E. Winslow Turner in American Bar Association National Institute, *Uniform Relocation Assistance and Land Acquisition Policies, Proceedings*, Houston, Texas, May 20-21, 1971, pp. 3 and 42, for reference to a great change in attitude on the part of many public interest organizations since 1968 including the American Association of State Highway Officials.

9. *Study of Compensation.*

10. Ibid., pp. 2-4.

11. U.S. Congress, House of Representatives, *Report of the Committee on Public Works, House of Representatives To Accompany S.1, Uniform Relocation*

Assistance and Real Property Acquisition Policies Act of 1970, 91st Congress, 2nd Sess., December 2, 1970, p. 2. (Hereafter cited as *Report to Accompany S.1.*)

12. Ibid., p. 105.

13. *Study of Compensation*, pp. 105-23.

14. Advisory Commission on Intergovernmental Relations, *Relocation: Unequal Treatment of People and Businesses Displaced by Government*, Washington, D.C., January 1965, pp. 114-5.

15. Ibid., p. 127.

16. *Report to Accompany S.1*, p. 2.

17. Ibid., p. 3.

18. American Bar Association National Institute, *Uniform Relocation Assistance and Land Acquisition Policies, Proceedings*, p. 3.

19. P.L. 91-646, 91st Congress, S.1, January 2, 1971. Considerations of the Real Property Acquisition Policies sections of the Act are beyond the scope of this work.

20. The analysis of this Act draws heavily from the Act itself, *ibid.*; a title by title summary in the *Journal of Housing*, no. 2 (February 1971); and Philip Schorr, "A Search for Social Equity: The Uniform Relocation Assistance and Real Property Acquisition Policies Act of 1970," *Right-of-Way* (February 1972):32-33.

21. Executive Order #11717, May 9, 1973, and correspondence with Joseph S. Cohen, Acting Director, Office of Property Management, General Services Administration, July 2, 1973.

22. See Administrative Procedures Act, 1946.

23. National Association of Housing and Redevelopment Officials, *Analysis of Proceedings of Relocation Institute*, edited by Philip Schorr, unpublished manuscript, Chicago, Ill., July 26-27, 1971, pp. 31-32.

24. Letter by President Nixon to Congress transmitting the Second Annual Report (1973) of the executive departments and agencies under the Uniform Relocation Assistance Act, undated.

25. Robert Beckham, "GAO Attacks Creating Public Housing Through Direct Acquisition," *Journal of Housing* 9 (1972):453-54.

26. U.S. Senate, Subcommittee on Intergovernmental Relations, Committee on Government Operations, *Differences in Administration Policies Act of 1970*, Comptroller General of the United States, June 1973, p. 34.

27. HUD, *Second Annual Report, Uniform Relocation Assistance and Real Property Acquisition Policies Act of 1970*, Introduction, unpaged.

28. Ibid., pp. 1-15.

29. Department of Transportation, *Annual Report, P.L. 91-646, Uniform Relocation Assistance and Real Property Acquisition Policies Act of 1970*, July 1, 1971, through June 30, 1972, p. 13.

30. Transmittal letter by President Nixon (1973 Second Annual Report), p. 1.

31. HUD, *Second Annual Report*, III-A-3; figures rounded.

32. U.S. Congress, House of Representatives, Committee on Public Works, *1971 Annual Report on Highway Relocation Assistance*, 92nd Congress, 1st Sess., April 1971, pp. v-x.

33. DOT, *Annual Report*, Exhibit II, unpaged.

34. Transmittal letter by President Nixon (1973 Second Annual Report), p. 2.

35. Chester W. Hartman, "Relocation: Illusory Promises and No Relief," *Virginia Law Review* 57, no. 5 (May 1971):805.

36. DOT, *Annual Report*, Exhibit II, unpaged.

37. See *Report to Accompany S.1*, p. 2: HUD data for families in their workload reveals that 36 percent are under $6,000 in home values or under $60 monthly rent value; 47 percent are from $6,000 to $15,000 and $60 to $110; and 17 percent are above $15,000 or $110.

38. HUD, *Second Annual Report*, p. III-A-2 and Exhibit I, unpaged.

39. See note 37.

40. Chester Hartman, "Relocation," p. 805.

41. Ibid., p. 817.

Chapter 8
The Impact of Planned Relocation
on People

1. *New York Post*, September 31, 1958, p. 3.

2. *The New York Times*, February 25, 1973, Section 8, pp. 1 and 6.

3. U.S. Congress, House of Representatives, Select Subcommittee on Real Property Acquisitions of the Committee on Public Works, *Hearings, Real Property Acquisition Practices and Adequacy of Compensation in Federal and Federally Assisted Programs*, 88th Congress, 2nd Sess., February 27-28, 1964, p. 9.

4. U.S. Congress, House of Representatives, Committee on Public Works, *Study of Compensation*, pp. 107-114.

5. Philip Schorr, *Final Report* (New York: Braislin, Porter & Wheelock, 1959), pp. 34-36.

6. Basil G. Zimmer, *Rebuilding Cities, The Effects of Displacement and Relocation on Small Business* (Chicago: Quadrangle Books, 1964), pp. 30-39.

7. Ibid., pp. 330-44.

8. Ibid., p. 347.

9. William Kinnard, Jr. and Zenon Malinowski, *The Impact of Dislocation From Urban Renewal Areas on Small Business* (Storrs: University of Connecticut, July 1960), p. 78.

10. Ibid., pp. 65-77. See also Brian Berry, Sandra Parsons, and Rutherford Platt, *The Impact of Urban Renewal on Small Business, The Hyde Park-Kenwood Case* (Chicago: Center for Urban Studies, The University of Chicago, 1968), p. 159, Table 4.11.

11. U.S. Congress, House of Representatives, Select Committee on Small Business, *Small Business Problems in Urban Areas*, no. 5, 89th Congress, 2nd Sess., 1966, p. 188. (Hereafter cited as *Small Business Problems.*)

12. See details in Chapter 7.

13. For financial details, see discussion of provisions of Uniform Relocation Assistance Act in Chapter 8.

14. HUD, *Second Annual Report, Uniform Relocation Assistance and Real Property Acquisition Policies Act of 1970*, July 1, 1971, through June 30, 1972, p. I-15.

15. Federal-Aid Highway Act, Sec. 505. See details in Chapter 7.

16. In a recent interview, Harris L. Present, Attorney for the Lincoln Square Chamber of Commerce in 1958, stated he had recommended that Section 106 of the Housing Act of 1949 be amended to provide for payment of good will when a business is required to move into a neighborhood where it is unknown. On this point see J. Anthony Panuch, *Relocation in New York City*, Special Report to Mayor Robert F. Wagner, 1959, pp. 38-39.

17. *Study of Compensation*, pp. 52-58 and 105-6. This is a valuable legal analysis of the concept of just compensation under the Fifth Amendment.

18. *Small Business Problems*, pp. 168-9.

19. Ibid., pp. 178-81.

20. Ibid., pp. 201-2.

21. U.S. Senate Report to the Subcommittee on Intergovernmental Relations, Committee on Government Operations, *Differences in Administration of the Uniform Relocation Assistance and Real Property Acquisition Policies Act of 1970*, Comptroller-General of the United States, June 1973, pp. 30-34.

22. HUD, *2nd Annual Report*, pp. I-6 and 7.

23. Jane Jacobs, *The Death and Life of Great American Cities* (New York: Random House, 1961), pp. 60-68.

24. Herbert Gans, *The Urban Villagers: Group and Class in the Life of Italian-Americans* (New York: The Free Press of Glencoe, 1962), pp. 117-9.

25. Relocation and Management Associates, Inc., *A Social Analysis of the City of Yonkers, N.Y.*, unpublished report, New York, 1970, pp. 260-2.

26. See Paul L. Niebanck and John Pope, *The Elderly in Urban Areas* (Philadelphia: Institute for Environmental Studies, University of Pennsylvania, 1965), p. 5.

27. Ibid., p. 6.

28. Charles Abrams, *The City is the Frontier* (New York: Harper and Row, 1965), p. 46.

29. Niebanck and Pope, *The Elderly in Urban Areas*, p. 14.

30. Ibid., p. 15.

31. Paul F. Niebanck, "The Residential Needs of Elderly Persons and the Effects of Relocation," in Chester Rapkin, ed., *Essays on the Problems Faced in the Relocation of Elderly Persons* (Philadelphia: University of Pennsylvania and National Association of Housing and Redevelopment Officials, 1963), pp. 26-45.

32. Wallace F. Smith, *Preparing the Elderly for Relocation, A Study of Isolated Persons* (Philadelphia: Institute for Environmental Studies, University of Pennsylvania, 1966), pp. 76-77.

33. R.N. Morris and John Mogey, *The Sociology of Housing* (London: Routledge & Kegan Paul, 1965), p. 163.

34. Niebanck and Pope, *The Elderly in Urban Areas*, p. 120.

35. Paul F. Niebanck and Mark Yessian, *Relocation in Urban Planning: From Obstacle to Opportunity* (Philadelphia: University of Pennsylvania Press, 1968), pp. 43-45.

36. Mercer L. Jackson, Jr., "A Report on Older Americans," *HUD Challenge*, May 1973, pp. 2-4.

37. Based upon the goals outlined by the President's Committee on Urban Problems in its report, *A Decent Home*, 1968, in U.S. Congress, Senate, Special Committee on Aging, *Developments in Aging, 1970*, 92nd Congress, 1st Sess., 1970, p. 36.

38. Jackson, "A Report on Older Americans," p. 4.

39. 1971 White House Conference on Aging, *Housing the Elderly* (Washington, D.C.: U.S. Government Printing Office, 1971), p. 3.

40. Ibid., p. 5.

41. Ibid., pp. 56-60.

42. Niebanck and Yessian, *Relocation in Urban Planning*, p. 49.

43. Martin Millspaugh, "Problems and Opportunities of Relocation," *Law and Contemporary Problems* 26, no. 1 (Winter 1961):14.

44. Ibid., pp. 20-21.

45. U.S. Commission on Civil Disorders, *Report of the National Advisory Commission on Civil Disorders* (Washington, D.C.: U.S. Government Printing Office, 1968), p. 216.

46. U.S. Congress, Report of the National Commission on Urban Problems, *Building the American City*, 91st Congress, 1st Sess., 1968, p. 44.

47. *The New York Times*, Letter to the Editor, October 26, 1959.

48. Robert Weaver, *The Urban Complex* (Garden City: Doubleday, 1964), pp. 46-49.

49. Ibid., p. 50.

50. Ibid., pp. 51-53.

51. Niebanck and Yessian, *Relocation in Urban Planning*, p. 21.

52. Alvin Mermin, *Relocating Families, The New Haven Experience, 1956 to 1966* (Washington, D.C.: National Association of Housing and Redevelopment Officials, 1970).

53. *Philadelphia's Skid Row, A Demonstration in Human Renewal* (Philadelphia: The Redevelopment Authority of the City of Philadelphia, 1965).

54. *The Homeless Man on Skid Row* (Chicago: The Tenants Relocation Bureau, City of Chicago, September 1961).

55. T.S. Settel, *The Wisdom of JFK* (New York: E.P. Dutton, 1965), p. 25.

56. Ibid., p. 26.

57. Ibid., p. 11.

58. *Norwalk CORE v. Norwalk Redevelopment Agency*, 395 F. 2 φ 920 (1968).

59. Ibid., pp. 920-1.

60. Ibid., p. 931.

61. Ibid., p. 937.

62. Chester Hartman, "Relocation: Illusory Promises And No Relief," *Virginia Law Review* 57, no. 5 (May 1971):5. See also *Powelton Civic Home Owners Association v. Western Addition Community Organization v. Weaver*, 294 F. Supplement 433 (1968).

63. *Green St. Assoc. v. Daley*, 373 F. 2d 1 (7 Cir.), cert. den. 387 U.S. 932 87 S. Ct. 2054 (1967).

64. *Garrett v. City of Hamtramck*, Civ. No. 32004, at 7 (E.D. Mich. March 7, 1969) as cited in Hartman, op. cit., p. 761.

65. Hartman thinks otherwise; See "Relocation," p. 758.

66. *The New York Times*, "L.I. Housing Plan Stirs Fear of Bias," April 30, 1967.

67. *Suffolk Sun*, "Bias Charges, Urban Project Under Attack," July 10, 1968.

68. *Long Island Newsday*, "U.S. Rejects Huntington Bias Claim," March 18, 1969.

69. Letter by the Fort Madison, Iowa Branch Administrative Secretary of the NAACP to the Department of Transportation, Federal Highway Administration, Equal Opportunity Division, Washington, D.C., June 30, 1970.

70. *Des Moines Register*, "NAACP Hits Road Plan at Ft. Madison; Cites Housing Loss for Minorities," January 29, 1972.

71. Letter by the Fort Madison, Iowa Branch of the NAACP to the Secretary of Transportation, October 10, 1972.

Chapter 9
The Deepening Conflict

1. Michael Harrington, "Slums Old and New," *Commentary* 30 (August 1960).

2. Staughton Lynd, "Urban Renewal—For Whom?" *Commentary* 31 (January 1961).

3. Harrington, "Slums Old and New," pp. 118-24.

4. Lynd, "Urban Renewal," pp. 34-44.

5. William Key, *When People Are Forced to Relocate, Final Report of a Study of Forced Relocation* (Topeka, Kansas: Menninger Clinic, May 1967), p. 161.

6. Leonard Duhl, ed., *The Urban Condition* (New York: Basic Books, 1963), pp. 95-96.

7. Marc Fried and Peggy Gleicher, "Some Sources of Residential Satisfaction in an Urban Slum," *Journal of the American, Institute of Planners* XXVII, no. 4 (November 1961):305-6.

8. Ibid., p. 308.

9. Ibid., p. 306-15.

10. Herbert Gans, *The Urban Villagers: Group and Class in the Life of Italian-Americans* (New York: The Free Press of Glencoe, 1962), pp. 11-12, p. 287.

11. Ibid., pp. 309-10.

12. Ibid., p. 328.

13. Ibid., pp. 329-30.

14. Marc Fried, "Grieving for a Lost Home: Psychological Costs of Relocation," in Leonard J. Duhl, ed., *The Urban Condition* (New York: Basic Books, 1963), pp. 151-6.

15. Ibid., p. 160.

16. Ibid., pp. 167-9.

17. Peter Marris, "The Social Implications of Urban Redevelopment," *Journal of the American Institute of Planners* XXVIII, no. 3 (August 1962):180-6.

18. A critical potpourri includes: Kurt Back, *Slums, Projects and People: Social Psychological Problems of Relocation in Puerto Rico* (Durham, North Carolina: Duke University Press, 1962); Chester Hartman, "The Housing of Relocated Families," *Journal of the American Institute of Planners* XXX, no. 4 (November 1964); Charles Abrams, *The City is the Frontier*; and Robert P. Groberg, *Centralized Relocation: A New Municipal Service* (Washington, D.C.: National Association of Housing and Redevelopment Officials, April, 1969).

19. Charles Vereker and John Barron Mays, *Urban Redevelopment and Social Change* (Liverpool, England: Liverpool University Press, 1961).

20. Ibid., pp. 1-67.

21. Ibid., p. 94.

22. Ibid., pp. 119-121.

23. Key, *When People Are Forced to Relocate*, pp. 58-64.

24. Ibid., pp. 144-5.

25. Ibid., pp. 162-3.

26. Ibid., p. 268.

27. Ibid., p. 278.

28. Ibid., p. 217.

29. Marvin Lipman, "Relocation and Family Life; A Study of the Social and Psychological Consequences of Urban Renewal," unpublished Ph.D. dissertation, University of Toronto, 1968.

30. Ibid., pp. 127-34.

31. Ibid., pp. 135-54.

32. Ibid., p. 179.

33. Eleanor Paperno Wolf and Charles N. Lebeaux, *Change and Renewal in an Urban Community* (New York: Frederick A. Praeger, 1969), p. 532.

34. J. Allen Williams, Jr., "The Effects of Urban Renewal Upon a Black Community, Evaluations and Recommendations," *Social Science Quarterly* 50, no. 1 (June 1969):708.

35. Laurence T. Cagle and Irwin Deutscher, "Housing Aspirations and Housing Achievement: The Relocation of Poor Families," *Social Problems*, no. 2 (Fall 1970):243.

36. Chester Hartman, "The Housing of Relocated Families," *Journal of the American Institute of Planners* XXX, no. 4 (November 1964):266.

37. Ibid., p. 270.

38. Ibid., p. 278.

39. Ibid., pp. 280-2.

40. Astrid Monson, "Urban Renewal Relocation: A Plea For Constructive Criticism," *Pratt Planning Papers* 3, no. 4 (October 1965):8-9.

41. Hartman, "The Housing of Relocated Families," pp. 325-32.

42. Housing and Home Finance Agency, *The Housing of Relocated Families* (Washington, D.C.: U.S. Government Printing Office, March 1965), p. 1.

43. Chester Hartman, "Omissions In Evaluating Relocation Effectiveness Cited," *Journal of Housing*, no. 2 (February 1966):88-89.

44. Ibid., p. 89.

45. Philip Schorr, "Relocation View Hit," *Journal of Housing*, no. 3 (March 1966):170.

46. Allan K. Campbell, "Book Review: Centralized Relocation," *Journal of Housing* (July 1969):369-70.

47. Robert P. Groberg, *Centralized Relocation: A New Municipal Service* (Washington, D.C.: National Association of Housing and Redevelopment Officials, April 1969), pp. 55-173.

48. Robert Moses' imperiousness is legendary. A vivid illustration of his character and administrative techniques is described by Roger Starr in "The City as a Work of Art: F. Scott Fitzgerald and Robert Moses," *New York Affairs* 1, no. 1, (1973):60-69.

49. *The New York Times*, "Unorthodox Title I Procedures Used by Moses Creates Disputes," June 30, 1959.

50. Groberg, *Centralized Relocation*, p. 151. See also *The New York Times*, "Housing Expert Replies to Moses," November 12, 1959.

51. *Tenant Relocation Report* (New York: New York City Planning Commission, January 20, 1954), p. 10.

52. City of New York, Office of the City Administration, *Tenant Relocation and the Housing Program*, May 1954, pp. 13-15.

53. The Mayor's Committee for Better Housing of the City of New York, *Report of Subcommittee on Problems of Relocation of Persons Displaced by New Housing and Other Public Improvements*, June 1955, pp. 17-20.

54. Groberg, *Centralized Relocation*, pp. 151-2.

55. J. Anthony Panuch, *Relocation in New York City*, Special Report to Mayor Robert F. Wagner, 1959.

56. Ibid., pp. 20-21.

57. Ibid., p. 21.

58. Ibid., pp. 41-42.

59. Based upon an interview with Selig Polayes, esq., former District Leader of the 5th Assembly District, which included the West Side Urban Renewal Area. He was also president of a local community group that was designated as a sponsor to develop two urban renewal sites.

60. City of New York, Department of Relocation, *Relocation Report for 1963-1965*, December 1965, p. 1. The new Department excluded independent authorities such as the New York City Housing Authority and the Port of New York and New Jersey Authority.

Chapter 10
The Implications of Economics

1. On economics and social analysis, see Martin Anderson, *The Federal Bulldozer, A Critical Analysis of Urban Renewal, 1949-1962* (Cambridge, Mass.: M.I.T. Press, 1964); on benefit-cost analysis, see especially Jerome Rothenberg, "Urban Renewal Programs," in Robert Dorfman, ed., *Measuring Benefits of Government Investments* (Washington, D.C.: The Brookings Institution, 1965); and on the relationship of education to productivity, see Edward F. Denison, *Accounting For United States Economic Growth 1929-1969* (Washington, D.C.: The Brookings Institution, 1974).

2. Anderson, *The Federal Bulldozer*, p. 52.

3. Ibid., p. 230.

4. Ibid., p. 4.

5. John C. Weicher, *Urban Renewal: National Program for Local Problems* (Washington, D.C.: American Enterprise Institute for Public Policy Research, 1972), pp. 46-47.

6. John Rawls, *A Theory of Justice* (Cambridge, Mass.: Harvard University Press, 1972), pp. 22 *et passim.*

7. Ibid., p. 15.

8. Roland N. McKean, "The Use of Shadow Prices," in Samuel B. Chase, ed., *Problems in Public Expenditure Analysis* (Washington, D.C.: The Brookings Institution, 1968), p. 36.

9. Otto A. Davis and Andrew B. Whinston, "The Economics of Urban Renewal," *Law and Contemporary Problems* XXVI (Winter 1961):105.

10. Nathaniel Lichfield, "Cost-Benefit Analysis in City Planning," in Wallace F. Smith, ed., *Land Using Activities* (Berkeley: University of California, 1970),

pp. 62-68. Originally published in the *American Institute of Planners Journal* XXVI, no. 4 (November 1960).

11. James C.T. Mao, "Efficiency in Public Urban Renewal Expenditures Through Benefit-Cost Analysis," *American Institute of Planners Journal* XXXII, no. 2 (March 1966):96.

12. Jerome Rothenberg, *Economic Evaluation of Urban Renewal* (Washington, D.C.: The Brookings Institution, 1967).

13. This is an application to housing of the "Prisoner's Dilemma" game described by Davis and Whinston, "The Economics of Urban Renewal," pp. 110.

14. Rothenberg, *Economic Evaluation of Urban Renewal*, pp. 32-57.

15. Ibid., pp. 115-27.

16. Ibid., pp. 223-9.

17. Ibid., pp. 160-1.

18. Ibid., p. 163.

19. Ibid., pp. 164-75.

20. Ibid., pp. 196-7. The subtotal in Rothenberg's benefit-cost analysis is represented by this equation:

$$TB = L_1 - L_0 + \text{spillover} + \Delta \text{ in social costs}$$

$$\underline{-TC = GPC - L_0}$$

where TB = total benefits;

L_1 = increased productivity of land after renewal;

L_0 = market value of land;

Spillover values are additional benefits to society beyond the direct and immediate ones due to individual changes;

Δ in social costs are the decreases in expenditures for fires, health, crime, and personal problems;

TC = total resource costs

GPC = gross project costs.

If the bottom line is positive, then the imputed values of the spillover effects and the savings in social costs exceed the costs of the project. If the figure is negative, then the imputed values assigned to spillovers and savings in social costs must be equal to or greater than the total costs in order for the project to be cost-effective.

21. Ibid., p. 249.

22. Anthony Downs, "Comments," in Robert Dorfman, ed., *Measuring Benefits of Government Investments*, pp. 342-61.

23. Theodore W. Schultz, "Investment in Human Capital," *American Economic Review* LI (March 1961):1-2.

24. Gary S. Becker, *Human Capital: A Theoretical and Empirical Analysis, With Special Reference to Education* (New York: Columbia University Press, 1964), p. 159.

25. Ibid., p. 1.

26. Schultz, "Investment in Human Capital," p. 2.

27. Burton A. Weisbrod, "Education and Investment in Human Capital," *The Journal of Political Economy* LXX, no. 5, Part 2, Supplement (October 1962):107.

28. Ibid., pp. 108-15.

29. Ibid., pp. 108-22.

30. Ibid., pp. 122-3.

31. Becker, *Human Capital*, p. 37.

32. Ibid., p. 115.

33. Ibid., p. 131.

34. Ibid., pp. 94-95.

35. Selma J. Mushkin, "Health as an Investment," *The Journal of Political Economy* LXX, no. 5, Part 2, Supplement (October 1962):130.

36. Ibid., p. 131.

37. Ibid., p. 138.

38. Ibid., pp. 139-52. These figures do not include estimates of the discounted value of future earnings nor the value of the product contributed by the increase in life expectancy.

39. Dorothy Rice, *Estimating the Cost of Illness* (Washington, D.C.: U.S. Department of Health, Education and Welfare, Public Health Service, 1966).

40. Ibid., p. 76.

41. Jacob Mincer, "On-The-Job Training: Costs, Returns, and Implications," *The Journal of Political Economy* LXX, no. 5, Part 2, Supplement (October 1962):59.

42. Ibid., pp. 53-63.

43. Lester Thurow, *Investment in Human Capital* (Belmont, Calif.: Wadsworth Publishing Co., 1970), pp. 96-97.

44. Ibid., pp. 98-102.

45. Larry A. Sjaastad, "The Costs and Returns of Human Migration," *The Journal of Political Economy* LXX, no. 5, Part 2, Supplement (October 1962):80-93.

46. Ibid., p. 85.

47. Ibid., pp. 86-93.

48. George J. Stigler, "Information In the Labor Market," *The Journal of Political Economy* LXX, no. 5, Part 2, Supplement (October 1962):94-104.

49. Denison, *Accounting For United States Economic Growth*, p. 16.

50. Ibid., pp. 131-5.

51. Thurow, *Investment in Human Capital*, pp. 103-11.

52. *The New York Times*, "World Bank Focuses on Educating Poor," December 29, 1974.

53. Neil W. Chamberlain, "Some Second Thoughts on the Concept of Human Capital," in Ronald Wykstra, ed., *Human Capital Formation and Manpower Development* (New York: The Free Press, 1971), pp. 205-11.

54. Ibid., p. 213.

55. Ibid., p. 214.

56. Ibid., p. 215.

Chapter 11
A Social Program for Enhancing the
Individual and Society

1. Frank S. Kristof, *The Housing and Community Development Act of 1974: Prospects and Prognosis*, mimeo. (New York: New York State Urban Development Corporation, October, 1974), p. 1.

2. P.L. 93-383, 93rd Congress, S. 3006.

3. U.S. Congress, Joint Economic Committee, Subcommittee on Urban Affairs, Donald N. Michael, "Urban Planning and Policy Problems," *Urban America: Goals and Problems* (Washington, D.C.: U.S. Government Printing Office, 1967), p. 69.

4. *The New York Times*, "Urban Crisis of the 1960's Is Over, Ford Aides Say," March 23, 1975, p. 1.

5. Citizens Housing and Planning Council of New York, Inc., *Policy Statement on Community Development Funds*, mimeo, October 25, 1974, p. 2.

6. Stephen D. Mittenthal and Hans B.C. Spiegel, "How Residents Perceive Participatory Planning," in Hans B.C. Spiegel, ed., *Citizen Participation in Urban Development* (Fairfax, Va.: Learning Resources Corporation, NTL, 1974), pp. 44-60.

7. This oversimplification of an open systems model is derived from Daniel Katz and Robert L. Kahn, *The Social Psychology of Organizations* (New York: John Wiley & Sons, 1966), p. 14 *et passim*. Their definition of an open system is one that ". . . includes the importation of energy from the environment, the through-put or transformation of the imported energy into some product form which is characteristic of the system, the exporting of that product into the environment, and the re-energizing of the system from sources in the environment" [p. 28].

8. Relocation and Management Associates, Inc., *A Social Analysis of the City of Yonkers*, unpublished manuscript, pp. 390-5.

9. *The New York Times*, "Citizens' Role in Revenue Sharing Urged," April 18, 1975, and *Journal of Housing* (March 1973):103.

10. Bruce Frankel and Diane Laughlin, "The Promise and Pitfalls of HUD's New Block Grant Approach: The First Thirty Days of Local Experience," *The MARC II News* (Winter 1975):6.

11. Mittenthal and Spiegel, "How Residents Perceive Participatory Planning," pp. 44-60.

12. For a description of the "entrepreneurial type," see David C. McClelland, *The Achieving Society* (New York: Free Press, 1961). The "change agent" concept is discussed by H. George Frederickson in Frank Marini, ed., *Toward a New Public Administration: The Minnowbrook Perspective* (Scranton: Chandler Publishing Company, 1971). Katz and Kahn take the position that leadership is a shared function (*The Social Psychology of Organizations*, p. 335).

13. J. George Chall, *Risk Behavior As An Emerging Bureaucratic Mode: Governing in the '70's*, unpublished paper presented before the National Conference of the American Society for Public Administration, New York, March, 1972.

14. Katz and Kahn, *The Social Psychology of Organizations*, p. 92.

15. Ibid., p. 88.

16. Ibid., p. 22.

17. One application of a systems approach is now in progress in Raleigh, North Carolina; see Emerson H. Snipes and David A. Norris, *Model Relocation Systems: A Systems Approach to Relocation Planning and Service Delivery* (Raleigh, N.C.: The Housing Authority of the City of Raleigh, North Carolina, 1974).

18. Henry Steele Commager, *Documents of American History* (New York: Appleton-Century-Crofts, 1963), pp. 484-5.

19. Ibid., p. 485.

20. Ibid., p. 553.

21. See Augustus F. Hawkins, "Planning for Personal Choice: The Equal Opportunity and Full Employment Act," *The Annals* 418, (March 1975):13-17. This bill is identified by Congress as H.R. 50.

22. Bertram M. Gross, "The State of the Nation: Social Systems Accounting," in Raymond A. Bauer, ed., *Social Indicators* (Cambridge, Mass.: The M.I.T. Press, 1966), pp. 216-71.

23. Hawkins, "Planning for Personal Choice," p. 19.

24. Ibid., p. 15.

25. Ibid., p. 16.

26. Hubert H. Humphrey, "Guaranteed Jobs for Human Rights," *The Annals* 418 (March 1975):24.

27. *The New York Times*, "U.S. Health Care Called Muddled in Senate Study," March 16, 1970, p. 1.

28. Department of Housing and Development, Office of Community Development Evaluation Division, *The Model Cities Program* (Washington, D.C.: U.S. Government Printing Office, July 1973), pp. 8-9.

Bibliography

Bibliography

Books

Abrams, Charles. *The City is the Frontier.* New York: Harper & Row, 1965.

The American Assembly. *The Population Dilemma.* Edited by Philip Hauser. Englewood Cliffs, N.J.: Prentice-Hall, 1963.

Anderson, Martin. *The Federal Bulldozer, A Critical Analysis of Urban Renewal, 1949-1962.* Cambridge, Mass.: M.I.T. Press, 1964.

Arnold, Joseph L. *The New Deal in the Suburbs: A History of the Greenbelt Town Program, 1935-1954.* Columbus: Ohio State University Press, 1971.

Back, Kurt W. *Slums, Projects, and People: Social Psychological Problems of Relocation in Puerto Rico.* Durham, N.C.: Duke University Press, 1962.

Baldwin, Sidney. *Poverty and Politics: The Rise and Decline of the Farm Security Administration.* Chapel Hill: The University of North Carolina Press, 1968.

Beales, H.L. *The Industrial Revolution.* New York: Augustus M. Kelley, 1967.

Becker, Gary S. *Human Capital: A Theoretical and Empirical Analysis With Special Reference to Education.* New York: Columbia University Press, 1964.

Berger, Curtis J. *Land Ownership and Use: Cases, Statutes and Other Materials.* Boston: Little, Brown and Co., 1968.

Beyer, Glenn H. *Housing and Society.* New York: The Macmillan Co., 1965.

Bollens, John C. and Henry J. Schmandt. *The Metropolis: Its People, Politics, and Economic Life.* New York: Harper and Row, 1965.

Boskoff, Alvin. *The Sociology of Urban Problems.* New York: Appleton-Century-Crofts, 1962.

Brezezinski, Zbigniew. *Between Two Ages: America's Role in the Technotronic Era.* New York: Viking Press, 1970.

Chamberlain, Neil W. "Some Second Thoughts on the Concept of Human Capital." In Ronald A. Wykstra, ed., *Human Capital Formation and Manpower Development.* New York: The Free Press, 1971.

Childe, Gordon V. *Man Makes Himself.* New York: Mentor Books, 1951.

_____. *What Happened in History.* England: Penguin Books, 1954.

Colean, Miles L. *Housing for Defense, A Review of the Role of Housing in Relation to America's Defense and a Program for Action.* New York: The Twentieth Century Fund, 1940.

Commager, Henry Steele. *Documents of American History.* New York: Appleton-Century-Crofts, 1963.

Conkin, Paul K. *Tomorrow a New World: The New Deal Community Program.* Ithaca, N.Y.: Cornell University Press, 1959.

Connery, Robert and Demetrios Caraley. *Governing the City: Challenges and Options for New York.* New York: Praeger Publishers, 1969.

Corwin, Edward S. *The President: Office and Powers, 1787-1957.* New York: New York University Press, paperback edition, 1964.

Davies, Richard O. *Housing Reform During the Truman Administration.* Columbia: University of Missouri Press, 1966.

Debo, Angie. *And Still the Waters Run: The Betrayal of the Five Civilized Tribes.* Princeton, N.J.: Princeton University Press, 1970.

Degler, Carl. *Out of Our Past, the Forces that Shaped Modern America.* New York: Harper & Row, revised edition, 1970.

Deloria, Jr., Vine, ed. *Of Utmost Good Faith: The Case of the American Indian Against the Federal Government of the United States.* San Francisco: Bantam Books, 1972.

Denison, Edward F. *Accounting for United States Economic Growth 1929-1969.* Washington, D.C.: The Brookings Institution, 1974.

DeRosier, Jr., Arthur H. *The Removal of the Choctaw Indians.* Knoxville: University of Tennessee Press, 1970.

Drucker, Peter F. *The Age of Discontinuity: Guidelines to Our Changing Society.* New York: Harper & Row, 1968.

Duhl, Leonard J., ed. *The Urban Condition.* New York: Basic Books, 1963.

Ferenbacher, Don E. *The Era of Expansion, 1800-1848.* New York: John Wiley & Sons, 1969.

Ferkiss, Victor. *Technological Man: The Myth and the Reality.* New York: George Braziller, 1969.

Fisher, Robert, ed. *The Metropolis in Modern Life.* New York: Russell & Russell, 1955.

Foreman, Grant. *Indian Removal: The Emigration of the Five Civilized Tribes of Indians.* Norman: University of Oklahoma Press, New Edition, 1953.

Frankfort, Henry. *The Birth of Civilization in the Near East.* New York: Doubleday, 1956.

Freedman, Leonard. *Public Housing: The Politics of Poverty.* New York: Holt, Rinehart, and Winston, 1969.

Gans, Herbert. *The Urban Villagers: Group and Class in the Life of Italian-Americans.* New York: The Free Press of Glencoe, 1962.

Gerth, H.H. and C. Wright Mills. From Max Weber: Essays in Sociology. New York: Oxford University Press, 1946.

Girdner, Audrie and Anne Loftis. *The Great Betrayal: The Evacuation of the Japanese Americans During World War II.* New York: The Macmillan Co., 1969.

Glick, Paul. *American Families.* New York: John Wiley & Sons, 1957.

Graves, Brooke W. *American Intergovernmental Relations: Their Origins, Historical Development, and Current Status.* New York: Charles Scribner's Sons, 1964.

Greer, Scott. *The Emerging City: Myth and Reality.* New York: The Free Press, 1962.

Grodzins, Morton. *Americans Betrayed: Politics and the Japanese Evacuation.* Chicago: University of Chicago Press, 1949.

Gross, Bertram M. "The State of the Nation: Social Systems Accounting." In Raymond Bauer, ed., *Social Indicators.* Cambridge, Mass.: M.I.T. Press, 1966.

Handlin, Oscar and John Burchard, eds. *The Historian and the City.* Cambridge, Mass.: M.I.T. Press, 1963.

Harmon, George Dewey. *Sixty Years of Indian Affairs: Political, Economic, and Diplomatic, 1789-1850.* Chapel Hill: The University of North Carolina Press, 1941.

Harrington, Michael. *The Other America, Poverty in the United States.* Baltimore: Penguin Books, 1962.

Hartwell, R.M. *The Causes of the Industrial Revolution in England.* London: Methuen & Co., Ltd., 1967.

Hauser, Philip M. *Population Perspectives.* New Brunswick, N.J.: Rutgers University Press, 1960.

Hawley, Amos H. *Human Ecology: A Theory of Community Structure.* New York: The Ronald Press, 1950.

_____. *The Changing Shape of Metropolitan America: Decentralization Since 1920.* Glencoe, Ill.: Free Press, 1956.

Heilbroner, Robert L. *Understanding Macroeconomics.* Englewood Cliffs, N.J.: Prentice-Hall, Fourth Edition, 1972.

Hodge, Clarence Lewis. *The Tennessee Valley Authority: A National Experiment in Regionalism.* New York: Russell & Russell, 1938, reissued 1968.

Hodge, Patricia Leavey and Philip M. Hauser. *The Challenge of America's Metropolitan Population Outlook, 1960 to 1985.* Prepared for the National Commission on Urban Problems. New York: Frederick A. Praeger, 1968.

Hoover, Edgar M. and Raymond Vernon. *Anatomy of a Metropolis: The Changing Distribution of People and Jobs Within the New York Metropolitan Region.* Cambridge, Mass.: Harvard University Press, 1959.

Hosokawa, Bill. *Nisei; The Quiet Americans.* New York: William Morrow, 1969.

Hoyt, Homer. *The Structure and Growth of Residential Neighborhoods in American Cities.* Washington, D.C.: Federal Housing Administration, 1939.

Jacobs, Jane. *The Death and Life of Great American Cities.* New York: Random House, 1961.

Johnson, Thomas F., James R. Morris, and Joseph G. Butts. *Renewing America's Cities.* Washington, D.C.: The Institute for Social Science Research, 1962.

Kirk, Dudley. *The Urban Scene.* New York: The Free Press, 1965.

Kirkendall, Richard S. *Social Scientists and Farm Politics in the Age of Roosevelt.* Columbia: University of Missouri Press, 1966.

Koenig, Louis. *The Chief Executive.* New York: Harcourt, Brace and World, Revised Edition, 1968.

Le Duc, Thomas. "History and Appraisal of U.S. Land Policy to 1862." In Howard W. Ohoson, ed., *Land Use Problems in the United States.* Lincoln: University of Nebraska Press, 1963.

Leighton, Alexander. *The Governing of Man.* Princeton, N.J.: Princeton University Press, 1945.

Lillienthal, David. *TVA: Democracy on the March.* New York: Harper & Bros., Twentieth Anniversary Edition, 1953.

McDonnell, Timothy L. *The Wagner Housing Act: A Case Study of the Legislative Process.* Chicago: Loyola University Press, 1957.

McKean, Roland N. "The Use of Shadow Prices." In Samuel B. Chase, ed., *Problems in Public Expenditure Analysis.* Washington, D.C.: The Brookings Institution, 1968.

Meier, Richard M. *A Communications Theory of Urban Growth.* Cambridge, Mass.: M.I.T. Press, 1962.

Meyerson, Martin, ed. *The Conscience of the City.* New York: George Braziller, 1970.

Mohl, Raymond and Neil Betten, eds. *Urban America in Historical Perspective.* New York: Weybright and Talley, 1970.

Morris, R.N. and Mogey, John. *The Sociology of Housing.* London: Routledge & Kegan Paul, 1965.

Mumford, Lewis. *The City in History.* New York: Harcourt, Brace & World, 1961.

Newton, Trevor. *Cost-Benefit Analysis in Administration.* London: Allen & Unwin, Ltd., 1972.

Niebanck, Paul L. and Pope, John. *The Elderly in Older Urban Areas.* Philadelphia: Institute for Environmental Studies, University of Pennsylvania, 1965.

Niebanck, Paul L. and Yessian, Mark R. *Relocation in Urban Planning: From Obstacle to Opportunity.* Philadelphia: University of Pennsylvania Press, 1968.

Park, Robert, Ernest W. Burgess, and Roderick D. McKenzie. *The City.* Chicago: University of Chicago Press, Sixth Edition, 1970.

Paxon, Frederic L. *History of the American Frontier, 1763-1893.* Boston: Houghton-Mifflin, 1924.

Post, Langdon W. *The Challenge of Housing.* New York: Farrar & Rinehart, 1938.

Presthus, Robert. *The Organizational Society.* New York: Vintage Books, 1962.

Quinn, James A. *Human Ecology.* Englewood Cliffs, N.J.: Prentice-Hall, 1950.

Rawls, John. *A Theory of Justice.* Cambridge, Mass.: Harvard University Press, 1971.

Reagan, Michael D. *The Managed Economy.* New York: Oxford University Press, 1963.

Reich, Charles A. *The Greening of America.* New York: Random House, 1970.

Reissman, Leonard. *The Urban Process.* New York: The Free Press, 1964.

Robbins, Roy. *Our Landed Heritage: The Public Domain, 1776-1936.* Lincoln: University of Nebraska Press, 1962.

Roosevelt, Franklin D. *Looking Forward*. New York: The John Day Company, 1933.

Rörig, Fritz. *The Medieval Town*. Berkeley: University of California Press, 1967.

Rothenberg, Jerome. "Urban Renewal Programs." In Robert Dorfman, *Measuring Benefits of Government Investments*. Washington, D.C.: The Brookings Institution, 1965.

————. *Economic Evaluation of Urban Renewal*. Washington, D.C.: The Brookings Institution, 1967.

Schnore, Leo F. *The Urban Scene*. New York: The Free Press, 1965.

Selznick, Philip. *TVA and the Grass Roots: A Study in the Sociology of Formal Organization*. New York: Harper Torchbooks. Originally published in 1949 by University of California Press, issued by Harper Torchbooks, 1968.

Settel, T.S. *The Wisdom of J.F.K.* New York: E.P. Dutton, 1965.

Shevky, Eshref and Wendell Bell. "Social Areas Analysis." In George Theodorson, ed., *Studies in Human Ecology*. New York: Harper and Row, 1961.

Sjoberg, Gideon. *The Preindustrial City*. Glencoe, Ill.: The Free Press, 1960.

Spiegel, Hans, G.C., ed. *Citizen Participation in Urban Development*. Fairfax, Va.: Learning Resources Corp., 1974.

Sternsher, Bernard. *Rexford Trowell and the New Deal*. New Brunswick, N.J.: Rutgers University Press, 1964.

Still, Bayard, ed. *The West: Contemporary Records of America's Expansion Across the Continent, 1607-1890*. New York: Capricorn Books, 1961.

Thurow, Lester. *Investment in Human Capital*. Belmont, Calif.: Wadsworth Publishing Co., 1970.

Tocqueville, Alexis de. In Richard D. Heffner, ed., *Democracy in America*. New York: Mentor Books, 1956.

U.S. Riot Commission, *Report of the National Advisory Commission on Civil Disorders*, New York: Bantam Books, 1968.

Vereker, Charles and John Barron Mays. *Urban Redevelopment and Social Change: A Study of Social Conditions in Central Liverpool, 1955-56*. Liverpool: Liverpool University Press, 1961.

Vernon, Raymond. *The Changing Economic Function of the Central City*. Committee for Economic Development, New York, 1959.

Von Eckardt, Wolf. *The Challenge of Megalopolis, A Graphic Presentation of the Urbanized Northeastern Seaboard of the United States*. New York: The Macmillan Co., 1964.

Weaver, Robert. *The Urban Complex*. Garden City: Doubleday, 1964.

Webber, Melvin. "The Urban Place and the Nonplace Urban Realm." In Melvin Webber, ed., *Explorations Into Urban Structure*. Philadelphia: University of Pennsylvania Press, 1964.

Weber, Adna F. *The Growth of Cities in the Nineteenth Century*. Ithaca, N.Y.: Cornell University Press, 1963. Date of original publication, 1899.

Weber, Max. *The City*. Translated by Don Martindale and Gertrud Neuwirth. New York: Free Press, 1958.

Wendt, Paul F. *Housing Policy: The Search for Solutions.* Berkeley and Los Angeles: University of California Press, 1963.

White, Leonard D. *The Jeffersonians: A Study in Administrative History, 1801-1829.* New York: Free Press Paperback, 1965.

Wilbern, York. *The Withering Away of the City.* Bloomington: Indiana University Press, 1964.

Wirth, Louis. In Elizabeth Wirth Marvick and Albert Reiss, Jr., eds., *Community Life and Social Policy.* Chicago: The University of Chicago Press, 1956.

_____. *The Ghetto.* Chicago: University of Chicago Press, Tenth Impression, 1969.

Wolf, Eleanor Paperno and Charles N. Lebeaux. *Change and Renewal in an Urban Community.* New York: Frederick A. Praeger, 1969.

Wood, Edith Elmer. *Recent Trends in American Housing.* New York: The Macmillan Co., 1931.

Zimmer, Basil G. *Rebuilding Cities: The Effects of Displacement and Relocation on Small Business.* Chicago: Quadrangle Books, 1964.

Articles

Beckham, Robert, "GAO Attacks Creating Public Housing Through Direct Acquisition." *Journal of Housing* 9, 1972.

Bell, Daniel. "The Post-Industrial Society." In Eli Ginzberg, ed., *Technology and Social Change*, N.Y.: Columbia University Press, 1964.

Blumenfeld, Hans. "The Urban Pattern." *The Annals, American Academy of Political and Social Science* (March 1964).

Cagle, Lawrence T. and Irwin Deutscher. "Housing Aspirations and Housing Achievement: The Relocation of Poor Families." *Social Problems* 18, no. 2 (Fall 1970).

Campbell, Allan K. "Book Review: Centralized Relocation," *Journal of Housing*, July 1969.

Chall, George J. *Risk Behavior As An Emerging Bureaucratic Mode: Governing in the '70's.* Unpublished paper presented before the National Conference of the American Society for Public Administration, New York, March 1972.

"City." *International Encyclopedia of the Social Sciences*, Vol. 2. New York: Crowell, Collier, and Macmillan, 1968.

Davis, Otto A. and Andrew B. Whinston. "The Economics of Urban Renewal." *Law and Contemporary Problems* XXVI (Winter 1961).

Downs, Anthony. "Comments," Robert Dorfman, ed., *Measuring Benefits of Government Investments*, Washington, D.C.: The Brookings Institution, 1965.

Duncan, Otis Dudley, and Stanley Liberson, "Ethnic Segregation and Assimilation." *American Journal of Sociology*, January 1969.

Dyckman, John. "The Changing Uses of the City." *Daedalus* XC (Winter 1961).

Frankel, Bruce, and Diane Laughlin. "The Promise and Pitfalls of HUD's New Block Grant Approach: The First Thirty Days of Local Experience." *The Marc II News* (Winter 1975).

Fried, Marc. "Grieving for a Lost Home: Psychological Costs of Relocation." In Leonard J. Duhl, ed., *The Urban Condition.* New York: Basic Books, 1963.

Fried, Marc and Peggy Gleicher. "Some Sources of Residential Satisfaction in an Urban Slum." *Journal of the American Institute of Planners* XXVII, no. 4 (November 1961).

Friedmann, John. "Cities in Social Transformation." *Comparative Studies in Society and History* 4 (November 1961).

Friedmann, John, and John Miller, "The Urban Field." *Journal of the American Institute of Planners* No. 4, November, 1965.

Harrington, Michael. "Slums: Old and New." *Commentary* 30 (August 1960).

Hartman, Chester. "The Housing of Relocated Families." *Journal of the American Institute of Planners* XXX, no. 4 (November 1964).

_____. "Relocation: Illusory Promises and No Relief," *Virginia Law Review* 57, no. 5 (May 1971).

_____. "Omissions in Evaluating Relocation Effectiveness Cited." *Journal of Housing*, no. 2 (February 1966).

Hawkins, Augustus F. "Planning for Personal Choice: The Equal Opportunity and Full Employment Act." *The Annals* 418 (March 1975).

Hershman, Mendes. "The Housing and Urban Development Act of 1968." *Real Property, Probate and Trust Journal*, 1968.

Housing and Home Finance Agency. *The Housing of Relocated Families.* Washington, D.C. U.S. Government Printing Office, March 1965.

Hughes, J.R.T. "Industrialization-Economic Aspects." *International Encyclopedia of Social Sciences*, Vol. 7. New York: Crowell, Collier and Macmillan, 1968.

"Human Ecology." *International Encyclopedia of the Social Sciences*, Vol. 4. New York: Crowell, Collier and Macmillan, 1968.

Humphrey, Hubert. "Guaranteed Jobs for Human Rights." *The Annals*, 418 (March 1975).

Jackson, Jr., Mercer. "A Report on Older Americans." *HUD Challenge* (May 1973).

Kirk, Dudley. "Population, the Field of Demography." *International Encyclopedia of Social Sciences*, Vol. 12. New York: Crowell, Collier and Macmillan, 1968.

Lichfield, Nathaniel. "Cost-Benefit Analysis in City Planning." *The Journal of the American Institute of Planners* XXVI, no. 4 (November 1960).

Lynd, Staughton. "Urban Renewal—For Whom?" *Commentary* 31 (January 1961).

Magrath, C. Peter. "The Supreme Court and a National Constitution." *Modern-*

izing American Government: The Demands of Social Change. Englewood Cliffs, N.J.: Prentice-Hall, 1968.

Marris, Peter. "The Social Implications of Urban Redevelopment." *Journal of the American Institute of Planners* XXVIII, no. 3 (August 1962).

Meltzer, Jack. "Relocation of Families Displaced in Urban Redevelopment: Experiences in Chicago," In Coleman Woodbury, ed., *Urban Redevelopment: Problems and Practices.* Chicago: The University of Chicago Press, 1953.

Millspaugh, Martin, "Problems and Opportunities of Relocation," *Law and Contemporary Problems*, 26, no. 1, Winter 1961.

Mintzer, Jacob. "On-The-Job Training: Costs, Returns, and Implications." *The Journal of Political Economy* LXX, no. 5, Part 2, Supplement (October 1962).

Monson, Astrid. "Urban Renewal Relocation: A Plea for Constructive Criticism." *Pratt Planning Papers* 3, no. 4 (October 1965).

Mushkin, Selma J. "Health As An Investment," *The Journal of Political Economy* LXX, no. 5, Part 2, Supplement (October 1962).

Nenno, Mary K. "Housing and Urban Development Act of 1969," *Journal of Housing*, no. 1 (January 1970).

"Population, the Field of Demography." *International Encyclopedia of the Social Sciences*, Vol. 12. New York: Crowell, Collier, and Macmillan, 1968.

Rodwin, Lloyd. "The Theory of Residential Growth and Structure." In William Wheaton, Grace Milgram, and Margy Meyerson, eds., *Urban Housing*. New York: The Free Press, 1966.

Rostow, Eugene V. "The Japanese-American Case: A Disaster." *Yale Law Journal* 54, no. 3 (June 1945).

Schnore, Leo F. "Social Mobility in Demographic Perspective." *American Sociological Review* 26 (June 1961).

Schorr, Philip. "Relocation View Hit." *Journal of Housing*, no. 3 (March 1966).
_____. "A Search for Social Equity: The Uniform Relocation Assistance and Real Property Acquisition Policies Act of 1970." *Right-of-Way* (February 1972).

Schultz, Theodore W., "Investment in Human Capital." *American Economic Review* LI (March 1961).

Sieber, Philip E. "Uniform Relocation Act Can be a Force for Citizen Support of Community Development." *Journal of Housing* (September 1972).

Sjaastad, Larry A. "The Costs and Returns of Human Migration." *The Journal of Political Economy* LXX, no. 5, Part 2, Supplement (October 1962).

Stigler, George J. "Information in the Labor Market." *The Journal of Political Economy* LXX, no. 5, Part 2, Supplement (October 1962).

"Uniform Relocation Assistance and Real Property Acquisition Policies Act of 1970." *Journal of Housing*, no. 2 (February 1971).

Webber, Melvin. "The Roles of Intelligence Systems in Urban Systems Planning." *Journal of The American Institute of Planners*, no. 4, November 1965.

Weisbrod, Burton A. "Education and Investment in Human Capital," *The Journal of Political Economy* LXX, No. 5, Part 2, Supplement (October 1962).

Williams, J. Allen, Jr. "The Effects of Urban Renewal Upon a Black Community: Evaluation and Recommendations." *Social Science Quarterly* 50, no. 1 (June 1969):703-12.

Reports and Studies

Advisory Commission on Intergovernmental Relations. *Relocation: Unequal Treatment of People and Businesses Displaced by Governments.* Washington, D.C., January 1965.

American Bar Association National Institute. *Uniform Relocation Assistance and Land Acquisition Policies, Proceedings*. Houston, Texas, May 20, 21, 1971 (published 1972).

Berkman, Herman G. "Delineation and Structure of Rental Areas: A Milwaukee Case Study." *Wisconsin Commerce Reports* IV, no. 5, August 1956.

Berry, Brian, Sandra Parsons, and Rutherford Platt. *The Impact of Urban Renewal on Small Business: The Hyde Park-Kenwood Case.* Chicago: Center for Urban Studies, University of Chicago, 1968.

Citizens Housing Council of New York, Committee on Rehousing of Tenants. *Report and Recommendations.* June 1938.

City of New York. Department of Relocation. *Relocation Report for 1963-1965.* December 1965.

_____. Office of the City Administration. *Tenant Relocation and the Housing Program*. May 20, 1954.

Darby, Roger M. "The Functional Housing Area: A Technique for Application to Residential Renewal Analysis." Unpublished Master's thesis, New York University, 1965.

Department of Housing and Development. Office of Community Development Evaluation Division. *The Model Cities Program.* Washington, D.C.: U.S. Government Printing Office, July 1973.

Final Report on Family Relocation-Government Center Project Area. Boston: Boston Redevelopment Authority. December 1963.

Groberg, Robert P. *Centralized Relocation: A New Municipal Service.* Washington, D.C.: National Association of Housing and Redevelopment Officials, April 1969.

Key, William. *When People Are Forced to Move: Final Report of Forced Relocation.* Topeka, Kansas: Menninger Clinic, 1967.

Kinnard, William, Jr., and Zenon Malinowski. *The Impact of Dislocation From Urban Renewal Areas on Small Businesses.* Storrs: University of Connecticut, July 1960.

Kristof, Frank. *The Housing and Community Development Act of 1974: Prospects and Prognosis*, mimeo. New York: New York State Urban Development Corporation, October 1974.

Le Gates, Richard T. *Can The Federal Welfare Bureaucracies Control Their Programs: The Case of HUD and Urban Renewal.* Institute of Urban and Regional Development, University of California, Berkeley, Working Paper #72, May 1972.

Levin, Jack. *Your Congress and American Housing: The Actions of Congress on Housing from 1892 to 1951.* Washington, D.C.: U.S. Government Printing Office, 1952.

Lipman, Marvin. "Relocation and Family Life: A Study of the Social Psychological Consequences of Urban Renewal." Unpublished doctoral dissertation School of Social Work, University of Toronto, 1968.

Mermin, Alvin. *Relocating Families: The New Haven Experience, 1956 to 1966.* Washington, D.C.: National Association of Housing and Redevelopment Officials, 1970.

National Association of Housing and Redevelopment Officials. *Analysis of Proceedings of Relocation Institute.* Edited by Philip Schorr. Unpublished manuscript, Chicago, Illinois, July 26-27, 1971.

National Highway Users Conference, Inc. *Tenant Relocation and the Highway Program.* Washington, D.C., May 1963.

New York City Housing Authority. *Fifth Annual Report.* 1938.

New York City Planning Commission. *Tenant Relocation Report.* January 20, 1954.

_____. *Tenth Annual Report.* 1942.

Niebanck, Paul, F. "The Residential Needs of Elderly Persons and the Effects of Relocation," in Chester Rapkin, ed., *Essays on the Problems Faced in the Relocation of Elderly Persons*. Philadelphia: University of Pennsylvania and National Association of Housing and Redevelopment Officials, 1963.

Panuch, J. Anthony. *Relocation in New York City.* Special Report to Mayor Robert F. Wagner, 1959.

Philadelphia's Skid Row: A Demonstration in Human Renewal. Philadelphia: The Redevelopment Authority of the City of Philadelphia, 1965.

Relocation and Management Associates, Inc. *City of Milwaukee, Community Renewal Program: A Relocation Analysis.* New York, March 1964.

_____. "A Social Analysis of the City of Yonkers." Unpublished manuscript, New York 1970.

Rice, Dorothy. *Estimating the Cost of Illness.* Washington, D.C.: U.S. Department of Health, Education, and Welfare, Public Health Service, 1966.

Schorr, Alvin. *Slums and Social Insecurity*, Washington, D.C.: U.S. Department of Health, Education and Welfare, 1963.

Schorr, Philip. Final Report. New York: Braislin, Porter & Wheelock, Inc., 1959.

Smith, Wallace F. *Preparing the Elderly for Relocation: A Study of Isolated*

Persons. Philadelphia: Institute for Environmental Studies, University of Pennsylvania, 1966.

Snipes, Emerson H. and David A. Norris. *Model Relocation System: A Systems Approach to Relocation Planning and Service Delivery.* Raleigh, N.C.: The Housing Authority of the City of Raleigh, N.C., 1974.

The Tenant's Relocation Bureau. *The Homeless Man on Skid Row.* City of Chicago, September 1961.

Tennessee Valley Authority. *Report of Relocation and Removal of Families From Reservoirs in the Tennessee Valley.* 1953.

_____. Reservoir Family Removal Section. *Norris Area.* September 1, 1937.

_____. *The Norris Project.* Technical Report No. 1. Washington, D.C.: U.S. Government Printing Office, 1940.

_____. Reservoir Property Management Department. *Population Readjustment, Wheeler Area.* February 1, 1937.

_____. *The Wheeler Project*, Technical Report No. 2, Washington, D.C.: Government Printing Office, 1940.

_____. *A Study of Population Relocation for Land Between the Lakes.* September 1970.

Tiebout, Charles M. *The Community Economic Base Study.* New York: Committee for Economic Development, 1962.

U.S. Commission on Civil Disorders. *Report of the National Advisory Commission on Civil Disorders.* Washington, D.C.: U.S. Government Printing Office, 1968.

U.S. Congress. *Fourth Annual Report on National Housing Goals: Message From the President of the United States.* 92nd Congress, 2nd Sess., June 29, 1972.

_____. House of Representatives, Committee on Public Works. *1971 Annual Report on Highway Relocation Asssistance.* 92nd Congress, 1st Sess., April 1971.

_____. House of Representatives, Committee on Public Works. *Report to Accompany S.1, Uniform Relocation Assistance and Real Property Acquisition Policies Act of 1970.* 91st Congress, 2nd Sess., 1970.

_____. House of Representatives, Committee on Public Works. *Study of Compensation and Assistance for Persons Affected by Real Property Acquisition in Federal and Federally Assisted Programs.* 88th Congress, 2nd Sess., 1964.

_____. House of Representatives, Select Subcommittee on Real Property Acquisitions of the Committee on Public Works. *Hearings, Real Property Acquisition Practices and Adequacy of Compensation in Federal and Federally Assisted Programs.* 88th Congress, 2nd Sess., Boston, Mass., and Providence, R.I., February 27-28, 1964.

_____. House of Representatives, Subcommittee on Housing of the Committee on Banking and Currency. *Slum Clearance and Urban Renewal.* Report No. 1. 84th Congress, 2nd Sess., 1956.

U.S. Congress, House of Representatives, Subcommittee of the Select Committee on Small Business. *Small Business Problems in Urban Areas.* No. 5. 89th Congress, 2nd Sess., 1966.

_____. Joint Economic Committee, Subcommittee on Urban Affairs. *Urban America: Goals and Problems.* 90th Congress, 1st Sess., 1967.

_____. Report of the National Commission on Urban Problems. *Building The American City.* 91st Congress, 1st Sess., 1968.

_____. Senate, Committee on Banking and Currency. *Hearings, Housing.* 80th Congress., 1st Sess., 1947.

_____. Senate, Special Committee on Aging. *Developments in Aging, 1970.* 92nd Congress, 1st Sess., 1971.

_____. Senate, Subcommittee on Housing and Urban Affairs, Committee on Banking and Currency. *Congress and American Housing, 1892-1967.* 90th Congress, 2nd Sess., 1968.

U.S. Department of Housing and Urban Development. *1971 HUD Statistical Yearbook.* Washington, D.C.

U.S. Department of Housing and Urban Development. *Second Annual Report, Uniform Relocation Assistance and Real Property Acquisition Policies Act of 1970.* Washington, D.C.

U.S. Department of Transportation. *Annual Report, P.L. 91-646, Uniform Relocation Assistance and Real Property Acquisition Policies Act of 1970,* July 1, 1971 through June 30, 1972.

U.S. Senate. Report to the Subcommittee on Intergovernmental Relations, Committee on Government Operations. *Differences in Administration of the Uniform Assistance and Real Properties Acquisition Policies Act of 1970.* Comptroller General of the United States, June, 1973.

Weicher, John C. *Urban Renewal: National program for local problems.* American Enterprise Institute for Public Policy Research, Washington, D.C., 1972.

Wood, Edith Elmer. "Slum Clearance—What? Why? How?" *Proceedings.* National Conference on Slum Clearance, 1933.

Newspapers

Federal Register. Vol. 37, no. 99, May 20, 1972; vol. 38, no. 109, June 7, 1973; vol. 38, no. 187, September 27, 1973.

Newsday. July 10, 1968; March 18, 1969.

New York Post. September 31, 1958.

The New York Times. September 14, 1958; June 30, 1959; November 12, 1959; March 16, 1970; July 21, 1971; October 15, 1972; February 25, 1973; December 29, 1974; March 23, 1975; April 18, 1975.

The New York Times. Sunday Supplement. "Population, The U.S. Problem, the World," April 30, 1972.

Suffolk Sun. July 10, 1968.

Index

Index

About the Author

Philip Schorr is President of the Relocation and Management Associates, Inc., and Rental and Management Associates, Corp. He has been involved in housing and relocation since 1946 and worked for the New York City Housing Authority after receiving the masters degree from New York University. Dr. Schorr received the Ph.D. degree in Public Administration from New York University and has published articles in the *Journal of Housing, Real Estate Review*, and *New York Affairs.*

Related Lexington Books

Barsby, Steve L., and Cox, Dennis R., *Interstate Migration of the Elderly: An Economic Analysis*, 176 pp., 1975

Birch, David; Atkinson, Reilly; Sandstorm, Sven; and Stack, Linda, *Patterns of Urban Change: The New Haven Experience*, 192 pp., 1974

Conroy, Michael E., *The Challenge of Urban Development: Goals, Possibilities, and Policies for Improving the Economic Structure of Cities*, 144 pp., 1975

Edmonston, Barry, *Population Distribution in American Cities*, 176 pp., 1975

Fredland, Daniel R., *Residential Mobility and Home Purchase: A Longitudinal Perspective on the Family Life Cycle and the Housing Market*, 144 pp., 1974

Friedly, Philip H., *National Policy Responses to Urban Growth*, 1974

Hunker, Henry L., *Industrial Development: Concepts and Principles*, 352 pp., 1974

Kinnard, William N. Jr., and Messner, Stephen D., *Effective Business Relocation*, 320 pp., 1970

Levin, Melvin R.; Rose, Jerome G.; and Slavet, Joseph S., *New Approaches to State Land-Use Policies*, 160 pp., 1974

Mills, Edwin S., and Oates, Wallace E., eds., *Fiscal Zoning and Land Use Controls: The Economic Issues*, 224 pp., 1975

Ottensmann, John R., *The Changing Spatial Structure of American Cities*, In Press

Rothblatt, Donald N., ed., *National Policy for Urban and Regional Development*, 368 pp., 1974